Faith For The Family

Jean Darnall

Elmer Darnall

LaDonna Elliott

Alan Elliott

Marshalls

We appreciate, more than we can say,

our dear friend
Florence Joseph

who painstakingly critiqued every word
and beautifully typed our manuscript.

Scriptures in *Faith For The Family* are selected from the Guide at the back of *Life In The Overlap*. They are study references from the book's themes: *Revelation, Redemption, Regeneration, Recognition, Reconciliation, Relinquishment.* Those who wish to pursue a personal study of these themes will find *Life In The Overlap* useful.

The Scripture quotations in this publication, except where otherwise stated, are from the *New International Version* of the Bible, copyrighted 1978 by New York International Bible Society.

All royalties from this book go to Christian Life College, London.

Marshalls Paperbacks
Marshall Morgan & Scott
3 Beggarwood Lane, Basingstoke, Hants., UK.

Copyright © 1983 by Jean Darnall
First published by Marshall Morgan & Scott 1983

Cataloguing in Publication Data
Darnall, Jean
  Faith for the family
  1. Christian life
  I. Title   II. Darnell, Elmer
  248.4   BV4501.2
ISBN: 0-551-01082-7
Typeset by PRG TypoGraphics, Cheddar, Somerset.
Printed in Great Britain by Anchor-Brendon Ltd., Tiptree.

INTRODUCTION

A nicely bound, green hard-backed book lies upon my desk. It is entitled in gold script 'The Family Altar Book'. Inside on the fly-leaf is written in my father's handwriting, 'Presented to J R Murphy and wife by Rev Glasgow, Charleston, West Virginia. May 10, 1919'.

I turn the page to a marriage certificate designed with blue ribbon and white orange blossoms across the top.

> This *Certifies* that on the 10th day of May in the year of our Lord 1919 John Robinson Murphy and Grace Pack were by me united in Marriage at Charleston according to the Ordinance of God and Laws of the State of West Virginia.
> Witnesses: Walter Murphy and Rosie Eith.
> Samuel M Glasgow, Presbyterian minister.

On the following pages is a month of daily readings and prayers given to help in '. . . the altar building and altar worship'.

When this special book was handed to my mother and father, neither one were Christian believers. For the next seventeen years they had little interest in God. I doubt whether they followed the instructions: 'Let the book be laid by the plate at the morning and evening meals. Quietly and reverently let one read the Scripture sentences . . . Let the hymn be sung or read . . . then kneeling, let the family be led in prayer . . .'

I do know the faith of Rev Glasgow was rewarded in 1936 when my parents and I came to the Lord in Toledo, Ohio. I've told their story in *Heaven Here I Come*'.

In the haste and strain of our modern lives, we may find it difficult to plan time and to keep the family together. But it is a thousand times worth the restraint in our rush and the firm, patient holding together, for a few minutes to be spent at the family altar. 'Altar' may seem an archaic word. By definition it is 'A table or other object which is the most important place in a building where a religious ceremony is held'. I well remember the big round oak table in my parents' dining room which became the most important place in our home.

Daily worship in households is of early origin. The Hebrew patriarchs built their altars where they pitched their tents. The disciples of Jesus in earliest Christian times had the church in the home. The blessing of God has rested upon the family altars continued through the ages.

May his blessing rest upon you as you gather around the most important place in your home, the place where the family prays.

FAITH FOR THE FAMILY is not a substitute for your own creative family worship. It is a stimulator, perhaps a starter for some. The prayers we include are only openers for spontaneous prayer.

FAITH FOR THE FAMILY will help parents to develop their priesthood. Our occasional instructions in the readings to sing, visualise, dramatize and even to hug and kiss each other are all part of the parent's privilege to present God to their children and their children to God.

Elmer and I, along with our daughter, LaDonna and her husband, Alan Elliott, have written this book together. Our son John, who lives in California, has conceived the cover. At the end of the book he and his wife, Ruby, have included their testimonies of faith.

God honours faith. Little did the Presbyterian minister, the Rev Samuel Glasgow in 1919 realise how far through the years ahead his faith would reach when he handed his gift book to my parents. We present FAITH FOR THE FAMILY, our gift to you, with prayers for the salvation of your family.

Jean Darnall with Elmer and LaDonna and Alan Elliott.
London, 1983.

PRAYER FOR REVELATION KNOWLEDGE

'For this reason I kneel before the Father, from whom his whole family in heaven and on earth derives its name. I pray that out of his glorious riches he may strengthen you with power through his Spirit in your inner being, so that Christ may dwell in your hearts through faith.'

Jean: I started this book by praying for the families who will be reading it. Perhaps you could start reading the book by praying for your family. A teenager once asked me 'Is God everybody's Father?' I replied, 'He wants to be'. The girl had not known her father and longed for a loving father-daughter relationship. I told her that God the Father, her Creator, had made a way for her to be part of his family. I spoke about Jesus' death on the cross and of the new birth. 'How can I be born again?' she asked. 'Just by a prayer'. She confessed her sin and placed her faith in Jesus. Her lonely heart was filled with the implanted, immeasurable love of Christ. She now knew Jesus by revelation knowledge.

Think of it! Just as your own father wants you to be known by his name, so God the Father wants us to be known as God's family.

Let's pray: Father, we pray our whole family will become part of your great family. May each one of us come to know Christ dwelling within our heart by faith. In Jesus' name, Amen.

THE HOLY SPIRIT REVEALS JESUS

'When the Counsellor comes, whom I will send to you from the Father, the Spirit of truth who goes out from the Father, he will testify about me; but you also must testify, for you have been with me from the beginning'.

Elmer: Jesus Christ has many names to depict the abundant grace he bestows upon us. The Holy Spirit also has many names, such as the Spirit of Christ, the Spirit of Holiness, the Spirit of Judgement, the Spirit of Life. In these verses he is called the Spirit of Truth because his testimony of Jesus is true.

The privilege of being with Jesus was not for the twelve disciples alone. Jesus promised 'I am with you always even until the end of the age'. (Matthew 28:20) Since he is with us, we should be testifying about what he means to us. The Spirit of Truth will help us, as he helped the disciples. We are always on the witness stand for Jesus. Our lives must always show the truth about him. The Spirit of Truth will confirm our words about Jesus as we share them. He will plant faith in the hearts of those who hear us testify.

Pause to think: Think of what your Lord means to you; what he has done for you; how much he loves you and how you feel about him. Allow the Holy Spirit to reveal to you how you can tell others about him.

Prayer: Dear God, may the Holy Spirit help us today to tell others about Jesus. We are thankful that he has revealed your Son to us. In Jesus' name, Amen.

JANUARY 3   **JOHN 16:13-15**

THE HOLY SPIRIT REVEALS THE SON, THE SON REVEALS THE FATHER

'But when he, the Spirit of truth, comes, he will guide you into all truth. He will not speak on his own; he will speak only what he hears, and he will tell you what is yet to come. He will bring glory to me by taking from what is mine and making it known to you. All that belongs to the Father is mine, that is why I said the Spirit will take from what is mine and make it known to you'.

LaDonna: I first encountered the venom of critical Christians at the age of fifteen in a church in Germany. According to them, the way I dressed was all wrong and displeased God. In their opinion I couldn't be 'saved'. Their accusations were devastating. I had always loved God and it had never occurred to me that the way I looked offended my heavenly Father. Isolated and rejected, I shrivelled into myself. In the depths of my unhappiness, I discovered the truth. The answer was in the inner recesses of my being, rooted like an oak. I knew my assurance was not based in my fleshly behaviour or adornment. It came from my spirit quickened to life by the Holy Spirit, who continually cried heavenward, 'Abba, Father'.

Think of it: The assurance the Holy Spirit gives to a spirit reborn, should never be stolen from a child of God.

Prayer: Lord, enable me to allow the Holy Spirit within to commune in love with you everyday. He will teach me the truth. Thank you Lord. Amen.

JANUARY 4   1 CORINTHIANS 2:12-13

THE HOLY SPIRIT REVEALS THE NEW LIFE

'we have not received the spirit of the world but the Spirit who is from God, that we may understand what God has freely given us. This is what we speak, not in words taught us by human wisdom but in words taught by the Spirit, expressing spiritual truths in spiritual words.'

Alan: When I was sixteen my best friend bought his first car. It liberated us! We had access to the world around us. We knew just enough about cars to check the oil level. When we discovered the car needed oil, we had the problem of how to get the oil into the engine. We didn't have a clue! When my father came around to check how we were doing, he found us trying to pour a quart of oil down the dip-stick tube! From that point on my father taught us how to maintain and operate the car. He did not start out with a thesis on engineering, but with a step-by-step, practical demonstration for us to gain experience.

My new spiritual life is rather like my experience with the car.

It gives me access to an enlarged life. But I need revelation knowledge to live it. I cannot understand how to use or maintain it unless the Holy Spirit teaches me. Nor can I understand everything all at once. God the Holy Spirit gives me just the right amount of revelation for each level of maturity I move into. He teaches me how to steer my new life along the road God has mapped out for me.

Question: Can you accept instruction from the Spirit of God? Would not his instruction, if heeded, make your life go more smoothly?

Prayer: Father God, I pray for all the wisdom I need now. I want to know what belongs in my new life and what doesn't, and how to make my choices. Amen.

JANUARY 5   **EPHESIANS 3:4-6**

REVELATION GIVEN BY THE HOLY SPIRIT

"In reading this, then you will be able to understand my insight into the mystery of Christ, which was not made known to men in other generations as it has now been revealed by the Spirit to God's holy apostles and prophets. This mystery is that through the gospel the Gentiles are heirs together with Israel, members together of one body, and sharers together in the promise in Christ Jesus."

Jean: An Old Testament mystery had kept the prophets guessing for centuries. The scriptures predicted a coming Messiah who would make a way for sinful man to be reconciled to a Holy God, and for men to be reconciled to one another. Who could do such a thing, and how would it be done?

St. Paul states that he had found the answer to the mystery. The Holy Spirit had revealed to him that Jesus Christ was the Messiah of the Jews and the Saviour of the world. Through him, Jew or Gentile could become a new man. Moreover, they were to be united in a new family, the church. Paul had seen the mystery turn to reality, the reality that through Christ enemies can become brothers.

Ask yourselves: Are there relatives separated from you by different beliefs and life-styles? Are you uncertain as to how they could ever change? Do you wonder how those who left you because of angry disagreements could ever return? Don't worry. If you have faith God can reveal his love to them. Christ can make them one with him and with you in his family.

Prayer: Dear God, thank you for the HolySpirit who can reveal Jesus Christ to people we could never change. Give us faith to believe and love and receive the answer to our prayers. In Jesus' name, Amen.

JANUARY 6   **1 JOHN 2:26-27**

REVELATION IS GIVEN BY THE HOLY SPIRIT

"As for you, the anointing you received from him remains in you, and you do not need anyone to teach you. But as his anointing teaches you about all things and as that anointing is real, not counterfeit, just as it has taught you, remain in him."

Jean: I shared with you on the first day my experience with a teenage girl who had never known a father's love. She accepted the Lord as we stood in a public park that very day. Her friends watched as we prayed. When she finished, I heard someone taunt her. Her reply was: 'Knock it off, will ya, this is the real thing!'

The apostle John taught people about Jesus, the Christ. They believed and were filled with joy. After John left, false teachers came, denying all he had taught and leading the people astray. When John heard of it he wrote to remind them of the Teacher who was their indwelling anointing. He would never leave them. He would help them discern truth from untruth. He was not counterfeit, but real.

Question: Is someone casting doubts on your faith in Jesus Christ? How is the Holy Spirit within you reacting? Does he affirm, or is he grieved? Listen to the Holy Spirit. Let him teach

5

you. He won't lead you astray. He'll stick with you until your doubts are settled.

Prayer: Father, I thank you for the Holy Spirit. He is real, not counterfeit. May he teach me to know the difference between truth and untruth. In Jesus' name, Amen.

JANUARY 7   LUKE 11:11-13

THE HOLY SPIRIT IS A GIFT FROM OUR FATHER

'Which of you fathers, if your son asks for a fish, will give him a snake instead? Or if he asks for an egg, will give him a scorpion? If you then, though you are evil, know how to give good gifts to your children, how much more will your Father in heaven give the Holy Spirit to those who ask him?'

Jean: In some manuscripts this passage reads – 'If the son asks for bread would he be given a stone? Stones, snakes and scorpions! Not a favourite dish at our house – how about yours?

A good father would never give such things to his son. Nor should a father give tobacco, alcohol, filthy films or foul language to the child who seeks knowledge, love and blessing. Good food for the soul's development is as important as good food for the body's health.

Our heavenly Father gives the Holy Spirit to those who ask him. Just as we are made to receive good food for body and soul, so we are made to receive the Holy Spirit. He is as necessary to the development of our spiritual selves as food is to our bodies. But remember that he is given to those who ask the Father.

A word to fathers: The promised Holy Spirit is a gift for all the family. '. . . The promise is for you and for your children . . .' (Acts 2:39). Is your Spirit-filled fatherhood encouraging a hunger in your child's heart for the Holy Spirit?

Prayer: (For fathers) Dear heavenly Father, help me to feed my child's hungry intellect and emotions with non-poisonous nourishment. Please God, help me to stimulate my child's hunger for the Holy Spirit. In Jesus' name, Amen.

JANUARY 8   1 JOHN 1:1

REVELATION THROUGH THE INCARNATION

'That which was from the beginning, which we have heard, which we have seen with our eyes, which we have looked at and our hands have touched – this we proclaim concerning the Word of life.'

Jean: One day my hairdresser said to me: 'It's hard to talk to someone you can't see and touch'.

He had looked into all kinds of religions to find some evidence for life after death. When I suggested he pray, he complained about God being too abstract. 'How would I know he was there?' he asked.

'Ask him to do something no one else could do for you, something consistent with his will, for your welfare; something not harmful to others. Do you have a need like that?'

'Yes, I surely do'. He gave me a wistful glance in the mirror. We planned a time when he would pray in his home and I in mine.

When I returned to the salon, he shouted, 'Hey, lady, it worked!'

Indeed it had. He had been an unhappy homosexual. He had planned to take his life; hence his interest in life after death! When he prayed, God changed him deeply. He found a new start and a new life. Today he is married and a father of three children.

Think about it! Jesus' disciples had hand-to-hand contact with the visible, audible, touchable God. Did they tell us how he looked and dressed, his mannerisms, his size, tone of voice, or how he combed his hair? Not a word. They proclaimed that Life had appeared . . . a life such as they had never known before.

Prayer: I want to tell others how I can hear, see and touch you by faith when I pray. I want to share what I know about you with my family, and with everyone. Amen.

THE HOLY SPIRIT GIVES US REVELATION

'I keep asking that the God of our Lord Jesus Christ, the glorious Father, may give you the Spirit of wisdom and revelation, so that you may know him better. I pray also that the eyes of your heart may be enlightened in order that you may know the hope to which he has called you, the riches of his glorious inheritance in the saints . . .'

Elmer: Our glorious Father has extended his divine plan for us beyond new birth. His blessed Holy Spirit remains the dynamic force in the life of every born again Christian. He endows our spirits with inspired wisdom and revelation so that we can know God the Father better and better. In this passage, Paul prays for believers to have the spirit of wisdom and revelation. Why? Not to become better witnesses, better pastors, or teachers or house-group leaders. Rather, his prayer is that the eyes of our hearts will be opened towards the Father.

To know the nature of our Father is to better understand the riches of his grace.

Consider this: As a family are we aware of the riches of our spiritual inheritance? Has he opened our eyes of faith?

Prayer: Dear Father, help us to realise the presence of the Holy Spirit within us. Help us to expect increased spiritual sensitivity as wisdom and revelation come to us from the Holy Spirit. We will then know you better and will know your will for each one of us better. In Jesus' name. Amen.

WE SEE GOD IN JESUS CHRIST

'He came to that which was his own, but his own did not receive him. Yet to all who received him, to those who believed in his name, he gave the right to become children of God — children born not of natural descent, nor of human decision or a husband's will, but born of God.'

LaDonna: I once worked in a home for emotionally disturbed children. The only world they knew was one of tears, anguish and abuse. Often a child would fly out of control, flailing his limbs in despair. I would wrestle the child to the floor, holding him safe in my arms. I felt tense muscles relax as he sensed my love flowing into him.

From eternity God poured out his heart of love incarnate in Jesus. On the cross, Christ wrestled for angry, sinful mankind, embracing all the ugliness of sin. He held this darkened world to his bosom so that we could experience the incomprehensible love of God. Many have recoiled in fear, but millions have recognised divine love and have reached up for more.

Respond: Let God embrace you today. Fall into his arms and learn what it means to be loved by God.

Prayer: Lord, I can only understand your love through letting you love me. Help me to receive your loving embrace and light in my life. Amen.

JANUARY 11   **JOHN 14:9-11**

JESUS REVEALS THE FATHER

'Jesus answered: "Don't you know me, Philip, even after I have been among you such a long time? Anyone who has seen me has seen the Father. How can you say, 'Show us the Father'? Don't you believe that I am in the Father, and that the Father is in me? The words I say to you are not just my own. Rather, it is the Father, living in me, who is doing his work. Believe me when I say that I am in the Father and the Father is in me; or at least believe on the evidence of the miracles themselves".'

Alan: I read a 'Letter to the Editor' in a daily newspaper the other day. It was from a clergyman who had been slandered in a previous article in that paper. The poor man refuted the harsh accusations. He had taken a stand which was unpopular with a large section of society. I say 'poor man', for he was publicly judged and condemned by people who had never heard of him.

People do the same thing to Jesus Christ many times. Those who have heard little of him and hardly know him will judge and condemn. Little do they know that he had a perfect relationship with Father God and was willing to surrender it upon the cross. He laid down his reputation so that they might live.

Think about this: Are we like Philip? He had been around Jesus a long time, but didn't really know him. At that stage, Philip saw Jesus as just another man. Later, he came to understand that Jesus was the Son of God. How do you see Jesus? Can you say you know him? Or are you seeking to know him?

Prayer: Father, we don't want to miss knowing you through your Son. The way he lived and spoke tells us who you are and what you are like. Thank you for Jesus. Amen.

JANUARY 12   JOHN 17:20-21

JESUS PRAYS FOR ALL BELIEVERS TO BE ONE

'My prayer is not for them alone. I pray also for those who will believe in me through their message, that all of them may be one, Father, just as you are in me and I am in you. May they also be in us so that the world may believe that you have sent me'.

Jean: The Father sent his Son, Jesus, from heaven to earth on an errand. He was to go to the cross, and return. While he was on earth, he was to tell his followers all the Father's words. In our reading today, Jesus was near the completion of his errand. He was approaching the cross. He had told his disciples all the Father had told him to say.

Little did the disciples realise that their belief in the truth and their acknowledgement that Jesus was sent by God would become the foundation for the future church of the Lord Jesus Christ. Soon, they too would be sent on an errand . . . to go into all the world as an evangelising fellowship. They would be people on an errand for Jesus.

Think of it! Jesus prayed for us, too. We who believe are also on an errand to tell others about God's love for them. When we obey, we are as close to Jesus and to one another, as Jesus was to his Father and to his followers. We are one in purpose and spirit.

Prayer: Father, help us to run the errands you have given us. May we take your word and your love to all we meet today. Amen.

JANUARY 13   **COLOSSIANS 1:15-18**

OUR INVISIBLE GOD BECAME VISIBLE

'He is the image of the invisible God, the first-born over all creation. For by him all things were created: things in heaven and on earth, visible and invisible, whether thrones or powers or rulers or authorities; all things were created by him and for him. He is before all things, and in him all things hold together. And he is the head of the body, the church; he is the beginning and the first-born from among the dead, so that in everything he might have the supremacy'.

Jean: Jesus is extraordinary. Anyone fitting the description above has to be more than of human origin and character. He must be God . . . and he is!

He is Creator — his creativity goes back long before the carpenter's workshop. He made all things, in heaven and on earth, visible and invisible. Everything we see came into being through him. Because of him, all we see has purpose and meaning. Life makes sense. Since he set everything in motion, then he existed before anything existed. Moreover, he is the power that keeps the universe running. That means God is in control. It also means that his nail pierced hand controls your life today.

Action: Go and look out the window. Everything you see is made and kept going by his power. Isn't God great! Now, whisper to yourself: "He has not forgotten our world. He won't forget me".

Prayer: Dear God, you hold the whole world in your hands. I thank you I am safe in the nail pierced hands of my Saviour. Amen.

THE SON REVEALS THE FATHER TO US

'At that time Jesus said, "I praise you, Father, Lord of heaven and earth, because you have hidden these things from the wise and learned, and revealed them to little children. Yes, Father, for this was your good pleasure". All things have been committed to me by my Father. No one knows the Son except the Father, and no one knows the Father except the Son and those to whom the Son chooses to reveal him'.

Jean: This week we have been reading scriptures about knowing God the Father through his Son, Jesus. He came to make the Father real and lovable to us.

A lot of people did not believe what Jesus said, especially the experts in religious matters, the professors and intellectuals. They had so much head knowledge, they found it difficult to believe with their hearts. Those who did come to believe Jesus' word with their hearts he called little children. They had a child-like faith.

A word to father and mother: There are many things hard to understand about God, even for adults. Your children, even though they may not understand with their minds, can believe with their hearts and love God deeply, just as you do. Trust the Son to reveal the Father and the Father to reveal the Son to your children.

Prayer: (For mother and father) Dear God, we love you and pray our children will love you with all their hearts. We trust you to reveal your love to each one of them. Amen.

JESUS IS THE LIGHT OF LIFE

'The true light that gives light to every man was coming into the world. He was in the world, and though the world was made through him, the world did not recognise him.'

Jean: Jesus, the true light, was a long time in coming. Eventually he came into our world. Not like a meteor, here one minute and gone the next. Nor like an explosion of sudden brilliance. He came like a gradual dawn . . . a child growing up among us. Sadly, he was unrecognised by most people, especially his own, the Jews.

Why? They were spiritually blind. A few perceived his nearness and asked for light. Others who once loved darkness and hated light were delivered and became children of the true Light. All who believed were touched by his transforming power.

Question: Shouldn't we be thankful Jesus' light continues to shine even when he is unrecognised?

Prayer: Father, help me to keep shining for Jesus, even when my closest friends seem blind to how lovely he is. Open their eyes, as you have mine. Amen.

JANUARY 16 1 PETER 1:22-23

LOVE ONE ANOTHER DEEPLY

'Now that you have purified yourselves by obeying the truth so that you have sincere love for your brothers, love one another deeply, from the heart. For you have been born again, not of perishable seed, but of imperishable, through the living and enduring word of God'.

Elmer: Purity of soul is achieved through obedience to the truth into which the Spirit leads us. Out of pure hearts can flow real deep feelings of love towards others.

Often we cannot freely express our true feelings of love towards another because our motives may be misunderstood. We hide honest feelings behind various masks of socially accepted hypocrisy. People to whom we are drawn in love are robbed of our care and companionship because of the fear of man.

There are two words for love used in verse twenty-two to emphasise an important teaching. One of the words used is 'philadelphia' – brotherly love. The other is 'agape' – deep affection with a conscious assent of the will which may entail great self-sacrifice. We are called here to progress from brotherly love to a love that rises deep within the heart that is pure and free from hypocrisy.

Discussion: Can you think of people in the Bible who seemed to have this extra special love which made them very close friends? Do you feel this way about some of your friends? Can you tell them how you feel and show your affection?

Prayer: Dear Father, we love you and we love Christians around us. We also love those who are not Christians, but differently. Help us to show our 'agape' love fervently. Let love grow into deep, honest devotion and lasting companionship. Amen.

JANUARY 17   **EPHESIANS 4:13-16**

GROWING UP IN GOD

'. . . Until we all reach unity in the faith and in the knowledge of the Son of God and become mature, attaining the full measure of perfection found in Christ. Then we will no longer be infants, tossed back and forth by the waves, and blown here and there by every wind of teaching and by the cunning and craftiness of men in their deceitful scheming. Instead, speaking the truth in love, we will in all things grow up into him who is the Head, that is, Christ. From him the whole body, joined and held together by every supporting ligament, grows and builds itself up in love, as each part does its work.'

LaDonna: Our modern world is a plastic world. We can see the discarded rubbish of our light-weight lifestyle in most any street. People try to fake durability by weighing themselves down with complex thought and activity.

We need not be confused and tossed about by men's opinions. Look to the Rock which is Christ. Receive his Word and be anchored in the unshakeable Body of Christ. Those who are in

Christ are joined to his Body — made up of believers from every era. When we meet God, through the Holy Spirit, we meet the Rock. The Rock is Jesus Christ, who sustains all things. He offers us durability.

A thought: People's opinions change. God's opinions are set down for us in his Word. Will he change his Word?

Prayer: Lord, help me to grow and become mature, stable and established in your truth. In Jesus' name, Amen.

JANUARY 18   **COLISSIANS 1:9-12**

QUALIFIED TO SHARE THE LIGHT

'For this reason, since the day we heard about you, we have not stopped praying for you and asking God to fill you with the knowledge of his will through all spiritual wisdom and understanding. And we pray this in order that you may live a life worthy of the Lord and may please him in every way: who has qualified you to share in the inheritance of the saints in the kingdom of light'.

Alan: The lighting man in a theatre stage crew has a responsible job. He must learn the techniques, safety precautions and general rules of stage lighting. He also must have patience, practical creativity and most of all, a deep sense of loyalty to the play, the director and the actors. They all depend on him to present them in the proper light. As an actor, I know that an inexperienced lighting man can cast shadows where they shouldn't be. He can also blind an actor, causing him to stumble.

Let's apply this thought to those occasions when someone is depending on us to help them. We need to ask: 'Do I understand the background of the problem? Am I committed to this person? Am I sure of what the Director, the Lord Jesus, wants me to do, if anything? Do I have a part?' Let us be certain we are qualified to deal with the problems of those who seek our help. We may cast more shadows than light upon them!

15

Discussion: Name friends who have asked you for help with their problems. Do you feel inadequate? What should you do? Should you send them to someone better qualified? What about asking a friend to pray with you? There may also be someone who can share the ministry.

Prayer: Thank you, Father, for St. Paul's great prayer. We pray that we may grow mature and qualify to help others to walk in the light. In Jesus' name, Amen.

JANUARY 19   **JOHN 8:31-32**

THE TRUTH SHALL SET YOU FREE

'If you hold to my teaching, you are really my disciples. Then you will know the truth, and the truth will set you free'.

Jean: My mother used to say of those who gave no heed to what they heard: 'They let it go in one ear and out the other'. Jesus realised that the Jews who said they believed were like that. They heard and agreed and then promptly forgot.

That is the difference between nominal Christians and committed ones. Nominal Christians hear the word, agree and forget it. Committed Christians hear the word, live with it in their hearts and are changed by it.

The Jews were unable to accept the implications of Jesus' word to them. They were enslaved to their religious traditions and national heritage, and relied on their ancestry. They were in bondage and didn't know it!

Think and discuss: Does being born in a certain country or into a Christian family make one a Christian? What kind of a Christian is the person who goes to church, hears the Word, but it never changes their life? Are they nominal, or committed?

Prayer: Lord God, set us free from the slavery of religious pride. Give us humility to commit ourselves to your Word. Your truth can set us free. Amen.

DISCERN WHAT IS BEST

*'And this is my prayer: that your love may abound more and
more in knowledge and depth of insight, so that you may be
able to discern what is best and may be pure and blameless
until the day of Christ, filled with the fruit of righteousness
that comes through Jesus Christ – to the glory and praise of
God'.*

Jean: When I was a child, our house would be full of the spicy
fragrance of the delicious fruit cakes mother baked every
Christmas. She packed them with lots of dried and glazed fruits
and nuts and decorated the tops with loads more. To this day, I
have little respect for dry, colourless, tasteless fruit cake with a
few stray raisins in it. I miss the big, red glazed cherries.

Paul's prayer is for Christians to be packed full of the fruit of
the Spirit, and especially love. A love-filled life is fragrant with
the fulness of Jesus. Love gives knowledge. Knowledge without
love becomes spiritual pride. But with love, knowledge can make
one a sympathetic teacher. Love makes us understanding. It
gives us insight, looking right into the heart. Without love, insight can become harsh judgment. Love, knowledge and insight
can make peacemakers of us.

Think about it: Love must come first. Have you been praying
for knowledge and insight to know what is best for you or
someone who concerns you? Perhaps God is waiting for more
love to grow in your heart.

Prayer: Father, we want to be a sympathetic, understanding
family. We want to discern what is best for each of us and all of
us together. May the Holy Spirit cause love to grow in us to make
us knowing and caring. Amen.

TO GROW WE HAVE TO EAT

*'Like newborn babies, crave pure spiritual milk, so that by it
you may grow up in your salvation, now that you have tasted
that the Lord is good'.*

Jean: This week we have considered how knowing Jesus can cause us to grow in truth, in love, in knowledge of the Lord and in wisdom, so we may help others.

To grow we have to eat. To eat properly we must have an appetite. There is nothing hungrier than a baby (well, perhaps a teenage boy). When babies feed on their mother's milk they are held very close to her body. They feel her nearness. As they grow they eat solids. No longer are they lying on her breast but she is still near, feeding them. The growing space between mother and child is evidence of the child's development. Sometimes one may not feel as near to the Lord as when he first believed. Perhaps God's child is growing and God is giving him space. But God is still there.

Discussion: In a Christian family everyone is at a different stage of spiritual growth. Some are mature and others may be babes in the Kingdom of God. The important thing is that each one is given the nearness or the space he needs to grow. A good gauge of where you are spiritually is to ask what you are hungry for.

Prayer: Father, I want to hunger for righteousness. I want to grow up to live as a son in your kingdom. Heal me of whatever takes away my appetite for your Word. Help us to encourage each other to feed and to grow. Amen.

JANUARY 22   **JOHN 12:37-40**

LET THE LOWER LIGHTS BE BURNING

'Even after Jesus had done all these miraculous signs in their presence, they still would not believe in him. This was to fulfill the word of Isaiah the prophet: "Lord, who has believed our message, and to whom has the arm of the Lord been revealed?" For this reason they could not believe, because, as Isaiah says elsewhere, "He has blinded their eyes and deadened their hearts, so they can neither see with their eyes, nor understand with their hearts, nor turn and I would heal them"'.

Jean: Have you ever been blinded by the bright lights of an on-coming car on the road at night? The same lights which give vision to the driver in one car blinds the driver in the other.

Christ, the Light of the world, caused some men to see, and blinded others! It depends on the direction in which they were going. If they were followers, as were some of the leaders who believed in him (v.42), then they were enlightened. If they were coming against him, as the leaders in our text did, they were unable to recognise him. So they did not turn to be healed of their blindness, but carried on in darkness.

Jesus was on his way to the cross. He could stay no longer. The unbelieving Jews were having their final chance to recognise Jesus. He slowed down for them.

Let's slow down and lower our lights so that others can see who he is, turn and follow him.

Talk it over: What do you think is meant by 'lower our lights'? Should we pass people with 'full head-lamps' or our 'dimmers' on? What about slowing down?

Prayer: Dear Father, help me as I rush around today, to sense where I need to slow down in order to give someone a chance to recognise your Son's life in me. It may be that they need to turn to you today. In Jesus' name, Amen.

JANUARY 23   **JOHN 3:3,6,19**

A NEW WAY OF SEEING THINGS

'. . . I tell you the truth, unless a man is born again, he cannot see the kingdom of God . . . Flesh gives birth to flesh, but the Spirit gives birth to spirit . . . How can this be? Nicodemus asked'.

Elmer: From the moment we are born we see, hear, feel, touch, and taste. Millions of sounds and sensations make impressions on our minds. We learn to react in accordance with the environment into which we have been thrust. We see things in relation to our needs and how we have been treated or mistreated. We build up a personal, biased and selfish view of the world. We respond positively to appreciation and negatively to disapproval. Aggression often becomes a way of life.

Most of us do not see far past 'the ends of our noses' in our selfish world. But Jesus taught that there is a whole new world to see. We have to be born again to see it. This is the miracle of the new birth, of regeneration. It is the miracle of seeing life differently. What we see is the kingdom of God. The blindness of our heart (Ephesians 4:18-20), where the eye seeks every kind of impurity, is taken away. Some outlooks change over-night. Other new views of life come into focus more gradually. So our Christian experience becomes an ever expanding panorama.

Discuss: How can we start our lives all over again? How can Christ wipe out of our minds the responses and attitudes built up over years of experience? What did Jesus say to Nicodemus when he asked 'How?' Can that happen to us?

Prayer: Father, thank you for the rapid changes I experienced when I believed. You changed my mind and my heart. Some things seem to be taking longer. Give me faith for those hardened attitudes and habitual reactions to change too. In Jesus' name, Amen.

JANUARY 24   JOHN 8:14-15

YOU JUDGE BY HUMAN STANDARDS

'Jesus answered, "Even if I testify on my own behalf, my testimony is valid, for I know where I came from and where I am going. But you have no idea where I come from or where I am going. You judge by human standards; I pass judgment on no one.

LaDonna: A baby snug inside its mother's womb is unable to comprehend the world outside. But once born, he experiences the puzzling combination of light, sound and sensation. In his first years, his main task will be to sort out those exciting impulses.

In the same way, God has come to us offering a world and kingdom our natural senses cannot perceive. His answer to our dilemma is birth into the spiritual kingdom. It takes a miracle from God. Nothing less will do. Once born, we are called to grow daily in spiritual understanding through the Holy Spirit: We cannot understand spiritual things with the natural mind. We must judge after the Spirit.

Question: Are there areas in our lives where we still judge by human standards, and not by God's?

Prayer: Lord, it took a miracle to give me birth into the Kingdom. Help me to grow in the joy of seeing the miracle of your Kingdom life at work in me, today. Amen.

JANUARY 25   2 CORINTHIANS 4:4-6

REVELATION IS RECOGNITION OF THE GOSPEL

'The god of this age has blinded the minds of unbelievers, so that they cannot see the light of the gospel of the glory of Christ, who is the image of God. For we do not preach ourselves, but Jesus Christ as Lord, and ourselves as your servants for Jesus' sake. For God, who said, "Let light shine out of darkness," made his light shine in our hearts to give us the light of the knowledge of the glory of God in the face of Christ'.

Alan: The memory of when I first saw the light of the gospel is as ever present in me as each breath I take. I can still feel the joy of that moment of conversion, when I passed from darkness into light.

I was driving on a Los Angeles freeway. Suddenly the spiritual darkness I was living in literally engulfed me. My natural vision was completely blacked out. Immediately, the light of Jesus Christ came flooding into my being. My sight returned. The world I saw about me was actually brighter. The difference was like a candle compared to a high intensity light. It was an illumination which still remains within me.

Think this over: Who is the god of this age who blinds the minds of unbelievers? What happens when the blindness goes? What power overcomes the god of this age? Can you think of someone who needs the darkness driven out of his life? Believe and pray for them.

Prayer: Father, we thank you for Jesus who overcomes the darkness in us. Make his light shine increasingly brighter in our hearts. We pray for . . . to come into light. Amen.

JANUARY 26   JOHN 14:19

I'LL BE SEEING YOU

'Before long, the world will not see me any more, but you will see me. Because I live, you also will live'.

Jean: Almost everyone has experienced sadness when someone they loved went away. Especially if they were going so far away, they would probably never return.

Jesus had told his disciples he was going back to his Father in heaven. Then he turned their sadness into joy when he said they would see him again in a little while. They didn't realise his words were an understatement.

His 'going away' meant that he was going to die on the cross and be buried. His 'coming back' would be his resurrection. When he returned he would bring them a surprise gift. It would be the surprise of the resurrection. He would share his life with them, resurrection life. What a wonderful gift!

Consider what this means now: Even though the world cannot see Jesus, we see him with the eyes of faith. I find that I can see Jesus better with my eyes closed. Close your eyes. See him on the cross far away. See him buried, in the sealed tomb. See him outside the tomb, risen. All that was long ago. Now, see him alive and with you. Accept his gift of resurrection life and live today in his power.

Prayer: Dear Father, the power that raised Jesus from the dead now quickens my mortal body. Thank you for the strength to live victoriously over all that seeks to overcome me. I thank you for eyes to see that Jesus is alive! Amen.

THINGS ARE DIFFERENT NOW

'So I tell you this, and insist on it in the Lord, that you must no longer live as the Gentiles do, in the futility of their thinking. They are darkened in their understanding and separated from the life of God because of the ignorance that is in them due to the hardening of their hearts. Having lost all sensitivity, they have given themselves over to sensuality so as to indulge in every kind of impurity, with a continual lust for more. You, however, did not come to know Christ that way'.

Jean: This scripture is rather stern and heavy, but it has something to say to us. It is a call to abandon the old way of living and learn the new way. Face the fact, once we have new life in Jesus, we are different from all those around us who do not have that new life. For the most part, they live aimless lives; we live purposeful lives. They live recklessly; we live carefully. They seek knowledge with darkened minds; we seek wisdom with enlightened minds. They are alienated from the life of God; we are united with and dependant upon his life. They become calloused; we become sensitive. They are shameless in the face of evil; we turn our faces from evil. They have deadened their consciences; we have the desire to please a holy God.

Think of it! Although all your good friends may not be dreadfully far away from God today, they are in a stream of death which daily becomes swifter. Show them how God helps you to stand against the undercurrents of evil. Show them there is another way to live.

Prayer: Father, may our Saviour teach us to be different, not so much in what we do or don't do, but the way we love. Give us compassionate concern for those who are perishing. Amen.

SEEING IS BELIEVING

'When Jesus rose early on the first day of the week, he appeared first to Mary Magdalene, out of whom he had driven

> seven demons. She went and told those who had been with him
> and who were mourning and weeping. When they heard that
> Jesus was alive and that she had seen him, they did not believe
> it'.

Jean: The first part of our Bible reading throbs with exciting
good news. Jesus is alive! Then, the last sentence drops like a
lead balloon. 'They did not believe it'.

Why do some people believe and others don't? The disciples
had heard an eye-witness account of Jesus' resurrection. Yet they
did not believe. Mary believed what she had seen.

Ah! There may be part of our answer. She had the revelation,
they had the report. It had happened to her, not to them.
Besides, they were afraid and discouraged. To the depressed,
good news is bad news. Even if it were true, they would be afraid
to believe in case they were let down again.

Later, Jesus made sure that each of those unbelievers had a
chance. He had a personal encounter with each of them. Then
they recognised him and believed.

Let's talk: When you tried to testify about Jesus, did your
friends react like the disciples did to Mary? Why do you think
they could not believe? Fear? Or disillusion? Many things could
have affected them. Have you tried again? Don't give up. Mary
didn't. She finally got the disciples to go and see for themselves.

Prayer: Father, I thank you that I know Jesus is alive. He has
done great things for me. I want my friends to meet him. Please,
Holy Spirit, help them to recognise Jesus when he reveals
himself to them. Amen.

JANUARY 29   GENESIS 1:1; PSALM 24:1;
                                            HEBREWS 11:3

REVELATION HELPS US TO
UNDERSTAND OUR WORLD

> 'In the beginning God created the heavens and the earth'.
> 'The earth is the Lord's, and everything in it, the world, and
> all who live in it . . .'

'By faith we understand that the universe was formed at God's command, so that what is seen was not made out of what was visible'.

Jean: Faith in God as our Creator and the Creator of our environment encourages confidence and security. God started it all. All that we see and can't see was God's idea in the beginning. Besides, he is the owner of all he has made. All the resources and potential of our world belong to the Lord. God has the maker's and owner's rights of control and use. He has also taken the responsibility of maintaining it all until his purposes are fulfilled.

Just think: God is responsible, and he has made us responsible, too. We have the privilege of living in an unparalleled world. We are stewards of it all. How do we live in our world? Do we vandalize or utilize our environment? Do we waste or save our resources? Let us use, rather than abuse, for we are accountable to our Master.

Prayer: Father, my Creator and my Owner, I recognise your rightful claims upon me. Even as you have taken the responsibility of caring for me and my environment, I want to take my respnsibility of caring for others and the world around them. Help me to discover your will and purposes for me in this universe, and make me trustworthy. Amen.

JANUARY 30   **2 CORINTHIANS 5:18-19**

RECONCILING LOVE

'All this is from God, who reconciled us to himself through Christ and gave us the ministry of reconciliation: that God was reconciling the world to himself in Christ, not counting men's sins against them. And he has committed to us the message of reconciliation'.

Elmer: Jesus wants us to love the world of people as he did. He wants us to go out into our world today with his love.

The lines of an old hymn say: 'Out of the ivory palaces into a world of woe. Only his eternal love made my Saviour go'. Since the first century, Christians have tried to create for themselves little heavens on earth. They have built their ivory towers. Drawn together in communities they would live separated lives. Such communities seldom lasted beyond the third generation.

Jesus prayed, 'My prayer is not that you take them out of the world, but that you keep them from the evil one'. As the Father sent him, so he sends us. We are sent, not to participate in the worldliness, but to love the worldlings.

What are we to do? There is only one mediator between God and man, the man Christ Jesus. But there are many intercessors. We can intercede by coming to God on the behalf of others. Yet, there is something more we can do. We who have been reconciled to God through Jesus Christ are given a ministry and a message of reconciliation. We can go out of our way, as he did, to draw people back to God. You can pray and reach out to someone today.

Prayer: Lord God, help me to love people so much that I will find myself reaching out to them and caring for them spontaneously ... before I know what I'm doing. Help me to love and forgive them so that they may see your loving compassion and seek your forgiveness and healing. In Jesus' name, Amen.

JANUARY 31   **LUKE 12:22-31**

WORLD OF THINGS

'Then Jesus said to his disciples: "Therefore I tell you, do not worry about your life, what you will eat; or about your body, what you will wear. Life is more than food, and the body more than clothes. Consider the ravens: They do not sow or reap, they have no storeroom or barn; yet God feeds them. And how much more valuable you are than birds! Who of you by worrying can add a single hour to his life? Since you cannot do this very little thing, why do you worry about the rest? Consider how the lilies grow. They do not labour or spin. Yet I tell you, not even Solomon in all his splendour was dressed

like one of these. If that is how God clothes the grass of the field, which is here today, and tomorrow is thrown into the fire, how much more will he clothe you, O you of little faith! And do not set your heart on what you will eat or drink; do not worry about it. For the pagan world runs after all such things, and your Father knows that you need them. But seek his kingdom, and these things will be given to you as well"'

LaDonna: Anxiety shows as people push and elbow their way from shop to shop in London's Oxford Street. Jesus probably viewed a similar scene. Here he remarks on the tranquillity of the birds and flowers. Why do we worry and strive and they do not? Christ's words provide the explanation. The birds and flowers never rejected God's care.

They lived constantly within the realm of God's rule. Their king faithfully provided everything for even the least of them.

Man's anxiety belies his separation from God. Christ urges us to seek the Kingdom of God where complete provision is available to every citizen.

Entrance to the kingdom is simple. Respond to God's call: Abandon your pride and independence, submit to the reign of God, and allow him to fill your life with his abundant care.

Children: Draw some birds or flowers – make them look happy.

Prayer: Father, help me to learn how to let you rule in my whole life, so that I can discover the joy of your provision for all my needs. Amen.

FEBRUARY 1   **1 JOHN 2:15-17**

REVELATION KNOWLEDGE
ABOUT THE WORLD OF THINGS

'Do not love the world or anything in the world. If anyone loves the world, the love of the Father is not in him. For everything in the world – the cravings of sinful man, the lust of his eyes and the boasting of what he has and does – comes not from the Father but from the world. The world and its

desires pass away, but the man who does the will of God lives for ever'.

Alan: During a group discussion with teenagers, I was asked, 'Why do men keep posters and books of nudes?' My reply was that we all keep around us the images we worship.

Mine was no quick answer to the teenager's question. I have found being a Christian is not a matter of giving up everything to live an austere, monastic life. He gives freedom to enjoy the good things of this world without coveting them; freedom to spend leisure time without temptation. Now I can spend time with people who attract me without having impure thoughts. I have had to choose who, or what, I would worship. And I heard God say 'Let that be me'. It is a matter of getting one's priorities sorted out.

Listen to the Lord: He's saying: 'Give me your worship'.

A prayer for men: Father, your word tells me the man who does the will of God lives forever. I want to be that man, by your grace. Amen.

A prayer for women: Father, your word says that the world and it's desires pass away. I want to love you more than the fading fashions of this world. Make me a woman who will live forever with you. Amen.

A prayer for children: Father, put your love in my heart and let me use it to love people more than things. In Jesus' name, Amen.

FEBRUARY 2   **2 CORINTHIANS 11:14-15**

THE MASQUERADE

'And no wonder, for Satan himself masquerades as an angel of light. It is not surprising, then, if his servants masquerade as servants of righteousness. Their end will be what their actions deserve.'

Jean: Have you ever gone to a fancy dress party? What fun it is to dress up, wear a mask and pretend you're somebody else. And when the mask comes off . . .!

In this passage of scripture, St. Paul says that Satan masquerades as an angel of light! Do you suppose it is because he was once an angel of light when he lived in heaven? He rebelled against God, lost his angelic glory and became a demon of darkness. Now he hides his evil nature under many disguises.

Evil people who work with Satan also masquerade. They imitate good people, hiding under many masks. It is often difficult to tell false men and women from true servants of God.

We don't have to be afraid, though, only watchful. We have the Holy Spirit inside us to give us discernment. If we're prayerful, no matter how clever the masquerader may be, we will sense where evil is present and avoid being deceived.

Family fun: Sometime soon, have a fancy dress party. Try to guess who the other person really is. Why not pretend you are a Bible character?

Prayer: Dear Father God, we are glad you have given us the Spirit of truth. Help us to hear his warnings in our hearts, through your Word and through those who pray for us. Thank you for his discernment. Amen.

FEBRUARY 3   **EPHESIANS 6:12; 1:3**

VICTORY IN THE HEAVENLIES

'For our struggle is not against flesh and blood, but against the rulers, against the authorities, against the powers of this dark world and against the spiritual forces of evil in the heavenly realms.'
'Praise be to the God and Father of our Lord Jesus Christ, who has blessed us in the heavenly realms with every spiritual blessing in Christ'.

Jean: Satan masquerades so cleverly that many people find it hard to believe he is real, even though the scriptures have plenty to say about a personal devil. The same people would never believe Satan has organised forces who are rulers of wickedness. Such things are spiritually discerned. In order to discern one must be indwelt by the Holy Spirit.

Christian families often have difficulty getting along amongst themselves. Relationships are sometimes under so much strain that they break. Could it be that we've fought with the wrong party? Perhaps we should have resisted spiritual authorities who have intruded into family relationships, rather than fought with each other. It is the devil's business to break up friendships, fellowships, partnerships, and family and he has organised forces to do so. Let us organise ourselves as a family to fight the devil, not each other.

Good News: Although there are evil powers 'in the heavenly realms', we have the victory. Read Ephesians 1:3. How can Satan curse what God has blessed?

Prayer: Dear God, we shout your word, the victor's shout, in the face of the enemy. (Now all read loudly Ephesians 1:3).

FEBRUARY 4   **MATTHEW 13:38-39**

SEEDS AND WEEDS

'The field is the world, and the good seed stands for the sons of the kingdom. The weeds are the sons of the evil one, and the enemy who sows them is the devil. The harvest is the end of the age, and the harvesters are angels.'

Jean: Jesus told a teaching story. He said there were two kinds of children: 'sons of the Kingdom' and 'sons of the evil one'. He described the children of the kingdom as 'Good seed' and those of the evil one as 'Weeds'. The seed-sons belong to Jesus, the Son of Man. The weeds are sown by the devil. Someday, at the end of time, God's angels will come and harvest the field, which is our world. God will sort out the seeds and the weeds. Sometimes it is hard to tell who is a seed-child and who is a weed.

The Holy Spirit will warn us inside if too many weeds crowd into our lives. Weeds are aggressive things and demand more and more room. They will take over if you give them an inch of ground. But God knows who are his, and so do the angels. They will sort things out and someday the sons of the kingdom will shine like the sun! (v.43)

Think it over: I heard a cassette recently of a children's singing group called 'The Kids of the Kingdom'. Are you a King's Kid? Why don't you look around and greet each other saying, 'Hello, I'm one of the King's Kids'. Go on, it'll make you feel good.

Prayer: Father, help me today to be a 'good seed-child', sharing your life. Please don't let me ever allow the weeds to crowd you out of my heart. Amen.

FEBRUARY 5   GENESIS 3:15 – GALATIANS 4:4-5
GENESIS 49:10 – MATTHEW 1:1-6; 16
PSALM 16:16 – MATTHEW 28:5-6
PSALM 22:6-8 – MATTHEW 27:39,40,43
PSALM 22:16 – JOHN 19:18; 20:24-27

REDEMPTION: PROMISED IN THE
OLD TESTAMENT, FULFILLED IN THE NEW

A family project: Look for the prophecy, and the fulfillment. One of you can look up the first Old Testament reference and read it aloud. Another look up the opposite New Testament reference and read it aloud. Do this with all five sets of references. We'll do this each day this week. You will be surprised how many prophecies about our Redeemer will be found fulfilled in the New Testament.

Jean: Today we start a new theme – Redemption. It means the act of buying back or getting back something.

Once I saw a sign on a building – "Redemption Centre". It turned out to be a place where people turned in trading stamps for merchandise.

The greatest Redemption Centre is the cross of Jesus. There, he paid the price to redeem us. Redemption was promised in the Old Testament and fulfilled in the New. It has been said: 'Jesus is concealed in the Old Testament and revealed in the New Testament'.

Prayer: Thank you, Father, for sending Jesus to redeem us. Thank you for keeping your word, even when it meant giving up your Son to die for us. Amen.

FEBRUARY 6   **PSALM 22:18 – MARK 15:24**
     PSALM 27:12 – MATTHEW 26:59-61
      PSALM 34:20 – JOHN 19:33

GOD PLANNED OUR REDEMPTION

A family project: Find the Old Testament prophecies in today's readings and the New Testament fulfillment. Perhaps someone else can read them aloud today. Go ahead, it won't take long.

Elmer: Jesus was even stripped of his underclothes, for we are told that his seamless robe was just that – a kind of long undershirt. Tradition has it that our Lord's mother wove it for her Son, but we don't know for certain. We do know, however, that our Saviour was afflicted and stripped of his clothes before they nailed him to the cross. The shame of nakedness came with sin. He who was made sin for us bore that shame to take away our reproach. He was stripped at Calvary, so that we might have 'white clothes to wear' (Revelation 3:18).

Discuss: What does the Bible mean in Revelation 3:18 by 'white clothes'?

Prayer: Lord God, help me to remember the suffering of my Saviour for my redemption. May I live today as one who has been redeemed and set free from the power of sin. In Jesus' name, Amen.

FEBRUARY 7   PSALM 41:9 – MARK 14:10,17-21
PSALM 68:18 – LUKE 24:50-51
PSALM 69:4,21 – JOHN 15:23-25; 19:29

GOD SEES OUR PRIDE

A family project: Find the Old Testament prophecies in today's readings and the New Testament fulfillment. Perhaps someone else can read them aloud today. Go ahead, it won't take long.

LaDonna: It came as no shock to God that society rejected Jesus Christ. God could predict man's response centuries before Christ's coming so anti-God was unregenerated human nature. History records in shame the crucifixion. Even the coldest cynic often admits the cross was a tragedy. How can we explain how reasonable people crucified Christ? They had hounded his steps, examined each miracle, and investigated his sinless life. They had seen it all. Yet, in the words of scripture, 'They hated him without reason'. They had no excuse.

While men gave the dying Christ vinegar and gall, foreseen by scripture, his blood bought forgiveness for all humanity. God would not be overwhelmed by man's sin.

Consider: Don't let pride prevent forgiveness flowing from God to you.

Prayer: Lord, it's hard to admit I am naturally sinful. But I don't want my pride to rob me of your complete love. Lord, I receive your forgiveness and love today. Amen.

FEBRUARY 8   ISAIAH 7:14 – MATTHEW 1:18
ISAIAH 9:1-2 – MATTHEW 4:12-16
ISAIAH 11:2 – LUKE 2:52

THE REDEEMER FORGIVES THE DISOBEDIENT

Family project: I hope you are still discovering how beautifully accurate the prophecies are concerning Jesus. Isn't it exciting to find how closely they are fulfilled in the New Testament. Who is going to look them up today?

Alan: The distressed people who lived in the land of Zebulun and the land of Naphtali were reaping the results of their disobedience to God's word. When the Israelites went into that land, they did not remove all the Canaanites, as God had told them to, and now they were under God's judgement. Their disobedience caused great hardship on everyone. The land became a place of gloom. Through their suffering they were humbled, but not forgotten. God sent the prophet to tell them that in the future they would be honoured . . . the people in darkness would see a great light. Centuries later, Jesus, the Light of the World, began his earthly ministry in that very place, thus fulfilling Isaiah's prophecy.

When I asked Jesus Christ to be the Lord and Saviour of my life at the age of twenty-four, I was living in the shadow of death. The lines of a popular rock song described my despair at that time: 'All that lives is born to die'. Then, I met Jesus who was truly born to die. He died to give me hope. He is the Light of my life.

Prayer: Let's repeat the 23rd Psalm today and particularly think of the phrase: 'Yea, though I walk through the valley of the shadow of death, I will fear no evil'.

FEBRUARY 9   **ISAIAH 50:6 – MARK 14:65**
ISAIAH 53:3 – JOHN 1:11; 5:43
ISAIAH 53:4,5 – MATTHEW 8:16-17

GOD THE FATHER KEEPS HIS WORD

Family project: I hope you are looking up the scriptures and getting excited about God's wonderful word.

Jean: Once I spoke in a public school for girls. Afterwards, the headmistress announced I would stay longer to talk with any who might have questions. Several girls came into the lounge where I waited.

A dark-haired, vivacious girl asked, 'Do you really believe God has a plan for this old world? Is there any future? It seems to me everything is pretty much out of control. I can't see anything ahead except self-destruction'.

I replied, 'I surely do. Jesus will return and reign on this earth. It is all prophesied right here'. I pointed to my Bible.

'Can you count on prophecy about the return of Jesus Christ?' she asked.

I explained how the prophecies concerning the first coming of Jesus were fulfilled so completely, I had little reason to doubt God's promises of his return should be inaccurate. Then I proceeded to give her some of the very verses you are reading this week. She was deeply touched. Suddenly she said 'I'm convinced Jesus Christ is my Messiah. I am a Jewess and I want to believe in him.'

Prayer: Thank you, Father, for your promises. I am depending upon your promise to keep me faithful until the coming of the Lord. I trust you for today. Amen.

FEBRUARY 10   ISAIAH 42:7 – MATTHEW 25:62-63
ISAIAH 53:9 – MATTHEW 27:57-60
ISAIAH 53:12 – MATTHEW 27:38

THE KING IS COMING

Family Project: Continue your exploration into prophecy.

Jean: Although separated by more than seven centuries, Isaiah and Matthew were brothers in their vision of Jesus. Both of them saw him as the Kingly Messiah. Isaiah (750 B.C.) had a vision of the enthroned Lord and was called to be a prophet when only a youth. Matthew (4 B.C.) a tax collector, was at work when Jesus called him to be a disciple.

Isaiah had a prophetic picture of the future, mission, titles and characteristics of Christ. Matthew had a witness' vision of the King. He looked back and saw the suffering Messiah who was victorious on the cross.

From where we are in history, we can have both the prophetic and witness vision. We can look back to Calvary and say by faith, 'There is my King'. We can look ahead into the future and say by faith, 'He will return King of Kings'. Best of all we can look up and, by faith, see him enthroned at the Father's right hand.

Just think! Your faith can span centuries. It can reach into eternity. Surely you can have faith for today.

Prayer: Yes, Father we will reign today, victorious in the name of Jesus Christ the King. Hallelujah!

FEBRUARY 11   MICAH 5:2 – MATTHEW 2:1
ZECHARIAH 11:12-13 – MATTHEW 26:15; 27:6,7
ZECHARIAH 12:10 – JOHN 19:34

JESUS OUR REDEEMER CAME
AS THE FATHER PROMISED

Family project: Today is our last day of prophetic readings.

Jean: The Bible is an amazing book. It is the very Word of God.

A missionary friend of mine lived in a remote village high in the mountains of Chile. She was alone one day in prayer when she heard a footstep behind her. There stood a tall young stranger.

'What is it?' she asked, not sure if he was friend or foe.

The youth told her that his father, a chief in another village, was very sick, dying. 'Bring your God and come with me'.

The missionary picked up her Bible and for several days she followed the youth many miles into territory she had not been in before. When they arrived she was told the chief had died three days before.

'Take your God and make him live' she was ordered.

She sat beside the chief and began to read Isaiah 53 over and over, prayerfully. Suddenly the man's eyes opened. He coughed. He was alive. When he spoke, he said to her, 'I have waited years to know the meaning of those words. I heard them in my heart when I was a boy. Now tell me their meaning.'

Through her teaching from the translated Scriptures and his healing, many villagers came to know Christ.

Don't forget: Take God's Word with you wherever you go. Do you have a pocket sized Bible or a New Testament? You may need it soon to tell someone about your God.

Prayer: We thank you Lord for your Word. We are thrilled with the prophecies and how they were fulfilled when you redeemed us. Now we wait for the prophecies of the future to be fulfilled. We have faith in you. In Jesus' name, Amen.

FEBRUARY 12 JOHN 8:43-47

REDEMPTION: GOD'S ANSWER TO THE SATAN PROBLEM

'Why is my language not clear to you? Because you are unable to hear what I say. You belong to your father, the devil, and you want to carry out your father's desire. He was a murderer from the beginning, not holding to the truth, for there is no truth in him. When he lies, he speaks his native language, for he is a liar and the father of lies. Yet because I tell the truth, you do not believe me! Can any of you prove me guilty of sin? If I am telling the truth, why don't you believe me? He who belongs to God hears what God says. The reason you do not hear is that you do not belong to God'.

Jean: These words of Jesus seem harsh. The truth can be hard to listen to. Actually the best friend is one who says it like it is, whether we want to hear it or not.

Jesus was speaking to hypocrites. They said one thing, but meant another. They had been arguing with Jesus for hours, pretending to believe, trying to trick him with clever questions. Jesus told them their attitudes were of the devil, who is a liar and a murderer. They were slaves to deceit.

Ever noticed how one lie leads to another? Lies are a net we get tangled up in. Once we start to lie, it gets harder to tell the truth. The Good News is that Jesus condemns lying, but not the liar. He can set liars free.

Ask yourself: Am I caught in a net of lies? Is the habit of lying growing in me? Do honest people make me angry?

Prayer: Dear Father, help me to accept the truth and to admit when I act more like the devil than like you. Keep me free by your Truth in my heart. In Jesus' name I pray, Amen.

FEBRUARY 13   JOHN 12:27-32

GOD WILL GET YOU THROUGH YOUR HOUR OF TRIAL

'Now my heart is troubled, and what shall I say? Father, save me from this hour? No, it was for this very reason I came to this hour. Father, glorify your name! Then a voice came from heaven, "I have glorified it, and will glorify it again". The crowd that was there and heard it said it had thundered; others said an angel had spoken to him. Jesus said, "This voice was for your benefit, not mine. Now is the time for judgement on this world; now the prince of this world will be driven out. But I, when I am lifted from the earth, will draw all men to myself." '

Elmer: Have you ever been in a tight spot where you prayed, 'God, get me out of this!'?

That is not what Jesus was saying. He wasn't trying to avoid what was about to happen, but asked, 'Help me to come safely through this hour'. Jesus knew he would soon be dying on the cross. He would take the judgement of all human sin upon himself. Satan would be defeated, driven out and deposed from usurped authority over this world. This world would not become his, though he had claimed to be the Prince of this world. He would have to yield to the crucified King.

God loved his Son, but he also loved the world of lost sinners. His love overpowered the prince of this world and defeated his forces. Satan had to recognise the victory of Jesus, the King.

Remember: Remember when you asked the Lord to help you out of a tight spot? Did he take you around it, or through it? One thing is sure, he didn't forsake you. Give him thanks.

Prayer: Dear God, we are grateful that as a family you are able to take us safely through the hours that are hard for us to face. Thank you. Amen.

THE SOLUTION TO GUILT

'For all have sinned and come short of the glory of God'.

LaDonna: Only recently I discovered the sentence continued '. . . and are freely justified by his grace through the redemption that came by Christ Jesus'.

When confronted with such an absolute, we like to remind God that there are greater sinners and lesser ones. God may seem unreasonable and unloving.

Yet in the same scripture he passes sentence, he declares pardon through Christ. Through God's justice all men become equal sinners and are given an equal chance for salvation. Entrance into heaven will be the same for all because everyone will have found grace through the same Redeemer. No one need miss out on the gift of God, even if he feels his sin is worse than others.

Remember: Don't let guilt of yesterday's failures – whether great or small – rob you of the joy of living in God's grace today. No matter how dark your sin is, God's forgiveness is greater.

Prayer: Dear Lord, thank you for your unlimited grace. Christ's sacrifice covers all our sins. Thank you I need not fear further punishment for sin. Take all my sins and cleanse me completely. In Jesus' name, Amen.

REDEMPTION: GOD'S ANSWER TO THE THE SIN PROBLEM

'Here is a trustworthy saying that deserves full acceptance: Christ Jesus came into the world to save sinners – of whom I am the worst'.

Alan: What's this? Paul, an apostle, pioneer, leader in the early church and writer of inspired scripture saying he is the worst of sinners! Is this false modesty or phony humility? I think it is an honest definition of us all!

We are all lost sinners. We can't change that fact ourselves, but Jesus can. Praise God that he has! He gave up his divine relationship in heaven with his Father to live on this earth and to die for us. Thus he paid the price of our redemption. So, when we feel guilty and want to somehow pay for our sins . . . remember the price has been paid in full. We have been bought back from the power of sin. In eternity we shall share with Jesus a perfect relationship with the Father. This is something he desires us to have. But we will have it, not by our own works, but by his grace.

Try this: Read 1 Timothy 1:15 out loud. Point to yourself and say, 'I am the worst of sinners'. Then declare: 'The worst thing is to be a sinner, but the best thing is to be a sinner saved by grace'.

Prayer: Thank you, Lord, that we are saved by faith and called to a holy life. I claim your grace today to live that life. Amen.

FEBRUARY 16   JOHN 8:34-36

GOD'S ANSWER TO THE SIN PROBLEM

'Jesus replied, "I tell you the truth, everyone who sins is a slave to sin. Now a slave has no permanent place in the family, but a son belongs to it for ever. So if the Son sets you free, you will be free indeed."'

Jean: Have you ever tried talking to someone about their need to believe in Jesus Christ for salvation? I have and here are some of the responses. 'I'm okay . . . I've got my own kind of religion.' 'My father was a vicar . . . Grandfather was a bishop!' 'Christian? Why, of course, I'm British!' I'm sure you can recall more.

In our Bible reading, the Jews were saying very much the same thing to Jesus. They counted on Abraham's righteousness to get them by. They also tried the old 'I'm as good as . . . probably better than' trick.

Satan rejoices when people say things like that. He has them fooled into thinking they are free from a sinful nature. It is sin to leave God out, assert our will, follow our own inclinations, and to please ourselves. When sin becomes a habit, we become slaves.

Question: In which direction should we look in order to see whether we are free from, or a slave to, sin? Backwards, towards our godly relatives? Remember, God has no grandsons! Should we be comparing ourselves with others – or looking to our Saviour?

Prayer: Father, we do not compare ourselves with saints or sinners, but with our Saviour. When we hold our hearts up to Calvary, we see that we need your forgiveness and salvation. In Jesus' name, Amen.

FEBRUARY 17   EPHESIANS 1:3-6

OUR HEAVENLY PLACE OF VICTORY

'Praise be to the God and Father of our Lord Jesus Christ, who has blessed us in the heavenly realms with every spiritual blessing in Christ. For he chose us in him before the creation of the world to be holy and blameless in his sight. In love he pre-destined us to be adopted as his sons through Jesus Christ in
accordance with his pleasure and will – to the praise of his glorious grace, which he has freely given us in the One he loves.'

Jean: I saw on a church bulletin board, 'Some people are so heavenly minded, they are of no earthly good!' I'd like to put it an opposite way. 'Some people are so earthly minded, they have no heavenly power'.

As believers, we need to raise our faith heavenwards and see our place with the Victor who has won the battle for us. We need to move into our seat of power and exercise a higher level of prayer. God has given us throne rights with his Son. How? By redemption! It wasn't cheap. Sin could not be set aside lightly. A sacrifice was required. Blood was shed for our release and for sin's defeat. Jesus fought the battle on earth so that we might share the victory in heaven. Let us praise God for the power in the blood of Jesus. Let us be seated in heavenly places with Christ Jesus. (2:6)

Let's declare: (and sing if you know the chorus.) 'We are heirs of the Father, we are joint-heirs with the Son. We are children of the kingdom. We are family, we are one'.

Prayer: Father, today let us be people who are so heavenly minded (or believing), that we can be of the greatest good on earth. Amen.

FEBRUARY 18
1 JOHN 3:4-5;
MATTHEW 22:35-37

THE LAW OF LOVE

'Everyone who sins breaks the law; in fact, sin is lawlessness. But you know that he appeared so that he might take away our sins. And in him is no sin'.
'. . . An expert in the law, tested him with this question: "Teacher, which is the greatest commandment in the Law?" Jesus replied: "Love the Lord your God with all your heart and with all your soul and with all your mind."'

Jean: We all complain about too many rules and regulations to follow. Why bother? The Old Testament Jews felt that way, too. Nothing but rules, rules and more rules! Not that the rules were bad. The Law was good, but no one was good enough to keep it.

That is exactly why God made the Law! It was his way of showing us that we are lawless. All of us are rule-breakers at heart and as such can never please God.

So what was the answer: no law? Imagine what kind of society we would have without God's laws! The answer was Jesus. He came not to destroy but to fulfill all the law. When we accept him as our Saviour he represents us at the throne of God . . . like a lawyer. Because of Jesus, we are forgiven. Then God writes upon our hearts the greatest law of all. 'Love the Lord your God with all your heart'. Do this, and you've done it all!

Discuss: This week we have looked at God's answer to the sin and Satan problem. His answer is redemption. Talk together about our Redeemer a few minutes before you pray.

Prayer: We love you, Lord. Thank you for writing your law upon our hearts. It is so much easier to obey you because we love you rather than because we fear you. Amen.

FEBRUARY 19   GENESIS 2:8-9; 3:6

GOD'S ANSWER TO MAN'S IRRESPONSIBILITY

'Now the Lord God had planted a garden in the east, in Eden; and there he put the man he had formed. And the Lord God made all kinds of trees grow out of the ground — trees that were pleasing to the eye and good for food. In the middle of the garden were the tree of life and the tree of the knowledge of good and evil'.

'When the woman saw that the fruit of the tree was good for food and pleasing to the eye, and also desirable for gaining wisdom, she took some and ate it. She also gave some to her husband, who was with her, and he ate it'.

Jean: Responsibility is a God-like characteristic. God was responsible for man. He planned and provided for his environment, giving man all he required to meet his physical, emotional and intellectual needs. Man was responsible. He worked as a gardener in Eden. He cared for his wife, and governed his environment. Woman shared equal responsibility with her husband.

However, when woman disobeyed God's commandment and involved her husband, they were guilty of extreme irresponsibility. Their sin changed their relationship to God, but did not release them from their responsibility to God, to each other, to their environment and fellow creatures. What changed were the conditions in which they had to live. Now there were thorns, sweat, toil, pain and sorrow.

But God, like a father, disciplined and punished their sin, covered their nudity, barred their way from the tree of life and gave them a model — a redemption model. The shedding of blood would be their ongoing means of forgiveness of sin.

Discuss: What are the responsibilities of different members of your family? Do they differ? What is irresponsibility?

Prayer: Father, help us to be a responsible family to one another, to our neighbours and most of all, to you. In Jesus' name, Amen.

FEBRUARY 20   PROVERBS 28:13

TAKING RESPONSIBILITY FOR OUR SINS

'He who conceals his sins does not prosper, but whoever confesses and renounces them finds mercy'.

Jean: Man and woman discovered in Eden when they sought to hide their sins, they hid themselves from God. From the beginning, human history has been a saga of 'cover-up's'.

As long as a smiling face of false piety hides evil within the heart, God is not allowed to forgive. God calls not the self-righteous to repentance, but those who will take responsibility and openly admit to their faults. Solomon declared when we confess and forsake our sins we will prosper.

It has also been said that we learn little from our successes, much from our failures. Through failure we gain valuable experience to help us in the future.

We can only profit from our sins as we recognise that they exist. Then, if we confess our sins openly, we make it possible for others to forgive us, as well as God. If we keep our sins secret and unconfessed, we hinder ourselves, and those around us from entering into the joy of reconciliation. Remember, we Christians cannot claim to be perfect, but can claim to be forgiven.

Thought: When we are responsible and confess our sins, God is responsible and forgives us. Let us also take the responsibility of forgiving others.

Prayer: Dear Father, help me to be honest with myself, with others and most of all with you. I know you will show me where I fail. You will also help me to admit it, if need be, to others. In Jesus' name, Amen.

FAITH TO LIVE RESPONSIBLY

*'So whatever you believe about these things keep between
yourself and God. Blessed is the man who does not condemn
himself by what he approves. But the man who has doubts is
condemned if he eats, because his eating is not from faith and
everything that does not come from faith is sin'.*

LaDonna: In travelling around the world with my family in
ministry, I have become aware of how standards differ from
place to place. One person may look over the rim of his beer
glass condemning your make-up, while elsewhere pious
teetotallers will approve the same.

The key to God's code of ethics is revealed in verse twenty-
three. 'Everything that does not come from faith is sin'. God is
not merely concerned with outward actions. He searches every
aspect of our convictions asking, 'Where is faith?' Are we confident God approves of our conduct? Is our life a moment by
moment relationship with the Father? When we cease to be
motivated by our responsibility and love to God, we are falling
into sin. If we call, God comes alongside to lift us out of our
unfaithfulness.

Project: Offer God your daily plans and he will show you what
you can do in faith; what he can bless.

Prayer: Lord, I offer you today all my plans – great and small.
Show me the things that are not blessed with your approval, and
that are void of faith. Show me what you approve and help me
to step forth in faith and joy. Amen.

WRATH EXPRESSED IN PAIN

*'Let no one deceive you with empty words, for because of such
things God's wrath comes on those who are disobedient'.*

Alan: God's wrath was expressed through the Son's agony on the cross. It was as though God cried out to, not against, the disobedient 'No! Please don't hurt me or yourself any more'. In the Old Testament God saw his beautiful creation corrupted by the evil boasting of man's empty words. He said he was sorry he made man. But God's intense sorrow and anger did not destroy man. Instead the Creator made himself responsible for man's redemption.

How can we alleviate his sorrow when we disobey him? We must admit to God and to ourselves that we have hurt both him, and his Son. We must not deceive ourselves nor allow others to deceive us. We need the cross where Jesus took God's anger against our sin.

Question: Anger needs to be expressed. How do you express yours? Can we learn from the example of God's wrath? How can we be honest without hurting, and offending others?

Prayer: Thank you, Lord, for loving me so much. Thank you for not giving up on me in anger, but drawing me to your Son. I don't want to hurt you, or myself or others, by my selfishness. Teach me how to love. Amen.

FEBRUARY 23   **1 JOHN 1:8-10**

LET'S BE RESPONSIBLE!

'If we claim to be without sin, we deceive ourselves and the truth is not in us. If we confess our sins, he is faithful and just and will forgive us our sins and purify us from all unrighteousness. If we claim we have not sinned, we make him out to be a liar and his word has no place in our lives'.

Jean: Do you know someone who is always getting hurt? Someone who goes silent when he is upset, who grunts 'Good morning', or 'Thanks', but not much more. Ever noticed how the family tiptoes around him? Before long, they start paying for all the tension with indigestion, migraines and arguments. Suddenly, it's all over! Somehow the family knows he's not mad any more. His strange behaviour is undiscussed, unconfessed. As if it didn't happen. Such conduct is dishonest and sinful.

God does not play games with us, and we can't play games with him. He is concerned about the quality of our lives. Good quality living means openness, honesty and confession. Poor quality living is secretiveness, dishonesty and a refusal to confess. We have a responsibility to own up when we are failing to live the life. Someone has said, 'What we cover up, we're left with; what we open up receives the revealing and the healing of God'.

Discussion: How do you handle unconfessed sin in your family? Do you hide it; pretend it hasn't happened; confess it; forgive it? How many times?

Prayer: Father, make us a good quality Christian family, open, honest and sincere. Cause us to help each other when we fail to accept reality and say 'I did it', so we can say to each other, 'Forget it'. In Jesus' name, Amen.

FEBRUARY 24   JAMES 1:13-14; 4:17

TEMPTATION AND SIN

'When tempted, no one should say, "God is tempting me".
For God cannot be tempted by evil, nor does he tempt anyone,
but each one is tempted when, by his own evil desire, he is
dragged away and enticed'.
'Anyone, then, who knows the good he ought to do and doesn't
do it, sins'.

Jean: There are tests, trials and temptations in every life. God tests us, life tries us and the devil tempts us. We have tests because we are God's children; we have trials because we are human; we have temptations because there is a devil who knows we are human. Nevertheless, we have triumphs because God knows we are human and that we are the children of his Kingdom. When God tests us, he uncovers our weaknesses in order to develop our character. When the devil tempts us, he uncovers our weaknesses in order to destroy our character.

Development, or destruction? We decide which it will be by taking responsibility for our desires, avoiding enticement and nipping sin in the bud — before it grows too big for us to handle.

Ask yourself: Is there an evil desire growing in me which if allowed to become full-grown would destroy my character and other's?

Prayer: Dear Father, help me to pass your tests, bear my trials, but please deliver me from the Tempter. In Jesus' name, Amen.

FEBRUARY 25   LUKE 15:21-22

GOD'S ANSWER TO MAN'S IRRESPONSIBILITY

'The son said to him "Father, I have sinned against heaven and against you. I sam no longer worthy to be called your son." But the father said to his servants, "Quick! Bring the best robe and put it on him. Put a ring on his finger and sandals on his feet".'

Jean: There are seven steps downwards for the irresponsible person. The prodigal son took them all. Here they are: Self-will (v.12); Selfishness (v.13); Separation (v.13); Sensuality (v.14); Self-affliction (v.15); Self-abasement (v.16); Starvation (v.17).

There are seven steps upwards for those who will take responsibility for their restoration: Realisation (v.17); Resolution (v.18); Repentance (v.19); Return (v.20); Reconciliation (v.20); Re-clothing (v.22); Rejoicing (v.23-24).

What a story! From ruin to reconciliation. God's wonderful love places a ring of reconciliation on the finger of everyone who decides to take responsibility for his sin and come to God for forgiveness. Redemption is God getting back what he had lost.

A quick Bible search: Take your Bible and follow the seven downward steps of the irresponsible son. Read each verse aloud. Now follow his seven steps back home.

Prayer: Father, thank you for your loving heart towards us. Today we wear the robe of your forgiveness and the ring of reconciliation. We are rich, we are loved, we are home. Praise God. Amen.

REDEMPTION: GOD'S ANSWER TO SEPARATION

*'You must not eat from the tree of the knowledge of good and
evil, for when you eat of it you will surely die'.*
*'Then the man and his wife heard the sound of the Lord God
as he was walking in the garden in the cool of the day, and
they hid from the Lord God among the trees of the garden.
But the Lord God called to the man, "Where are you?"'*

Jean: When I was a child, my mother set limits as to where I
went to play and how long I stayed. Now and then an odd thing
would happen. When I was beyond my boundaries of time and
space, I'd hear my mother's voice call clearly, 'Jean, Jean! It's
time you came home!' I'd run home as fast as I could, fearing a
scolding. Instead, mother seemed surprised to see me. I would
ask, 'Didn't you call me?'

She'd smile and say, 'No, but it was time I did'.

God set limits for man and woman in the garden of Eden.
Although they didn't understand the reason for those limits,
they were expected to obey them. Their obedience would be the
best way for them to show their trust in their heavenly Father's
wisdom and love. But they did not obey and went beyond the
limits. Afterwards, they felt guilty and were afraid of God.
Although they tried to hide, God came and called 'Where are
you?' Sin had separated them from God, but sin could not
separate God from them.

Discussion: Talk together about the different limitations each
of you has to accept. Do you trust the one who has made them?
Do you understand the reason for all of them? Are you free to
disobey those who have authority over you?

Prayer: Father, we thank you for your love which will not
allow us to run free and be hurt. Help us to trust those whom
you have set around us. May the limitations we set others always
be prompted by love. Amen.

NO FEAR OF DEATH

'Since the children have flesh and blood, he too shared in their humanity so that by his death he might destroy him who holds the power of death − that is, the devil − and free those who all their lives were held in slavery by their fear of death'.

Elmer: When Jesus breathed his last breath on the cross and said, 'Father into your hands I commend my spirit', the devil must have thought it was all over. But it wasn't . . . it had only just begun. A whole new era of spiritual dynamics began. By his death, he put down the control of the devil over death. By his resurrection he brought in a new age of spiritual blessing to the whole world. We may now accept God's blessing, realising that Satan's work in our lives is destroyed.

There are many to whom these verses in Hebrews speak. They are people who have lived all their lives with the fear of dying. It actually is fear of the unknown. If you are one of these people, fear no more. Final victory over the one who held the power of, death has been accomplished. Christ's redemptive work on the cross has done it. We can look with great hope to the future . . . here and hereafter.

Project: If you have a copy of Jean's book 'Heaven here I come' in your home, I suggest it would be a blessing to all if your family read chapter four. It tells the remarkable story of her mother's experience with death. It will make heaven very real.

Prayer: Dear God, thank you for taking the fear of death away. I know that when death comes, I will see Jesus. I will know complete joy. So I look forward to that time with peaceful faith. In Jesus' name, Amen.

HOW GOD FACED THE SIN PROBLEM

'But the gift is not like the trespass. For if the many died by the trespass of the one man, how much more did God's grace

and the gift that came by the grace of the one man, Jesus
Christ, overflow to the many! Again, the gift of God is not
like the result of the one man's sin: The judgement followed
one sin and brought condemnation, but the gift brought
justification. For if, by the trespass of the one man, death
reigned through that one man, how much more will those who
receive God's abundant provision of grace and of the gift or
righteousness reign in life through the one man Jesus Christ'.

LaDonna: Some claim to be right with God because they
belong to the church congregation. But Romans 5 considers
reconciliation an individual matter. God didn't solve our sin
problem by sending a hundred thousand angels to sweep sinners en masse into heaven. No! Sin began with one individual
choice, so God sent one individual – an obedient, faithful,
sacrificial Son – who was Jesus Christ.

'God so loved the world' . . . he didn't send a committee!
Through Christ, God reaches towards man. Jesus, one solitary
individual, touched people one at a time, listened to one at a
time. God touches each of us in the same way. He desires an individual response.

Comment: Do you feel treated as if you were a digit?
Remember, God knows and cares for you personally.

Prayer: Lord, it is wonderful to know that you understand how
I feel. Thank you for accepting me as I am, and help me to
understand your personal word to me today. Amen.

FEBRUARY 29   **ROMANS 6:20-23**

ONE JOB – ONE BOSS

'When you were slaves to sin you were free from the control
of righteousness. What benefit did you reap at that time from
the things you are now ashamed of? Those things result in
death! But now that you have been set free from sin and have
become slaves to God, the benefit you reap leads to holiness,
and the result is eternal life. For the wages of sin is death, but
the gift of God is eternal life in Jesus Christ our Lord'.

51

Alan: Some people try to hold down two jobs. It's called 'Moon-lighting'. It can be done, but not well and not for long!

Nor does it work too well for anyone to try and serve God and the devil. That is why the Bible calls us to renounce sin. Instead, we are to take on full-time employment under God's management. Such a switch may be more practical than expected.

A person employed in a business that has questionable policies or a shady reputation may well find that he is not free to be as honest as he would like to be. His knowledge of the truth may force him to quit such employment. In the struggle to win earth's prizes and places, we dare not temporize with sin. Even if man doesn't observe, God does. As Christians, our greatest incentive to live clean and straight lives is grace. But we are free to choose whom we will serve.

Sin pays a wage. On the other hand, God gives a gift — eternal life through Jesus Christ our Lord.

Think it over: Today's reading is more for the adults in the family and for those who are planning their careers. Try to make the choices which will be compatible with the truth as you know it from God's Word.

Prayer: Father, we are your love-slaves. By your grace we want our whole lives to be full-time employment under your management. In Jesus' name, Amen.

MARCH 1   **EPHESIANS 2:1-5**

AMAZING GRACE

'As for you, you were dead in your transgressions and sins, in which you used to live when you followed the ways of this world and of the ruler of the kingdom of the air, the spirit who is now at work in those who are disobedient. But because of his great love for us, God who is rich in mercy, made us alive with Christ even when we were dead in transgressions — it is by grace you have been saved'.

Jean: When we were in our twenties, Elmer and I were missionaries in the small interior town of Santiago, Panama. We lived with the Gonzalez family . . . mom, dad and ten children. Their house was our church and the Gonzalez family most of our congregation. Curious townspeople would crowd around the doorways and windows to listen. Mrs Gonzalez, a pleasant, plump, good-looking woman with a powerful voice would stand in her doorway, pointing over the dirt road to a tumbled-down mud hut.

'Look! That is where we used to live. We thought we were living, but we were dead in sin's darkness. Then, we heard about Jesus. He forgave us our sins. Now we are alive! Once we had nothing. My husband was lazy. But now God has given him ambition'.

She would smile at her husband with loving pride as her voice rose. 'See! We're living with Jesus in our hearts and home!'

Mrs Gonzalez' words are the best illustration of what the apostle Paul wrote: 'You were dead . . . you used to live . . . like the rest . . . BUT GOD . . . made you alive . . . it is by grace you have been saved'.

Sing together: Amazing grace, how sweet the sound, etc. First verse only.

Prayer: Sing the melody of Amazing Grace, only this time sing these words: 'Praise God, praise God, praise God' through to the end. Amen!

MARCH 2   EZEKIEL 18:19-20

NOT GUILTY

'Yet you ask, "Why does the son not share the guilt of his father?" Since the son has done what is just and right and has been careful to keep all my decrees, he will surely live. The soul who sins is the one who will die. The son will not share the guilt of the father, nor will the father share the guilt of the son. The righteousness of the righteous man will be credited to him, and the wickedness of the wicked will be charged against him'.

Jean: Guilt is a terrible burden for any adult to carry, much less a child. When a parent places guilt upon a child he is crippling his future development. Words like 'You'll never amount to anything – you're just like your father' are most destructive to a child's self-image.

No parents are perfect, whether they be Christian or non-Christian. Good parents often want to live out their unfulfilled dreams in their children. Over-done, that causes a child to feel guilty if they fail. Some thrust upon their children the guilt they feel about their, or others', past sins. Guilt can go on for generations propagating fear of suicide, mental illness or sickness. God does not do this. 'The son will not share the guilt of the father, nor will the father . . . the guilt of his son' (Read vv.21-23).

It is surprising how sometimes a lily will grow up out of a garbage heap. Just as strange, is how now and then an honest civic leader will emerge from a family with a long criminal record; a scholar from illiterates; a missionary from atheists!

Parents: God treats us all as individuals with special destinies hidden within. Start your children out with a light heart. Embrace them, lay your hands on their heads and bless them.

Prayer: Father, today we claim your pardon for us and your power to release us from the guilt of our fathers' sins. Help us to train our children to turn easily from sin and live free from guilt. Amen.

MARCH 3   **JAMES 5:20**

WE ALL NEED A LITTLE HELP SOMETIMES

'Remember this: Whoever turns a sinner away from his error will save him from death and cover over a multitude of sins'.

Jean: Yesterday we read that our heavenly Father is pleased when a person turns from sin and lives. He has no pleasure in the death of the sinner.

Often it is hard to turn from deception even when we see the dangerous consequences. A rabbit hypnotised by a snake will stay rigid when otherwise he would flee. Something has to break the spell, make the move or make a sound which releases the victim.

Our Bible verse is like a P.S. on the end of James' letter. He has written about the prayer of faith saving the sick, the power of Elijah's prayer which closed and opened heaven, and then he adds: 'Oh yes Brother, if any one of you goes wrong and gets caught under a spell of lies (my paraphrase!) and someone makes the effort to tell him the truth and doesn't go around saying "Look at what so-and-so did", that person has saved his friend from being wiped out by the enemy'.

Let's think about it: If there is someone you know who has strayed into a dangerous deception, don't tell everybody about it. That person may want to turn and run from it, but can't. Pray for them first. Then perhaps you should go and speak the truth in love.

Prayer: Lord God, your Word says love covers a multitude of sins. May we be good 'cover' for those who have strayed into error. In Jesus' name, Amen.

MARCH 4   **GENESIS 3:21; 4:4; 8:21a**

THE ELEMENTS OF ATONEMENT

'The Lord God made garments of skin for Adam and his wife and clothed them'.
'But Abel brought fat portions from some of the firstborn of his flock. The Lord looked with favour on Abel and his offering'.
'The Lord smelled the pleasing aroma and said in his heart: "Never again will I curse the ground because of man. . ."'

Jean: (excerpts from my book 'Life in the Overlap') 'Was there no healing for the sin-sick pair? Did not God say something, do something to reveal mercy in the judgement he pronounced? Was there no covering to protect the exposed couple? . . . Yes! . . . Somewhere in the garden something was slain; blood was shed to provide a covering for the two sinners. God himself provided the sacrifice and supplied the covering . . .

55

Altars appear in the very next chapter of human history, where the acceptable sacrifice was Abel's firstling of the flock. Adam's son with his offering was the first to say, 'Have faith. God has made a way for man to come back forgiven. It is by the blood of the Lamb. Noah shared more of God's plan with man ... He built his altar to the Lord and made a blood offering. God made his covenant with Noah unforgettable by setting a rainbow in the clouds.'

Suggestion: My book 'Life in the Overlap', is a study on the great themes we are discovering in our daily readings. It may be of interest at some stage to read chapter four, 'How God Got Into The Overlap'.

Prayer: Thank you, Father, that we have restored fellowship with you by the blood of the Lamb. Thank you for your family plan of redemption which included our family. Amen.

MARCH 5   **HEBREWS 11:8-10**

ABRAHAM'S ALTARS

'*By faith Abraham, when called to go to a place he would later receive as his inheritance, obeyed and went, even though he did not know where he was going. By faith he made his home in the promised land like a stranger in a foreign country; he lived in tents, as did Isaac and Jacob, who were heirs with him of the same promise. For he was looking forward to the city with foundations, whose architect and builder is God*'.

Elmer: Abraham's altars became monuments to his faith. By faith he went out from his own country, not knowing where he was going; by faith he made his home in a foreign land, lived in tents and looked forward to see a city built by God; by faith he became a father in his old age. Afterwards, when faced with his greatest test — to build an altar upon which to offer his son — he proved he loved God more than even the life of his own son. God honoured Abraham's faith.

How was this amazing faith sustained? It was kept alive by his altars. Through sacrificing by faith he became father of the faithful. Obedience, unselfishness, benevolence, uncorruptibility and mighty faith were all blessings God bestowed on a man who built his altars and made his sacrifices. Abraham knew nothing of atonement, but by faith he continued the blood-line which had begun in Eden – a line which would reach to Calvary.

Think about it: Your sacrifices and your faithfulness to the Lord will not only sustain your own faith and your family's, but all those who are blood-brothers and sisters with you will be blessed. For we are one in the new covenant sealed with the blood of the Lamb of God.

Prayer: Help us today, dear Father, to see how important it is for us to be faithful in our prayers. Help us to make whatever sacrifices you want us to make in order that we might be a blessing to others. Amen.

MARCH 6   HEBREWS 9:28

CHRIST, THE SIN BEARER

'So Christ was sacrificed once to take away the sins of many people; and he will appear a second time, not to bear sin, but to bring salvation to those who are waiting for him'.

Jean: Some of the most exciting stories have been written around the theme of the secret love letter, documents with intimidating evidence, photos or IOU notes. Usually there is a villain who holds the dreadful evidence of scandal, debt or crime. Then there is the poor victim who has a life-long fear of being found out. What anguish he suffers, until the hero comes. He is able to seize and destroy the damning evidence – and win the favour of the formerly distressed victim!

Once there was a pile of evidence against the human race. The devil, man's accuser, constantly harassed man with condemnation. Man was threatened with the knowledge of his sin. At the same time the Holy Spirit would not let up his constant, conviction upon hearts. When there seemed no way out . . . Jesus came. He took the world's sins, carrying them to the cross. Then he discharged the debts. Paid them off by his blood. He gathered all the IOU's and evidence of man's guilty past and destroyed it all.

Will our sins come back to us with demands for payment when Jesus returns? No. All he'll bring are the final touches of his priceless gift of love to us – our salvation.

Remember: If you feel guilty over sins you have confessed, just tell the devil to go. You're cleared. Send him to the Judge, who is your Saviour.

Prayer: Father, Jesus your Son is all in all to me. Without him I would be in constant fear of judgement. Thank you for setting me free. Amen.

MARCH 7   ROMANS 4:7-8

REDEMPTION ACCOMPLISHED THROUGH THE ATONEMENT

'Blessed are they whose transgressions are forgiven, whose sins are covered. Blessed is the man whose sin the Lord will never count against him'.

Alan: There is a difference between transgression and sin. A transgressor is one who comes up to a marked limit and deliberately goes beyond it. A sinner is one who by nature is unable to make the mark of acceptance. He cannot please God in his own moral strength, and is often ignorant of the demands of righteousness. So to transgress is to be guilty by a deliberate decision of the will, and to sin is to be guilty by the lack of will to even try to seek God or please him.

Both attitudes produce much unhappiness. Our record of what we do and what we are can be changed by the Lord. That does not mean that he has said: 'Oh, forget it . . . it was nothing'. No, sin had to be judged and punished. Jesus took the judgement and the punishment for us. So now God can pardon us when we put our trust in the Lord. It has been said, 'God is not forgetful . . . he CHOOSES to forget our sins and to remember our faith in his Son'.

Question: Are you happy, because your sins are forgiven? Say so to each other.

Prayer: Father, help us to resist the temptation to step over the line. We thank you for a new nature so that we do not want to sin. For this we are happy. Thank you, Amen.

MARCH 8   **JOHN 1:29**

REDEMPTION ACCOMPLISHED BY
THE REDEEMER

'The next day John saw Jesus coming towards him and said, "Look, the Lamb of God, who takes away the sin of the world!"'

LaDonna: When Alan and I walk down the street, or watch TV, he will see things I completely overlook. Only one man noticed the arrival of Christ at the beginning of his public ministry: John the Baptist, at the River Jordan. At waters of baptism for the repentance of sins. John cried: 'Look! The Lamb of God who takes away the sin of the world'. His heart had been prepared. He saw the Saviour. No doubt many glanced Jesus' direction in response to the prophet's cry. But who could perceive this man would die not only for their sin, but for the sins of the whole world? It would take a lot more looking to see that.

Remember: The Saviour is present in all your circumstances. Don't overlook him nor underestimate him. Let him redeem every part of your life. Take another look at Jesus. He can mean much more to you.

Prayer: Lord, let me see you in the things I do today. Help me to allow you to be the Lamb of God, Redeemer and Saviour of every part of my life. Amen.

MARCH 9   **HEBREWS 10:11-14**

BE SEATED!

'Day after day every priest stands and performs his religious duties; again and again he offers the same sacrifices, which can never take away sins. But when this priest had offered for all time one sacrifice for sins, he sat down at the right hand of God. Since that time he waits for his enemies to be made his footstool, because by one sacrifice he has made perfect for ever those who are being made holy'.

Jean: 'Man's work is from sun to sun; woman's work is never done'. I suppose we all of us feel that way sometimes. We're always glad for a chance to take a break and sit down.

The Old Testament priests must have felt like that once in a while. Their job was to accept the sacrifices people brought, prepare those sacrifices for the altar, offer them to God and perform the appropriate ceremonies for each one. Although the priests took their duties by turn, they must have become very tired. But they couldn't sit down . . . there were no chairs in the tabernacle.

'This priest . . . sat down'. Jesus, our great high priest offered his blood upon the cross, his altar, and when he finished, sat down at the right hand of God in heaven. Why did he sit down? There was no further need for sacrifice. His was the last, the perfect sacrifice. He forgives all who come to God by him, and will keep doing this until his intercession days are over and he will return as king.

Discussion: St Paul says we are seated with Christ Jesus in heavenly places (Ephesians 2:6). What do you think that means in the light of our reading today?

Prayer: Father, help me to stop working so hard to make up for

my wrongs. It is tiresome, trusting in my own righteousness.
Forgive me. For Jesus' sake. Amen.

MARCH 10   **EXODUS 12:3,11**

GETTING READY FOR A JOURNEY

*'Tell the whole community of Israel that on the tenth day of
this month, each man is to take a lamb for his family, one for
each household.'*
*'This is how you are to eat it: with your cloak tucked into your
belt, your sandals on your feet and your staff in your hand.
Eat it in haste; it is the Lord's Passover'.*

Jean: There was great commotion the night of the Passover. The
children were so curious. They overheard their parents whispering with the neighbours about how much lamb was needed. They
counted over and over again how many were in each family.
When the children started asking questions, they were sent on errands to gather wood and find herbs. Mothers had washed
everything and had packed. The lamb was slaughtered and
cooked. Bread was baked. The children were told to get their
coats and sandals on and to stand up while they were eating! It
was more mysterious when they saw the men painting the door-
sides and tops with the blood of the lamb.
  'Why are you doing that, father?'
  Mother hushed them. 'It's the Lord's Passover. That's all we
can say now. We'll tell you more later'.
  To this day, Jewish parents tell their children how Israel was
saved by the blood of the lamb. It is the Exodus Story.

Fathers: God said each man was to take a lamb for his family.
You can appropriate the shed blood of Christ for your family's
salvation by faith.

Family project: Someday soon, why not get together as a
family and dramatize the night of the Passover (From Exodus
12:1-50).

Prayer: Dear Lamb of God, we receive the power of your blood by faith for the salvation of our family. Thank you, Father, for Jesus. Amen.

HOW TO MAKE AN ALTAR

'Make an altar of earth for me and sacrifice on it your burnt offerings and fellowship offerings, your sheep and goats and your cattle. Wherever I cause my name to be honoured, I will come to you and bless you. If you make an altar of stones for me, do not build it with dressed stones, for you will defile it if you use a tool on it. And do not go up to my altar on steps, lest your nakedness be exposed on it'.

Jean: A new convert was told by his pastor that he should have a family altar in his home. Some days later he returned to say he had looked everywhere, but couldn't find one in any furniture store in town!

Every family needs an easy-to-get-at place where everyone can pray. It can be around the kitchen table, or by the bed, or in the lounge, but a place in the home where all the family can take a few minutes (with this book, I hope!) to share, read and pray.

The altar is for God. He wants a place where his name is honoured, a place to come and bless you. It should be an altar of sacrifice. You'll have to sacrifice the best time; give of yourself and your heart to God. It is to be a place of fellowship offerings, or peace offerings. There needs to be time to talk things over prayerfully and to forgive one another. The Catholics said it well: 'The family that prays together stays together!'

Family fellowship: Why not draw a picture of an altar made with stones. Make them big so you can put words in them. Name the 'stones' you think are needed to make a permanent place of prayer in your home, like 'love', etc.

Prayer: Father, we would rather have a family altar in our home than family idols. We welcome you to come and bless us. We honour your name here. Amen.

LIFE IN THE BLOOD

'For the life of a creature is in the blood, and I have given it to you to make atonement for yourselves on the altar; it is the blood that makes atonement for one's life'.

Elmer: The question is often asked, 'Why did God demand the shedding of blood for the remission of sins?' Our verse today answers the question. 'The life of a creature is in the blood . . .'

Isaiah wrote (Isa. 53:12), 'He has poured out his life unto death'.

In Old Testament times the life blood of bulls, goats, sheep and doves was shed as an atonement for sin. The word atonement means to cover. So, the blood was a cover for man's sin. When the offering was made the life of the animal covered the guilt of the sinner. That is why John the Baptist prophesied when he saw Jesus, 'Behold, the Lamb of God who takes away the sins of the whole world'. When Jesus cried out from the cross, 'Father, into your hands I commend my spirit', he was pouring out the most precious commodity the earth had ever known . . . his life-giving blood. It was poured out in perfect love. When we accept it for cleansing from our sins, we receive eternal life.

Question: Have you ever heard someone say as they pray, 'I plead the blood of Jesus'? Now you know they meant they were counting on the power of his life, which was in his blood.

Prayer: Father, today we live in the power of the life Jesus gave for us. Amen.

REDEMPTION THROUGH THE ATONEMENT

'We all, like sheep, have gone astray, each of us has turned to his own way; and the Lord has laid on him the iniquity of us all'.

LaDonna: Scotland is one of my favourite places. I was a teenager when I first visited the North of Scotland with friends. Flocks of sheep on the purple slopes ribbed by thousands of narrow sheep paths, brought certain metaphors of scripture to life. Such as, 'All we, like sheep, have gone astray'. Overlapping paths criss-cross the highlands. Sheep have determined to abandon the well-worn paths to seek their very own patch of green grass. Often their pursuit from one tasty patch to another has isolated them on a perilous cliff edge. There, they have no sense of direction. Often there is no path to follow back. Then the hills echo with their bleating.

Like sheep, human beings quite often abandoned God's ways to pursue their own desires. They isolate themselves from those who follow God. Some, try a lifetime to get back to where they were. They cannot do it.

Through Christ everyone who has gone astray can have a new beginning. On his shoulders he will carry us away from our old life and give us a new start.

Listen: Don't waste time trying to retrace all the wrong turns and mistakes you've made. Simply submit them all to Christ and take the greatest gift he offers us – a new start.

Prayer: Father, wash away all of yesterday's willful mistakes. I receive your forgiveness and a new beginning for today. Amen.

MARCH 14   1 CORINTHIANS 5:7-8

A NEW BATCH OF DOUGH

'Get rid of the old yeast that you may be a new batch without yeast – as you really are. For Christ, our Passover Lamb, has been sacrificed. Therefore let us keep the festival, not with the old yeast, the yeast of malice and wickedness, but with bread without yeast, the bread of sincerity and truth'.

Alan: Before I came to Christ I had a lot of negative emotions working inside of me; self-defence, anger, aggression. My barbed-wire behaviour was my way of keeping people from the part of me that hurt. The day I was saved, that action stopped spreading inside of me and started to recede.

I'm still yielding my defences up to the Lord. I'm discovering my real self. Now I am like new dough, free of active malice and wickedness. Sincerity and truth have come to stay.

The more confident we become in our new relationship with God, the less we need to struggle with the old self. God wants us to be like plain unleavened dough — sincere and true. That is the life of the Holy Spirit in us. When we accept Christ, our Passover Lamb, then we can be what we really are . . . a new batch of dough!

Try this: Make some unleavened bread . . . that's bread with no yeast. See how simple it is and remember God wants us to be simply sincere and true. Let the children try making some bread.

Prayer: Father, your word says to get rid of the old yeast — the things that are churning inside. I know Jesus can do this for me. Change me inside and take away the anger, the need to fight . . . and heal me where I'm hurting. Amen.

MARCH 15   **1 CORINTHIANS 6:19-20**

TOO GOOD FOR THAT

'Do you not know that your body is a temple of the Holy Spirit, who is in you, whom you have received from God? You are not your own; you were bought at a price. Therefore honour God with your body'.

Jean: A young American Christian was invited by her non-Christian friends to a party. She was a very popular girl who enjoyed fun. This party would be different, though . . . There were plans to tell their parents they'd be one place, when in fact they would be at another, and there would also be lots of drink and probably pot. When she heard this she said, 'Sorry, I'm made for something better than that!'

Her remark may have sounded a bit super-spiritual, but was it? It seems to me that she refused to sell herself cheap. She knew her value. She was so precious to God; he bought her salvation with the blood of Jesus. She knew her worth. She had a look at Calvary. She not only knew her value. She knew that she was the temple of the Holy Spirit. She had a precious gift from God and she didn't want to lose him. So she honoured God by keeping her body free from that which would grieve the Holy Spirit and cause her to lose her self-esteem.

Fathers and mothers: Your children are to be nourished and developed as future men and women of God. Pray they will soon be filled with the Spirit.

Children: Since your body belongs to the Holy Spirit and you are a very valuable person to God, you'll want to take good care of yourself, won't you? Keep this in mind the next time you are tempted to do things that would be harmful to your body.

Prayer: Father, you have shown us how valuable we are to you by the cross of Jesus. Help us to realise we are too precious to be wasted by those things which harm both body and soul. Thank you for the Holy Spirit. In Jesus' name, Amen.

MARCH 16   **EPHESIANS 5:1-2**

LIVE A LIFE OF LOVE

'Be imitators of God, therefore, as dearly loved children and live a life of love, just as Christ loved us and gave himself up for us as a fragrant offering and sacrifice to God'.

Jean: Paul, the apostle, called believers to not only be followers of God, but imitators of God.

Those of us who have become children of God, by his grace, are by constant practice to become more like the heavenly Father. If we're going to imitate God, then we will have to live a life of love. Our love is to answer his love. Jesus gave up his life for us. That is easy enough to accept, but giving up our lives for others is not so acceptable. Does that mean we should die for each other? It means not holding back our lives, ourselves, from being available. It means being helpful, lovable, touchable. Live and love and let yourself be used up. That's what it means. Give your life up and practice being like Jesus.

Who needs you? Is someone asking for your help, time, friendship? Won't you give some of yourself away – today? Love makes you last longer.

Prayer: Lord God, fountain of love, let your love flow through me. Help me to take time to listen, to give my attention to those who need me. Teach me Lord, to love in deed and in spirit. Amen.

MARCH 17   **1 PETER 1:18-19**

PILGRIMS PASSING THROUGH

'For you know that it was not with perishable things such as silver or gold that you were redeemed from the empty way of life handed down to you from your forefathers, but with the precious blood of Christ, a lamb without blemish or defect'.

Jean: Last week we've noticed the importance of a family altar; the significance of the blood sacrifices in the Old Testament; to appreciate Jesus our Lamb who can change us on the inside. We have realised our bodies are valuable temples of the Holy Spirit because of the atonement, and that we are to give up our lives for others since Christ gave up his for us. What a lot in one week!

To finish off this week, let's notice how St Peter reminds us to live as pilgrims in this world. Neither things nor people have redeemed us. So let us not become too dependent upon earthly things or relationships. These make us want our heaven here on earth. Live with heaven in view. Then you won't mind if you're not rich or don't have influential contacts in this world. If you do have them, by the grace of God, then don't hold on too tightly. Keep a light touch on them. Use things and love people . . . not the other way around. Christians should always be just a little homesick for heaven.

Discuss: Talk together a bit about heaven. What do you think heaven will be like? Where is it?

Prayer: Father, thank you for all you have given us in this world. But we know heaven is better than this. Let us celebrate your love today by living with heaven in our hearts. Amen.

MARCH 18   MARK 10:45

THE MAN WHO CAME TO SERVE

'For even the Son of Man did not come to be served, but to serve, and to give his life as a ransom for many'.

Jean: The Son of Man came to serve. He was a life-giver. He made a commitment to us and expressed it by his ministry, his mission and the relationship he established with us. Jesus exemplified the real meaning of ministry. He served, instead of asking to be served, and said that his followers were to do the same. He made himself approachable and available to men. Yet it was not a hit and miss affair; he had a mission and goal, and each day's serving took him closer to it. Every act of love was part of the major purpose of his coming. He was here to redeem us and he would have to give his life to accomplish it. So as he went his way to the cross he healed all who were oppressed.

He demonstrated the kind of relationship he wanted us to have with the Father. He had come because the Father had sent him. We are to be obedient, also. He also demonstrated servanthood. He was born to serve. But he couldn't do it alone. He drew around him followers who would learn by their relationship with him to love the Father, one another and to be servants of the Lord. We learn to serve the Lord by serving together.

Parents: Your parenthood is servanthood. Under God you can make a commitment to your children to serve them; to complete the goals you have set yourselves for their sakes; to develop your relationship with them in such a way that they will love you, each other and their heavenly Father.

Prayer: Father, help us today to see that the little things we do

68

and the people we touch today are part of the larger mission of love you have given us − to live our whole lives as your faithful servants. Amen.

MARCH 19   LUKE 19:5-10

THE SEEKER

'When Jesus reached the spot, he looked up and said to him, "Zacchaeus, come down immediately. I must stay at your house today." So he came down at once and welcomed him gladly. All the people saw this and began to mutter, "He has gone to be the guest of a sinner". But Zacchaeus stood up and said to the Lord, "Look, Lord! Here and now I give half of my possessions to the poor, and if I have cheated anybody out of anything, I will pay back four times the amount". Jesus said to him, "Today salvation has come to this house, because this man, too, is a son of Abraham. For the Son of Man came to seek and to save what was lost"'.

Elmer: It seems that tax collectors have never been well-liked. The ancient Roman system of tax collecting tended to make thieves of the officials. The people had placed Zacchaeus in a little stereo-typed box of prejudice. Jesus looked up and saw the very kind of person he was sent to find . . . the lost.

The great difference between Jesus' message and that of the religions of the East is the identity of the 'seeker'. In Eastern religions man is the seeker; seeking a better way, another step further in philosophy. They are forever seeking, never finding, always asking, never discovering the answer. In the Christian religion, God is the seeker. God comes seeking man.

Consider this: Let's think of people we know who for some reason are like Zacchaeus . . . disliked because of their job, colour, where they live or how they speak. Jesus seeks them through us. Try to show them a little personal attention, today.

Prayer: Thank you, Father, for sending Jesus to find the lost. Be the invited guest in our house, even if it means we have to do some things differently. In Jesus' name, Amen.

REVELATION KNOWLEDGE IS SPIRITUAL LIGHT AND SIGHT

'The true light that gives light to every man was coming into the world'.

LaDonna: 'Identity crisis', 'Low self-image', 'Understanding yourself' are some terms which signal the cries of people desperate to define the meaning of their existence. In an over-populated, over-explored world one of the last frontiers of discovery has become the depths of the human psyche. But the paths of self-investigation often lead to deep, dark chasms of inner meaninglessness, emptiness and loneliness.

Into this kind of darkness the Redeemer descended. He came to people without light, without a reasonable existence. He not only had a lamp to illumine their path; he was Light. He shed light on the significance of man.

When Jesus, the Light, declared that man was made to have a central place in the heart of God, it terrified the men of darkness. They crucified the one who offered this message of human significance. But in his death and resurrection, Christ the Light illuminated the way to God's heart. He fulfilled the promises he gave. Jesus is the light of our life. He is our identification. He gives us understanding of ourselves.

Remember: God himself has a special, tailor-made plan for your life. Look at the cross and the great price paid for your soul. Let the brightness of his love light up your life.

Prayer: Father, thank you for showing me how precious I am to you. Help me to live in the light of your love today. Amen.

HOW TO GET ON GOD'S TEAM

'But now a righteousness from God, apart from law, has been made known to which the Law and the Prophets testify. This righteousness from God comes through faith in Jesus Christ to

all who believe. There is no difference, for all have sinned and fall short of the glory of God, and are justified freely by his grace through the redemption that came by Christ Jesus'.

Alan: When I was eight years old I joined my first and last little league baseball club. It was a lesson in humiliation. I could not hit the ball. Every now and then the coach would throw caution to the winds and allow me up to bat. Every time I would let him down, except on one unforgettable occasion: I managed to hit the ball. I was so surprised I almost forgot to run! It wouldn't have done any good anyway, for I hit the ball straight into the hands of the first base man. I stumbled back to the bench, head bowed under the jeers and the laughter. I never went to bat again.

I'm sure each one of us feels we have somehow failed to become all God requires a man to be. We can't make first base. God feels the hurt of every soul who has tried to please him and failed. That is why he gave his Son . . . so we could be accepted into his family team. Jesus brings us into right standing with a holy God. How is such righteousness obtained? By faith. We have all fallen short . . . missed the ball . . . but Jesus brings us back to win.

Remember: More important than making any ball teams, is accepting Jesus' love and becoming part of the family of God. You can't lose when God is on your side.

Prayer: I thank you dear Jesus that when I throw down the bat of my own self-righteousness, you accept me just as I am and bring me into your family. Help us to demonstrate your love to others who are striking out. In Jesus' name, Amen.

MARCH 22   **1 CORINTHIANS 1:30-31**

LET'S TALK ABOUT JESUS!

'It is because of him that you are in Christ Jesus, who has become for us wisdom from God — that is, our righteousness, holiness and redemption. Therefore, as it is written: "Let him who boasts boast in the Lord".'

Jean: I've sometimes heard kids boasting about their homes, their family car, their possessions . . . like TV games, collections of records, stamps, rocks or insects. Adults boast too, about more or less the same things. Probably not the insects!

St Paul talks about boasting in the Lord. A lot of religious people in his day boasted about their nationality (racists), about their superior knowledge ('know-it-alls'), their family names (snobs), their schools (the old school tie bit), and their mature characters ('I have arrived!'). Well, Paul was not impressed. He said none of that nonsense counts once believers know the Redeemer. Not that Christians never boast anymore. They don't boast about themselves. That's boring, anyway. Now they boast about the Lord. He is their wisdom. There's no one smarter than Jesus! He is their righteousness. No one can be in better standing with God than Jesus. He is their redemption, which makes every believer very humble.

Next time: When someone starts boasting, why don't we start boasting about Jesus!

Prayer: Father, we are so proud of Jesus that it makes us feel ashamed of ourselves for not telling others about him. May the Holy Spirit give us power to witness. In Jesus' name, Amen.

MARCH 23   1 TIMOTHY 2:3-6

GOD WANTS EVERYBODY TO BE SAVED

'This is good, and pleases God our Saviour, who wants all men to be saved and to come to a knowledge of the truth. For there is one God and one mediator between God and men, the man Christ Jesus, who gave himself a ransom for all men – the testimony given in its proper time'.

Jean: When I was a teenager I memorized these verses in the New Converts Class I attended in the church. 'God wants all men to be saved. . .' Those words were the first seeds of my call to take the gospel to the world.

'One mediator between God and men'. How simple. No indirect, complicated system to approach God. Just one name. One crucified saviour with one nail-pierced hand reaching toward sinners while the other reached to his Father to make reconciliation for all who came.

That was my testimony then and it still is. The truth never changes.

Think of it: God wants your friends to be saved. Do you? Have you told them of the Redeemer? Paul writes to Timothy of 'the testimony given in its proper time'. Let us pray for the right time to tell our friends.

Prayer: Father, may the Holy Spirit give his signal inside our hearts when the time is right to tell . . . (you put in the name). Amen.

MARCH 24   **TITUS 2:14**

EAGER TO DO GOOD

> '. . . Who gave himself for us to redeem us from all wickedness and to purify for himself a people that are his very own, eager to do what is good'.

Jean: For what purpose has Jesus redeemed us? Our text gives us three. First: to release us from all wickedness. Wickedness is 'badness'. In James 1.21 it means 'naughtiness'. Second: 'To purify for himself a people who are his very own'. In other words, to form a family. In the AV it says 'a peculiar people'. That doesn't mean odd acting, strange people whose funny ways make others whisper about them. No one wants to belong to a family like that. It means he redeemed us so we could be a clean-living, loving, laughing people. The kind of people Jesus would be glad to call 'my very own'. But that is not all. He redeemed us, set us free from being bad and made us special, so we could do good and enjoy it. Being good is hard for bad people. Being good is not enjoyable for impure people. But the Lord's very own people are eager to do good, and enjoy it!

Talk it over: As part of God's family, living together in your family, are you eager to do good? Chapter three, verse two tells us what that means.

Prayer: Hallelujah, Jesus. We thank the Father you have redeemed us. Now purify us so we can find that doing good comes easy because we are good. In your name, Amen.

MARCH 25   MATTHEW 26:17-18,28,30

OUR PLANS FIT INTO GOD'S APPOINTMENT

'On the first day of the Feast of Unleavened Bread, the disciples came to Jesus and asked, "Where do you want us to make preparations for you to eat the Passover?" He replied, "Go into the city to a certain man and tell him, The Teacher says: My appointed time is near. I am going to celebrate the Passover with my disciples at your house".'
'This is my blood of the covenant, which is poured out for many for the forgiveness of sins'.
'When they had sung a hymn, they went out to the Mount of Olives'.

Jean: The disciples had done it all before: selecting an eating place; shopping for the lamb, herbs, bread; setting the table. For them it would be the Passover, for Jesus it was the Last Supper. The ordinary tasks were part of the extraordinary mission.

Much that we do today, with our limited understanding, blends into the larger unknown plan of God. We look backward, celebrating the past; he looks forward, celebrating the future. We remember what he has done; he anticipates what he will do. As he is in our past, we are in his future. Time and eternity meet at his table.

What everyday tasks he gives us in preparation for eternity. He asks so little . . . 'Go into the city . . . see a certain man' . . . A place, a meal is ours to give. He does so much.

His gift is a covenant, a cup, bread and finally, himself on the cross. His intentions and mine all combine, like a small stream emptying into an ocean, when we are at his table. 'His table'! Lord, make my table yours, my house, your own. You alone know the greater meaning.

Let's sing: 'When they had sung a hymn, they went out'. Jesus sang with his disciples. Choose a hymn about the cross and sing with Jesus.

Prayer: Dear Lord, let us be aware today of how the most simple things we do for you are part of a far grander purpose. Father, we thank you for Jesus in our home. Amen.

MARCH 26   LUKE 9:30-31; 22:42-43; 23:24-25

JESUS CHOSE TO DIE

'Two men, Moses and Elijah, appeared in glorious splendour, talking with Jesus. They spoke about his departure, which he was about to bring to fulfillment at Jerusalem'.
'Father, if you are willing, take this cup from me; yet not my will, but yours be done. An angel from heaven appeared to him and strengthened him'.
'So Pilate decided to grant their demand. He released the man who had been thrown into prison for insurrection and murder, the one they asked for, and surrendered Jesus to their will'.

Elmer: Jesus knew he was born to die. It must have been on his mind most of the time. Not because he was morbid, but because he was on a mission. He was not the victim of circumstances; he was the Victor. Yet, as the son of Man, it would appear that he needed added confirmation and affirmation of the Father's will.

In our reading today we read of his conversation with Moses and Elisha. We do not know the details of the discussion, but we know he talked about 'his departure' (his death). Later, in Gethsemane, a final decision had to be made. 'Father, not my will, but thine be done'.

The very night as angels strengthened him, Pilate surrendered to the will of the mob. Jesus went on to lay down his life and to take it up again. Pilate, according to the historian Eusebius, later committed suicide. Pilate took his life; Jesus gave his.

Let's talk about it: Dying is like taking the slip-road off the motorway. Our road of life gets narrower, but it takes us into another world! Take a minute and name as many beautiful things as you can think of about going to be with Jesus.

Prayer: Father, we thank you for giving Jesus the chance to talk about his death to Moses and Elijah. Thank you for sending the angel to help him — we know you will help us when it is hard for us to understand why we have to die. In Jesus' name, Amen.

MARCH 27   JOHN 3:14-15

REDEMPTION COMPLETED AT THE CROSS

'Just as Moses lifted up the snake in the desert, so the Son of Man must be lifted up, that everyone who believes in him may have eternal life'.

LaDonna: Why did Christ say he had to be lifted up like the brazen serpent in the wilderness? The serpent represented both judgement and salvation. The cross of Christ is likewise the place of judgement and salvation. It has broken Satan's power over us.

All we have to do is look and believe. There is nothing beautiful about the cross. It is the spectre of sin tried and judged. There the bleeding Christ took our sin and our judgement, but salvation requires that we look. God will not honour the pride of man which looks away from sin. But when one looks, one experiences divine love. The power of the cross is Christ dying in man's place. There is complete redemption from the horror of sinful nature. The cross of Christ is horrible, yet powerful, the place where judgement and mercy meet.

Think about it: Have you allowed yourself to see the horror of the cross? Look, identify with sin, with the Saviour and rise redeemed by Christ's salvation.

Prayer: Father, I acknowledge that Christ suffered in my place. I also accept your forgiveness and the daily victory over the power of sin which Christ secured on the cross for me. In Jesus' name, Amen.

MARCH 28   JOHN 14:30

THE CROSS, GOD'S PLUS SIGN

'I will not speak with you much longer, for the prince of this world is coming. He has no hold on me, but the world must

learn that I love the Father and that I do exactly what my Father has commanded me. Come now; let us leave'.

Alan: The cross is God's plus sign. When Jesus died on the cross he gave to this world the Church of the living God and himself as its head. By his death he changed the most negative event in human history into the most positive phenomenon this world has ever witnessed.

Hell rejoiced when Jesus died, for Satan seemed to have won a victory over Christ. He has been pressing for the kill and thought he'd made it. But he had no control over Jesus, the sinless Lamb of God. He didn't take Jesus' life. Jesus gave it willingly to save men from the terror of death. Jesus established his victory over hell and set the prisoners free. Just as it was promised in Eden, he bruised the serpent's head. The powers of darkness thought they had subtracted the Saviour from this world. But the cross added to mankind the Saviour of the world.

A little arithmetic: If you add Jesus, the Cross and yourself, what do you get? Answer: a Christian! What if you subtract Jesus and the Cross from yourself?

Prayer: Father, I praise you for the victory of the cross. Jesus has added so much joy to my life. Help me to multiply it everywhere I go. Amen.

MARCH 29   **ACTS 4:28-31**

GOD'S FORETHOUGHT

'They did what your power and will had decided beforehand should happen. Now, Lord, consider their threats and enable your servants to speak your word with great boldness. Stretch out your hand to heal and perform miraculous signs and wonders through the name of your holy servant Jesus. After they prayed, the place where they were meeting was shaken. And they were all filled with the Holy Spirit and spoke the word of God boldly'.

Jean: This passage takes us right into a first century house-church prayer meeting. The apostles Peter and John had returned from a cross-examination before the Sanhedrin, the supreme court of the Jewish nation. When the people heard the report they started to pray loudly. They did what we often do when we pray. They went back over everything . . . way back, all the way to creation! They told God everything.

Why did they do that? I think it was because they needed to affirm their faith in the continuity of God's powerful will. They knew that nothing had happened just by accident. It was not God's afterthought, but God's forethought. Those praying people seemed to know God's purposes. Ever noticed how much better we understand God's plan and purposes when we pray?

Think it over: Redemption wasn't your idea nor mine. It certainly wasn't the devil's. Whose was it, then?

Prayer: Father help us to talk everything over with you until our faith is released. In Jesus' name, Amen.

MARCH 30   1 CORINTHIANS 1:17-18

THE POWER OF THE CROSS

'For Christ did not send me to baptise, but to preach the gospel – not with words of human wisdom, lest the cross of Christ be emptied of its power. For the message of the cross is foolishness to those who are perishing, but to us who are being saved it is the power of God'.

Jean: I was leading a prayer service in my home church in Toledo, Ohio. In the quietness I heard a voice say softly, 'The cross! The cross! I see it. I see the cross!' Bowed heads lifted to see who spoke. All of us knew the sweet-faced, silver-haired gentleman. We watched as he lifted his hands, tears streaming down his face, his lips trembling as he spoke. 'I knew there was a cross up there near the centre of the altar, somewhere. I couldn't see it, but I just kept praying and believing. Then just now, suddenly it was there. I see it!' He rose to his feet and, as I embraced him, he sobbed with joy. We all wept with him. Our brother who had been completely blind for most of his life could see.

The cross has never lost its power. Its message has to be heard with an ear of faith, and seen with the eyes of faith, as the Holy Spirit reveals it with power. Revelation knowledge produces spiritual sight. Whether blindness is physical or spiritual, the power of God can remove it from those who keep praying.

Have faith: If you have someone in your family who needs a miracle from the Lord, direct them to put their faith in the power of the cross. Then, pray for them.

Prayer: Father, we pray for revelation to be given to those we love who are blind to the meaning of the cross. We love you, crucified Jesus, and we want them to love you too. Amen.

MARCH 31   HEBREWS 13:20-21

FOLLOW THE SHEPHERD

'May the God of peace, who through the blood of the eternal covenant brought back from the dead our Lord Jesus, that great Shepherd of the sheep, equip you with everything good for doing his will, and may he work in us what is pleasing to him, through Jesus Christ, to whom be glory for ever and ever. Amen'.

Jean: The letter to the Hebrews was written to converts who were in constant danger of going back to the old ceremonial observances of Judaism. The writer tried to show them the glory of the gospel of Jesus far outshines the light they had before in the Old Testament. He reminded them of all those men and women of faith who didn't give up, even though they died without seeing the day of grace. He implored the reader to get his eyes on Jesus and not look back. 'Finish the race' he seemed to say. 'Hang in there . . . don't give up, for God has not given up on you. He has made a blood covenant with you and he's not going to break it'.

Finally, after comparing Jesus to prophets, angels and priests,

the writer of Hebrews held Jesus up before those who were in-
clined to stray from truth, as the great Shepherd of the sheep.
That got right down into their Hebrew hearts, for they knew he
had been sent to the lost sheep of Israel.

He has also been sent to us . . . and he is able to keep us by the
blood of the eternal covenant.

In silence think of this: It takes two parties to make a covenant. God is the first party. He is keeping his promise to me. Am
I, the second party, keeping my promise to him? Listen, do you
hear your Shepherd's voice? He has a word to say to you today.

Prayer: Father, I'm trusting the Holy Spirit who brought
Jesus back from the dead to keep me from straying from your
will. Amen.

APRIL 1   2 CORINTHIANS 5:14-15

CHRIST DIED FOR ALL

*'For Christ's love compels us, because we are convinced that
one died for all, and therefore all died. And he died for all,
that those who live should no longer live for themselves but for
him who died for them and was raised again'.*

Jean: My missionary friends had brought me out into the bush
to see how they worked with the nomads of the Australian out-
back. There they were . . . a bunch of Aborigine on walk-about.
Young men and women gathered around the missionaries, the
older ones and mothers with children leaned against the worn
out van. Old men stood warily aside from the rest. They were
half-clothed, dark and dusty, feet bare. There was a mixture of
gentleness and fear in their eyes. None of them smiled. Miles
from nowhere, they had found an oasis of kindness. They
negotiated with the missionaries about their children. They
wanted to leave them with the missionaries. They talked of
some sick folk they had left behind. When some of the women
moved away from the van I saw painted on the side these words,

'Christ died for all'. He died for all; for the Aborigine, for the missionaries, for me.

Consider this: The love of Christ can become a master passion, gripping us with an unshakable conviction that Christ died for all. Such conviction becomes the force that sends men and women to the ends of the earth to tell others the good news. What if such conviction gripped you? Would you allow it to master you?

Prayer: Father, you so loved the world you gave your son. May we be willing to give our dearest loved one, if you should ask, for the sake of those for whom Christ died. Amen.

APRIL 2   PSALM 119:176

STRAY SHEEP

'I have strayed like a lost sheep. Seek your servant, for I have not forgotten your commandments'.

Elmer: Sheep don't get lost intentionally. Absent-minded, intent only upon what is under its nose, a sheep wanders farther and farther away from the flock, unmindful of danger.

People who end up far from their originally intended goals find it hard to explain how they went astray. We are like sheep. Too much attention is placed upon the present and not enough upon the future. Often, we are unaware of the dangers we may encounter when we stray from Christ and his Church. We are exposed to temptations, unexpected calamities, unseen enemies without the protection of praying friends and the close presence of Jesus, our Shepherd.

Shall we allow the delinquency of our nature, the tendancy to go our own way, destroy us? Or shall we ask him who came to seek and to save that which was lost to bring us back to where we belong?

David's prayer was for God to seek him, his servant. He humbled himself before the truth that he could not find his way back. God must bring him back. David remembered God's commandments. The word of the Lord had come to him; it went with him wherever he went. It warned him and gave him hope.

Helplessness is the most sincere form of prayer. Let the Lord bring us back, no matter if we have strayed for a long time or have just begun to draw away.

Question: If I were on my own would I stay true to God and myself?

Prayer: Father, you alone know my heart. Don't leave me to go my own way. Help me to follow you, rather than my own selfish inclinations. I have not forgotten your word. Keep me close to you. In Jesus' name, Amen.

APRIL 3   ROMANS 5:10-11

RECONCILED BY LOVE

'For if, when we were God's enemies, we were reconciled to him through the death of his Son, how much more, having been reconciled, shall we be saved through his life! Not only is this so, but we also rejoice in God through our Lord Jesus Christ, through whom we have now received reconciliation'.

LaDonna: The awful realism and terminology of warfare is thrust upon most of us today. Through the media we are invaded by the reports of violent carnage occurring in other hemispheres. With horror we hear of armies who shoot their deserters.

But there is a war which is seldom reported. Its front line runs through the heart of every individual. Mankind is locked into Satan's opposition against God. In this war's front line, there is a chance to desert the enemy and come over to God's side. Through Christ's death Satan no longer has power to restrain deserters against their wishes or punish them. We are free to choose either side. No line of hostility exists on heaven's side, only a frontier of love. If we accept reconciliation, lay down our arms, and come to God we will be saved from destruction through Christ's life.

Comment: Are there conflicts in your life? As Romans 5:11 says: 'Rejoice in God', because the greatest barrier − the hostility between you and God − can become a frontier of love. Enter into his love today.

Prayer: Father, thank you for your willingness to take the first step of reconciliation. I receive your love and take joy in your complete forgiveness. Amen.

APRIL 4   COLOSSIANS 1:21-22

REDEMPTION RECONCILES

'Once you were alienated from God and were enemies in your minds because of your evil behaviour. But now he has reconciled you by Christ's physical body through death to present you holy in his sight, without blemish and free from accusation'.

Alan: I overheard a youth witnessing to other passengers on an underground train in London. Quietly, but joyfully, he sought to share his new life. He was met with ridicule and bitter hostility. Those who overheard were the most caustic. I don't think their hostility came out of hearing the name 'God', whatever that name may have meant to them. They resented it when the youth spoke of Jesus Christ and his atoning death on the cross.

I was like that myself until I was twenty-four. Although I had teaching in my church as a child, I had not yielded my life to God for forgiveness and cleansing by the blood of Christ. I had no peace with God. My constant hostile reaction to Jesus was my way of protecting myself from guilt. This reaction continued until sorrow for my sins overcame my hostility and brought me to repentance. I turned my heart over to God and through Jesus was reconciled to him.

Discuss: Does hearing about Jesus make you feel happy or hostile inside? Tell others about your feelings.

Prayer: Father, we are glad for the cross where we find peace with you. May we not be afraid to speak your name to others, even when it makes them angry. Amen.

YOU ARE WELCOME!

'Remember that at that time you were separate from Christ, excluded from citizenship in Israel and foreigners to the covenants of the promise, without hope and without God in the world. But now in Christ Jesus you who once were far away have been brought near through the blood of Christ'.

Jean: We stopped to worship in a village church one Sunday morning while on holiday in the country. We chose a back pew. We were a little early. There were no ushers. A few minutes later a happy group of young people came in. It was obvious they were strangers, like us. They looked around and sat in the very front pew which had a door at the end of it. Later an elderly man, obviously an usher, arrived. He saw the young people, hurried up the aisle and spoke in low tones to one of them. Murmuring among themselves, they all filed out of the pew, came down the aisle and sat near us. A portly, well-dressed woman was then ushered down the aisle and with a flourish, a little door was opened for her to sit in her own pew.

The Gentiles were excluded from a lot of privileges the Jews enjoyed in their covenant relationship with God, until Jesus came. When he came to them, they came to each other. Jews and Gentiles became blood brothers through the new covenant of the cross. Their God was no respector of persons.

Draw a picture: Outline a cross so you can write inside of it. Then take the word: 'Reconciliation' and print it down the upright bar. Make sure the 'o' is in the centre where the other bar crosses. Then print on the cross-bar 'Relationships'. Make the 'o' be the same one as the 'o' in reconciliation. Do you see a lesson in this little illustration?

Prayer: Father, help us never to make people feel unwelcome who come to our church or to our house. May we be willing to give up our place for them. Amen.

APRIL 6   2 CORINTHIANS 5:19

A NEW MESSAGE

'. . . that God was reconciling the world to himself in Christ,
not counting men's sins against them. And he has committed
to us the message of reconciliation'.

Jean: The message of reconciliation is really the most wonderful news in the world. It is not a message about a lot of rules to follow. It is not a long list of penances. It is not mystical. It is the simple and easy to understand fact that God was in Christ, reconciling the world unto himself. As one little boy put it, 'God sent Jesus to tell us he's not mad at us'. God clears our record. But that is not all!

He gives us a new nature, so that we don't have to do the things that made God sad with us in the first place. Second, he does not hold anything against us to bring up later. Third, he changes us inside so we can keep things straight between him and us.

There are a lot of people who don't know that they can have a relationship with God like that. They think God is angry with them and will never forgive them. Or, even if he did forgive, how could they keep from doing something to make him angry again! We must not keep such good news to ourselves when so many people need to know God loves them and has made a way for them to love him, too.

Talk it over: If God forgives us, is not angry with us and helps us keep a good relationship with him . . . don't you think we should do the same for one another? Why don't you look at one another now and say with a smile, 'I'm not mad at you. I love you' (This is good for grown-ups too!).

Prayer: God, you are so good. It makes my heart sing with joy. I'm not angry with you, either. Why should I be? Thank you, Jesus, for enabling me to help others to love you. Amen.

BY HIS WOUNDS YOU HAVE BEEN HEALED

'He himself bore our sins in his body on the tree, so that we might die to sins and live for righteousness; by his wounds you have been healed. For you were like sheep going astray, but now you have returned to the Shepherd and Overseer of your souls'.

Jean: This passage reminds us of the fifty-third chapter of Isaiah. The punishment that brought us peace was upon him, and by his wounds we are healed.

Isaiah believed by looking forward to the cross. Peter believed by looking back at the cross. Both of them saw the Innocent One who died for the guilty and was the great Physician. As he suffered for our sins, he also suffered for our sicknesses.

Peter knew Jesus could heal. Had he not healed him of his back-sliding, when his heart was broken? He had seen Jesus heal many of physical illnesses, too. Peter would never forget the joy of the crippled man who was healed the day he and John stopped to speak to him at the Gate Beautiful. Nor would he ever understand the grace of God who gave people so much faith that as he, Peter, walked by, they were healed.

Above all, Isaiah and Peter saw Jesus as the great Shepherd who watches over us. He cares for those he heals.

Prayer for the sick: Today, if there are any sick in the family, take a few moments to pray for one another. In Jesus' name be made whole.

THE YEAR OF LIBERATION

'The Spirit of the Sovereign Lord is on me, because the Lord has anointed me to preach good news to the poor. He has sent me to bind up the broken-hearted, to proclaim freedom for the captives and release for the prisoners, to proclaim the year of the Lord's favour and the day of vengeance of our God, to comfort all who mourn'.

Jean: The Year of Jubilee! Once in fifty years slaves in Israel were released, debtors were freed and a general restitution took place (Leviticus 25:8-16). The bondage of years was broken for those who had sold themselves in order to pay off debts, and for those who had been born into slavery. It was a once-in-a-lifetime chance to be free. The prophet foresaw the Liberator, the one who would some day bring spiritual liberty.

Centuries later in his home town, Jesus actually stood in his church and read the very words Isaiah wrote. When he finished he said, 'Today this scripture is fulfilled in your hearing!'

There are three things a person who wants to be free should remember. First, he has to make the decision to accept his freedom. Second, he has to walk out of his slavery and live the new life. Third, he has to allow time for development in his new freedom. It doesn't all happen at once. Decision, departure and development. Remember, it was the YEAR of Jubilee.

Reflect on this: If someone you know has broken away from a former life of unhappiness after being in bondage for years, give them time to heal, and to adjust to a new way of living. Let us be tolerant and understanding of those who seem slow in developing Christian attitudes.

Prayer: Father, let this be a year of liberation for those we know who have been hurt, broken and bruised. Help us to be patient so that healing may be deep and complete. In Jesus' name, Amen.

APRIL 9   LUKE 13:16

THIS WOMAN OUGHT TO BE HEALED

'Then should not this woman, a daughter of Abraham, whom Satan has kept bound for eighteen long years, be set free on the Sabbath day from what bound her?'

Elmer: Jesus called the devout Jewess a daughter of Abraham. He saw her as a covenant woman. As such she had a right to be set free from her bondage, for Jesus said Satan had bound her. In Matthew 15:26, Jesus said healing belonged to the Jews; it was 'the children's bread'.

Although she had been crippled for eighteen years, she was eligible for a miracle. Bowed over, at the back of the women's court, she was visible to the compassionate eyes of Jesus. Neither her age, sex, nor the length of time she had been crippled could hinder his love. When Jesus called her to come forward to the rostrum where the teachers were seated, he saw a daughter of Abraham . . . a covenant woman. God's covenant is everlasting. Time, age and circumstances cannot alter God's word. We are children of the kingdom, under the new covenant of his shed blood. We too are called of the Lord to be liberated from the intrusion of Satan's power.

Think of it: Next time you go to church ask the Lord to show you someone who is bowed over because of their affliction. The Lord can give you spiritual discernment. You can go and bring them to the Lord, who delivers from the bondage of Satan.

Prayer: Father, thank you that you set the captives free. Help us to be sensitive to those who are in bondage, and bring them the good news of liberty to the captives. In Jesus' name, Amen.

APRIL 10   **JOHN 8:34**

REDEMPTION RELEASES THE CAPTIVE

'Jesus replied, "I tell you the truth, everyone who sins is a slave to sin"'.

LaDonna: Freedom was the cry of the 'Flower People' and the hippies in the drug culture in the sixties and early seventies. Around then I journeyed to Afghanistan with a Youth With a Mission team in search of hippies who would receive Christ's love. We found them suffering from malnutrition, hepatitis and various regional diseases in dingy, dirty hotels. They boasted that they were 'free' — free to stagger from one drug-induced experience to another.

Christ faced a similar challenge with first century Jewish

culture, as we see from John 8. He challenged people who boasted of their great heritage, ancestry and tradition – and ignored the fact that they were under Roman occupying forces. Freedom under tyranny! Christ pointed to the sin factor. If they sinned, they were slaves. If they did not sin, they were free.

The fact that when we do not want to sin, we do, proves our slavery to sin. Only one who is free can set another free. That One is Christ. He breaks our bondage.

Take stock: Acknowledge your unwanted habits and wrong behaviour traits. Submit them to the Lord, do what he tells you to do about them, and watch him set you free.

Prayer: Lord, release me from the present bondages in my life, and show me how they can become things of the past. Amen.

APRIL 11   ACTS 10:38

THE CURE FOR OPPRESSION

'. . . *God anointed Jesus of Nazareth with the Holy Spirit and power, and how he went around doing good and healing all who were under the power of the devil, because God was with him*'.

Alan: When Jesus walked this earth, injustice, cruelty, poverty, religious bigotry and political graft were rife. He saw the people were not only oppressed by Rome, but by Satan.

There are many problems today of the same order. The greatest, however, are those caused by Satanic power. Oppression makes people feel ill and sad. Their frustration is like someone walking into a small room with an extremely low ceiling, so low and so small that all one can do is sit or crawl. When one is oppressed, he doesn't think straight. The lasting cure for oppression, whatever its cause, is not a new job, or a change in government, or industrial action, but a touch from the anointed Jesus. He will do you lasting good. When he delivers from oppression, he releases you to think and act with deep-down, joyous faith. He changes you so that you can change the circumstances.

Today. If you or someone you know is oppressed, seek some spiritual help. Prayer can change things, and it can change you.

Prayer: Dear Father, let us see the spiritual causes of oppression. Thank you that we need not walk in bondage. Amen.

APRIL 12   **ROMANS 6:11-14**

THE SUM TOTAL IS VICTORY

> *'In the same way, count yourselves dead to sin but alive to God in Christ Jesus. Therefore do not let sin reign in your mortal body so that you obey its evil desires. Do not offer the parts of your body to sin, as instruments of wickedness, but rather offer yourselves to God, as those who have been brought from death to life; and offer the parts of your body to him as instruments of righteousness. For sin shall not be your master, because you are not under law, but under grace'.*

Jean: Let's take stock today of where we stand with the Lord. An accountant determines the exact state of his accounts and from these accounts, the condition of his business. Let's add up what we are in Christ. We are 'dead to sin', we are 'alive to God'; free from the mastery of sin and free to offer ourselves to God. Add these up and the sum is a victorious Christian life. 'Dead to sin' means identification with Christ at the cross. He died for our sins, so we are dead to sin. 'Alive to God' means identification with the risen Lord. Because he is alive, so are we. We are free to offer to the Lord our body, soul and spirit. Our bodies are the temple of the Holy Spirit, full of praise and worship.

A young man decided to be a missionary. His friends reminded him of the dangers he faced in the place he planned to go, dangers such that he might lose his life. He replied, 'I died when I decided to go'.

Discuss it: What did the young man mean by those words? Was such an attitude a loss or a gain for him? How does your life add up?

Prayer: Dear Lord, we look at your cross and say 'For me to live is Christ, and to die is gain'. Amen.

APRIL 13   COLOSSIANS 1:13-14

THE STORY OF THE PRINCE OF PEACE

'For he has rescued us from the dominion of darkness and brought us into the kingdom of the Son he loves, in whom we have redemption, the forgiveness of sins'.

Jean: Long ago the Kingdom of Darkness was ruled by an undefeated evil ruler, Satan. The whole human race was in blind darkness. They could not see their sad surroundings nor their ugly master.

But Father God, with his All Seeing Eyes, saw them and observed their cruel slavery. His All Hearing Ears heard the cries of broken hearts as they struggled under heavy burdens. Finally, God's All Loving Heart was so deeply touched, he sent his dear Son to rescue them.

The Prince bravely fought enemy forces all the way to the Kingdom of Darkness. A few companions who started to follow him gave up and fled. One of them betrayed him to the enemy. The Prince was nailed to a cross where he hung helpless, and soon died. When he was buried behind a big stone in a cave, all the rulers of The Darkness shrieked with glee. The blind inhabitants drew back into their darkness. A fearful, heavy silence hung over the land.

Suddenly, the Prince of Peace reappeared! He gathered up those who had hoped against hope for a rescue. Before the Evil One knew what was happening, he swept them out of reach and took them into his Father's Kingdom. The Prince was exalted to be King and Lord over all.

To this day, the Father God still sends heralds and soldiers into the Kingdom of Darkness. They fight back the evil powers, and get through to the inhabitants to tell them of the Prince's victory over Satan. Someday the King himself will return, when the last battle will be fought. A shout will fill the earth . . .'Long live the King. Hallelujah!'.

Try this: Make a banner and pretend you are a herald or a soldier for the King. Mother or Dad will help you. You can paint on it crosses or crowns. I'm sure you have some good ideas.

Prayer: Let's shout aloud in unison Revelation 11:15!

APRIL 14   PSALM 23:4,6

FOR THE OLDER CHILDREN OR SENIOR SAINTS

'Even though I walk through the valley of the shadow of death, I will fear no evil, for you are with me; your rod and your staff, they comfort me'.
'Surely goodness and love will follow me all the days of my life, and I will dwell in the house of the Lord for ever'.

Jean: A psychiatrist said, 'I have never seen a case of senile psychosis in the aged when they have faith in God and are free from the fear of death and are active'.

The fear of death is usually wrapped up in the fear of old age. Such fears, when surrendered into the hands of God, can release faith for an exciting adventure in old age and in death.

Inner fears cannot be concealed. They show. Pretending they are not there is like putting make-up on wrinkled cheeks. Are your fears showing through your attempts to hide or ignore them? Get alone with the Lord and say, 'Dear God, you have promised to deliver those who fear death and are subject to bondage. I will be in fear of old age unless you deliver me. I surrender this inner torment for you to take away. I believe it is now gone. Thank you'.

To the rest of the family: Today, make some Senior Saint feel beautiful and needed.

Prayer: Father, as a family we thank you for those who have shared their love and faith with us over the years. Please God, may we give back to them something of what they have given us. May we all live free from fear. Amen.

WHERE ARE YOUR ACCUSERS?

'Who is he that condemns? Christ Jesus, who died – more than that, who was raised to life – is at the right hand of God and is also interceding for us'.

Jean: God has already ruled in our favour! No matter how guilty you or I may feel, the fact is we are pardoned. The Lord's forgiveness covers all our past and future sins. The case is closed. It's hard to believe, because we know we've sinned. How could the record be changed?

Jesus our Advocate has pleaded for us and won the case. He took the punishment for our sins. His death met the requirements of the Righteous Judge. How can we be sure?

By his resurrection. It is proof that his death was enough to clear our record. Not only is Jesus Victor over the judgement on our sins, but he is exalted on the throne and there pleads for us. The Holy Spirit echoes his intercession in our hearts.

So, who is there to condemn us? The devil? His accusations are silenced by the Victor. Who else condemns us? We ourselves, most of the time. Every time we speak against ourselves we grieve the heart of him who intercedes for us in heaven. Start telling the accuser within yourself, 'Silence! Jesus has won the case for me. I'm forgiven. Go see my lawyer!'.

Let's declare right now: 'Not guilty!' Say it to yourself and to one another. Go ahead, it will do you good.

Children: You may like to act out a court scene. Choose a guilty prisoner, a judge, a prosecutor (the one who says the prisoner is guilty) and a defender. Everybody else can be spectators in the court. Try the prisoner. When the judge pronounces him 'Not guilty', applaud and hug the prisoner. Thank the defender, and ignore the prosecutor!

Prayer: Father, we are sometimes harder on ourselves than even you are. Help us to see ourselves from your point of view – forgiven, and free to love. In Jesus' name, Amen.

FOR THOSE WHO ARE BEING SAVED

'*For the message of the cross is foolishness to those who are perishing, but to us who are being saved it is the power of God*'.

Elmer: Someone said, 'I have been saved, I am being saved, I will be saved'. It means that once we enter salvation we are on the way to salvation in salvation! Often salvation is thought of as an experience; something that happened at a certain place and at a specific time. Such an experience is a good starting point, but it is only the beginning. Salvation is not a frozen lake but a flowing river.

It is true that the message of the cross calls for a definite decision, but once that decision is made, it continues to be an unfolding message of God's expanding grace. We are not saved into an eternal state, but into eternal life. God has an infinite plan for his children and all of eternity will reveal it. His inexhaustible provision for us will never run out.

Think of it: Dear friends, today you are being saved. Grace is at work in you, saving you from perishing. The outer, destructive forces which threaten are not greater than his inner power.

An idea for the children: Or maybe for the adults, too! Make a badge or write these letters on a piece of paper: PBPWMGI-NTWMY (Please Be Patient With Me, God Is Not Through With Me Yet!) Place this where you can see it and others, too.

Prayer: Father, I thank you that when I was saved you did not leave me on my own. Thank you that my life flows within the river of eternal life forever. In Jesus' name, Amen.

FREED FROM THE WORLD'S STANDARDS

'*May I never boast except in the cross of our Lord Jesus Christ, through which the world has been crucified to me, and I to the world*'.

LaDonna: Introductions can be awkward, unsettling experiences. 'What was your surname again?' 'What do you do?' 'Are you married?' I used to find myself longing for a really 'significant' personal achievement that would justify my presence in this world and would identify me. After working through numerous projects seeking to achieve, I stopped, disheartened and exhausted.

The Lord in his compassion spoke to me. 'You don't have to "do" anything to be significant. YOU ARE SIGNIFICANT. The whole of your existence – tasks great and small – is graced with the touch of my significance.'

What peace that brought. His significance made me significant. The demands of those around me became irrelevant. The world with its demands has been crucified to me. Its transitory awards, its false and changing values could never give me the permanent significance I desired. I now have a new value standard: the cross of Christ.

How do you assess yourself? By the standards of the world; status, financial success, personal achievement? Competition will increase and challenge you. Let God's love give you priceless value. Then watch as your whole life takes on a new meaningfulness.

Project: Make it stick. Write out the words 'YOU ARE SIGNIFICANT', add a cross (+) and sellotape it where you can see it.

Prayer: Father, thank you that I mean something to you. My life is worth more to you than treasure. You give me worth and significance. I praise you for this. Amen.

APRIL 18   2 CORINTHIANS 5:17

SOMETHING NEW FOR SOMETHING OLD

'Therefore, if anyone is in Christ, he is a new creation; the old has gone, the new has come!'

Alan: Much of the housing in today's London is a legacy of its Victorian past. Some of it is beautiful and well-kept; other parts are in varying states of decay or total ruin.

So it is with people and the legacy of their past lives. Some are in good shape, some are frayed and many are in ruin.

Jesus comes into our lives as a master carpenter to make all things new. He has a perfect plan for each 'property' he has purchased by his blood shed on the cross. The price was steep, but we're paid for in full! Construction commences, according to the blueprint for a temple; a temple of the Holy Spirit. God hasn't promised a face-lift, he makes something completely new out of something old, worn-out and decayed – something beautiful.

Comment: The Lord as master carpenter, makes the plans that best suit him. Have we the right to tell the Lord what he should be doing in our lives, and how he should be doing it?

Prayer: Master Carpenter, build me anew! Help me to be submissive to the new creation you are making of me. Show me those areas not yet yielded to your plans, so that construction may not be held up. Amen.

APRIL 19   **2 CORINTHIANS 4:16**

THE INNER SECRET

'Therefore we do not lose heart. Though outwardly we are wasting away, yet inwardly we are being renewed day by day'.

Jean: St Paul knew the secret of spiritual power. He faced tremendous pressures but did not faint. The constant onslaught wore down his physical strength. Yet, the inner life grew stronger. He lived life on two levels at once. While he talked with people, he talked with God. When he walked with his friends, he walked with God . . . He was being renewed all the time. His secret? A day by day communion with God. A strong Christian life by the year, month or week is an impossibility. I'm sure we can identify with Paul when he speaks of troubles, but can we agree with him that they are light and momentary?

He kept them light by daily casting his care on the Lord. That is day by day renewal.

For the children: Make up seven heaps of books, toys, anything. Line them up a couple of feet apart. Then one of you go along and pick up these heaps . . . one, two, three, four . . . through to the end. What a load! Then, another stack them up again. This time go along from one heap to another with someone walking beside you. Take each load and pass it over to the other person. The other person can take it out of sight. This is an illustration of how heavy our burden gets unless we unload it day by day.

Prayer: Father, thank you that we have Jesus the Burden-bearer travelling with us all the time. Help us as a family not to let problems accumulate in our lives. In Jesus' name, Amen.

APRIL 20   **1 PETER 1:23**

BORN AGAIN!

'For you have been born again, not of perishable seed, but of imperishable, through the living and enduring word of God'.

Jean: One of the most beautiful songs in Jimmy and Carol Owen's musical 'The Witness', is the song 'Born Again'. The term has been popularized in recent years. Famous people have claimed to be born again. For instance, ex-president Jimmy Carter. Chuck Colson wrote a book called 'Born Again' to tell his personal experience which came out of the Nixon trial. In fact, ex-president Nixon claimed to have been born again! Who should judge, but God? Perhaps he was.

One thing is sure: the Word of God is one of the powers that operate in the new birth experience. The other is the Holy Spirit. The two work together to sustain an on-going regenerated life. To be incorruptible, one must abide in the imperishable living Word of God.

Learn a verse: Memorize our verse for today. It will be good seed to carry in your heart.

Prayer: Dear Father, we will hide your Word in our hearts so that we will not sin against you. Amen.

APRIL 21   **1 JOHN 5:1**

HOW DO I LOVE GOD?

'Everyone who believes that Jesus is the Christ is born of God, and everyone who loves the father loves his child as well'.

Jean: A young man during a pre-marital counselling session said this: 'I can't stand her family. But that doesn't matter. I'm not marrying her family . . . just her'. He was in for a surprise.

When we're born again we're born into God's family. '. . . Everyone who loves the father loves his child as well'. That doesn't mean loving the Child Jesus, but loving the child of God near you who needs you. Our flow of love for God is not simply up towards him, but outwards to one another. How do I love God? By loving you, God's little child.

Let's draw a picture: Draw a smiling face and write below 'Smile!' God loves you and so do I!' Give it to one of God's children today.

Prayer: Father, when I say I love you, may people know it is true by the way I love them. Make our family a loving family. In Jesus' name, Amen.

APRIL 22   **PSALM 32:5-7**

A SONG OF DELIVERANCE

'Then I acknowledged my sin to you and did not cover up my iniquity. I said, "I will confess my transgressions to the Lord" – and you forgave the guilt of my sin. Therefore let everyone who is godly pray to you while you may be found; surely when the mighty waters rise, they will not reach him. You are my hiding place; you will protect me from trouble and surround me with songs of deliverance'.

Jean: One of the most difficult things for us to do is to admit we are wrong. I guess that is why confession of sin is so hard. To confess sin is to know one has failed to do right . . . and to say so to God. Often we know we have failed, but cannot say so to ourselves, much less to God. To accept the reality of sin in one's life is to take a big step towards total well-being. Concealed sin is a devourer. One act of sin can eat away at one's insides for years.

A university student remarked: 'Contact with religion deepens the guilt complex. I think it is unhealthy . . . downright dangerous.' That is true if the contact stops there. But the difference between religion and Christianity is that contact with Christ introduces you to forgiveness. Guilt does breed disease. Forgiveness, especially God's forgiveness, breeds health. When we weep because of sin, let us not weep alone, but before God. He will give us a song of deliverance.

Let's sing: Can you think of a song of deliverance? Make up one of your own. The Holy Spirit will help you, he loves singing!

Prayer: Thank you, Jesus. When I have stopped hiding and have sought you, you have never hidden from me. I'm glad we have this openness with you. Amen.

APRIL 23   **LUKE 5:8-11**

TAKE TIME TO TURN

'When Simon Peter saw this, he fell at Jesus' knees and said, "Go away from me, Lord; I am a sinful man!" For he and all his companions were astonished at the catch of fish they had taken, and so were James and John, the sons of Zebedee, Simon's partners. Then Jesus said to Simon, "Don't be afraid; from now on you will catch men". So they pulled their boats up on shore, left everything and followed him'.

Elmer: Repentance means turning from sin towards God. There can be a considerable time lapse between the first encounter with the Lord and a final decision to turn and follow him. Even the turning and the following may come in stages. Simon Peter's experience was like that. Peter met Jesus when John was baptizing converts in the Jordan River. When he returned to Galilee he was with Jesus for a short time.

But Peter went back to his fishing trade. He may have thought he was through with Jesus, but Jesus was not through with him. Our Lord turned up again in Peter's life when he was at a low ebb. He had fished all night and caught nothing. Peter wanted fish and Jesus gave him fish. It was a miracle. The nets were so full, they broke. So did Peter's heart. In the presence of the miracle he forgot fish and thought of his sins. Jesus wanted Peter to turn from his nets and follow him. And he did. He became a follower of Jesus and a leader of the church. As Jesus predicted, he became a fisher of men.

If we listen, we will hear the Lord speak to us in language we can understand. It may have to do with our work, our family, or our friends. He will cause us to be more concerned about our sins and our commitment to him, than about what seems important to us now.

Discussion: How might God speak to us through daily circumstances?

Prayer: Lord, help us to hear you speaking in our everyday lives. May we turn and follow you and become what your will is for us. Amen.

APRIL 24   **MATTHEW 3:8**

LET'S HAVE THE REAL THING

'Produce fruit in keeping with repentance'.

LaDonna: Christians must beware of mechanical faith. We sometimes act as though we have learned how to switch on faith and manipulate God himself. Spirituality sometimes becomes an equation – 'If I do this, God will do that'.

John the Baptist confronted mechanical faith. The Pharisees came to the water's edge along with the Sadducees garbed in the garments of religious tradition. They were professional manipulators of Scripture. John the Baptist's sharp reply was a rebuke. He demanded, 'Live it. Breathe it. Be it'.

Fruit is the product of a living organism. The Lord does not require a mechanical faith which is easily turned on and off. He asks for humility and reality – the real fruit.

Think about it: Is your faith based on outward actions and equations? Allow yourself to respond to the Lord each day like a living plant which moves and adjusts to changing light.

Prayer: Father, each day is different, always holding surprises. Help me to hear your word in each situation and give me the strength to have a living, growing faith. In Jesus' name, Amen.

APRIL 25   ACTS 2:38-39

REPENTANCE THE FIRST STEP

'Peter replied, "Repent and be baptised, every one of you, in the name of Jesus Christ so that your sins may be forgiven. And you will receive the gift of the Holy Spirit. The promise is for you and your children and for all who are far off – for all whom the Lord our God will call"'.

Alan: People often pray, 'Lord, I've repented of this thing but it keeps coming back. Why can't you take it away?' In frustration the formula St. Peter outlined for us is missed.

Repentance is the first step. We must not stop there, but be cleansed, as in baptism, and rise above it, claiming the promise of forgiveness. Then openly receive the power of the Holy Spirit. Allow him access to work in particular areas of our lives. This formula – repentance, baptism, forgiveness and the gift of the Spirit – begins at conversion and should continue to be appropriated throughout our new life.

Today: Let's look at the one particular thing we want to repent of and follow through these steps to Christ's victory by the power of the Spirit.

Prayer: Lord Jesus, please point out to me today that area in

me which needs your victory. In all things, make me more than
a conqueror. Amen.

APRIL 26 **ACTS 8:22-24**

I WANT TO BUY A MIRACLE

*'Repent of this wickedness and pray to the Lord. Perhaps he
will forgive you for having such a thought in your heart. For
I see that you are full of bitterness and captive to sin. Then
Simon answered, "Pray to the Lord for me so that nothing
you have said may happen to me"'.*

Jean: A little girl went into a chemist's, placed some money on
the counter and said, 'I want to buy a miracle'. 'A miracle?'
asked the chemist. 'What do you mean?' She explained. 'My
little brother is very sick and the doctor said only a miracle
would save him. So I want to buy a miracle'.

God has miracles to give, but none for sale. The power of God
is a gift, but it is not cheap. We can't bargain with God. 'We'll
do this if you do that'. Don't pray for power. There is plenty of
power available. Pray for a heart that is right with God. There
is a cost in Pentecost. It is a broken and contrite heart. Ask
Peter, the man who spoke to Simon in this passage. He would
tell you that miracles flow through a forgiven heart.

Question: Are you hungry for the Holy Spirit's power in your
life? Would you give anything to be used of God? All he wants
is you.

Prayer: Father, we have friends who need your miracle power.
Please help us all to realise that repentance releases the power of
the Holy Spirit. Amen.

APRIL 27 **ROMANS 2:4**

GOODNESS AND GRATITUDE

*'Or do you show contempt for the riches of his kindness,
tolerance and patience, not realising that God's kindness
leads you towards repentance?'*

Jean: I recall an eleven year old girl covered from head to toe with broken, bleeding watery eczema. A kindly neighbour had brought her for prayer. The next time I saw her she was like a different child. Her skin was clear and smooth. I went to see her parents. Her father met me at the door. I asked him if he was pleased about his little girl. 'Yes, but we owe you nothing!' he said. I was embarrassed and said, 'Oh, I didn't come to collect anything. Divine healing is a gift. I just thought . . .' He interrupted. 'Look, it is nice what's happened to her. But we didn't ask for it and we don't want to be obligated'. 'But don't you feel some gratitude to God?' I asked. 'No' he moved to shut the door. 'We don't owe anybody anything'.

It was ten years later when I saw his daughter. She was beautiful. She had not lost her healing. 'I'll never forget what you did for me' she said when she recognised me. 'Oh, but I didn't do it! It was the Lord. Do you ever thank him?' I asked. But her father's ingratitude to God had affected her. She smiled. 'Mrs Darnall, you are the one I'll always be grateful to'.

God's goodness is meant to lead us to repentance. It does not drive us. If we won't be led, his goodness waits and waits and waits.

Think about it: Is there someone you know who has received a wonderful miracle from the Lord? Have they given thanks to the Lord? I hope so. If not, you can thank him and pray they will still be led to repentance.

Prayer: Father, give us grateful hearts. May we always love Jesus and remember your goodness to us as a family. In Jesus' name, Amen.

APRIL 28   LUKE 15:18-20

YOU CAN'T RUN AWAY FROM LOVE

'"I will set out and go back to my father and say to him: Father, I have sinned against heaven and against you. I am no longer worthy to be called your son; make me like one of your hired men". So he got up and went to his father. But while he was still a long way off, his father saw him and was

filled with compassion for him; he ran to his son, threw his arms around him and kissed him'.

Jean: A young girl was found wandering the streets in a state of amnesia. Her home life was so unhappy, she didn't want to remember it. Amnesia was her escape.

The younger son in our Bible reading wanted to be free. He escaped from a good home. After he left he thought he was free . . . He was free to get into trouble. He couldn't escape from himself. When he realised he didn't really want to be on his own, but needed his father, he went back.

Many try to run away from God by various means. They think God's will is bondage, and their own will is freedom. That is an illusion. God the Father's will, and our well-being are one. When we set our will against God's will we go against our own happiness. When we don't want to live with God the Father, we soon don't want to live with ourselves. Repentance is a long road, but it leads home. Regret doesn't lead home; it makes the guilty feel more guilty. The repentant returns, asks forgiveness and offers to stay.

Talk about it: Discuss how you feel about each other in your family.

Prayer: Father, help us to be such a close family, joined together in love, that even when we are grown and separated, we will feel near each other. Amen.

APRIL 29   **TITUS 3:5-7**

'NATURALLY, SUPERNATURALLY'

'He saved us, not because of righteous things we had done, but because of his mercy. He saved us through the washing of rebirth and renewal by the Holy Spirit, whom he poured out on us generously through Jesus Christ our Saviour, so that, having been justified by his grace, we might become heirs having the hope of eternal life'.

Jean: Doing good is not to be mistaken for being good. 'Do-gooders' are disliked by most people and not approved by God, unless their doing springs from their being. When the Holy Spirit dwells in us we are good because we are washed and renewed. Under his cleansing, unnatural evil washes out and we become supernaturally natural. Goodness is a very simple way to behave. Evil is complex. Ever noticed how mixed up we get when we lie or cheat? When we are reborn or renewed we are for the first time doing what comes naturally. We are made for the Holy Spirit. A Spirit-centred person does everyone good.

Think it over: Shouldn't we try to impress people with how good our God is, rather than how good we are?

Prayer: Father, let any good that we do today bring glory to you. Let us be so filled with the Spirit, we'll be 'supernaturally natural'. In Jesus' name, Amen.

APRIL 30   **1 JOHN 4:7**

LOVE COMES FROM GOD

'Dear friends, let us love one another, for love comes from God. Every one who loves has been born of God and knows God'.

Elmer: A man in Panama once said to me, 'English is the language for business, Spanish is the language for love'.

There are several words in Spanish to express love. The English word 'love' may be used in many ways. We love food, friends and Mickey Mouse!

St John used a special Greek word for a special kind of love. He himself had that kind of love for Jesus. It was a love that survived the shock of the crucifixion. What kind of love was that?

It was God-Love. God has many characteristics . . . mercy, justice, holiness, grace and others. But love is not a characteristic of God. God **is** love. Everyone who is born of God has this inner God-love. To know God is to know love; to love my brother is to love God.

Some years ago I was on an ocean freighter travelling from San Francisco to Australia. Other passengers noticed how I was met at every port by friends. 'How is it you know so many people in so many places?' they asked. They didn't realise I had never seen these people before! Yet when we met there was an instant bond of love. We were family. People are often afraid of love, even God's love. They keep at a distance with their affections bottled up inside. They cannot trust love to be real and lasting. Remember, God's love, perfect love, will cast out all fear. Let it happen to you.

Question: How can you as a family express love openly to each other? Mothers and fathers have a wonderful privilege to teach children how to express love. Such teaching will enable them to have a living relationship with God. And . . . do you express love to others, outside the family?

Prayer: Father, please let us express affection to one another. Also help us to express the special God-love which helps us to go through anything together. In Jesus' name, Amen.

MAY 1   JOHN 3:5-8

NEW LIFE A 'MYSTERY'

'Jesus answered, "I tell you the truth, unless a man is born of water and the Spirit, he cannot enter the kingdom of God. Flesh gives birth to flesh, but the Spirit gives birth to spirit. You should not be surprised at my saying, You must be born again. The wind blows wherever it pleases. You hear its sound, but you cannot tell where it comes from or where it is going. So it is with everyone born of the Spirit" '.

LaDonna: The words 'miracle' and 'mystery' are not common expressions of today. It is more fashionable to suggest something is a phenomenon or inexplicable. The mystery of regeneration is reflected in the miracle of birth. Just as natural birth is a gift of parental love, so one must receive the gift of new life from the Father of Life. Christ baffled Nicodemus by his statement that true spirituality cannot be attained by self-effort.

Our mysterious life in the Spirit is accomplished by the miracle of new birth. Yet, there are those regenerated by the Spirit, who deny the possibility of further miraculous events in their lives!

Think about it: Is your spiritual life manifesting the miraculous, powerful presence of the Spirit? or is it a system of well-established routine actions and beliefs? If the second is true, ask the Lord to open your heart to the mystery of faith and accept his miraculous gifts.

Prayer: Lord, I want your presence in my life to show through. Help me to allow the power of the Holy Spirit to flow out of me. By faith, I expect a miracle in my life today. Amen.

MAY 2   **2 CORINTHIANS 3:3-6**

STONE TURNS TO FLESH

'You show that you are a letter from Christ, the result of our ministry, written not with ink but with the Spirit of the living God, not on tablets of stone but on tablets of human hearts. Such confidence as this is ours through Christ before God. Not that we are competent to claim anything for ourselves, but our competence comes from God. He has made us competent as ministers of a new covenant – not of the letter but of the Spirit; for the letter kills, but the Spirit gives life'.

Alan: Sometimes I have the opportunity to watch the Lord work in a new believer. One of the first marks of change is his facial appearance. He beholds the world with new eyes. Hard, staring eyes under a creased brow, which avoid contact with others, give way to a new direct softness. Lips clamped tight, wrinkled like stitches over a wound, relax. The joy of Jesus brings a smile, and even a laugh. Stone turns to flesh as the Holy Spirit writes upon the heart that very special message from Jesus Christ: Peace with God. Those who believe become competent and confident in a new love.

Question: Does your face reflect a relationship with God? We CAN be confident in God — He relaxes us and makes us smile. Especially when we realise we can do nothing of ourselves, but all things through him.

Prayer: Lord, help me to recognise any hardness in my heart. Make me soft and pliable, full of joy and confidence in you. Amen.

MAY 3   1 PETER 1:22-23

HOW DOES YOUR GARDEN GROW?

'Now that you have purified yourselves by obeying the truth so that you have sincere love for your brothers, love one another deeply, from the heart. For you have been born again, not of perishable seed, but of imperishable, through the living and enduring word of God'.

Jean: Seeds in the package won't grow. They must be planted. Seeds need soil. The Bible on the bookshelf will not release life. The Word of God needs the soil of the human heart. Once planted, its hidden power is released to produce the fruit of the Spirit. The predominant fruit is love. Love from the heart (v.22) grows out of a life renewed by the living Word of God. Such love lasts; it is as enduring as the Word of God. Wild flowers wilt; grass withers, but the Word of God will not die.

Plant God's Word in your heart. Outgrow the old life. Un-nurtured, our natural love and affections wither. We need the Word of God to revitalize our natural affections and draw them out towards those who need us. Let love grow from the inside.

Growing time: Start something growing today in your garden, or window box or flower pot! Plant some seeds. Watch them grow.

Plant the seed of God's word in your heart and observe how you grow more loving. Today memorize verse 25 'But the word of the Lord stands for ever!' It will only take a minute. Do it now. Say it together. 'Amen'.

EVERYTHING WE NEED

*'His divine power has given us everything we need for life and
godliness through our knowledge of him who called us by his
own glory and goodness. Through these he has given us his
very great and precious promises, so that through them you
may participate in the divine nature and escape the corruption in the world caused by evil desires'.*

Jean: God is the great Giver. He has more to give than any
other person. He gathered his glory and goodness into his Son
and sent him with all we need for a godly life. To be godly means
to be like God. To be like God is to share in his holiness and
goodness. He invites us to share his divine nature. How do we
do that?

We must claim the great and precious promises he has given
us. We need to read the word of God and use it in our daily life.
Cultivate the desire to be good for the glory of God. The word
will divert us from soul-destroying influences.

God has promised joy in the morning to those who weep,
deliverance for the afflicted, divine care and healing for the sick.
He will see us through when we are threatened by disaster. In
all things he works for good and according to his purposes. His
divine grace is sufficient. He has promised us everything we
need for life and godliness.

Today: Claim a promise in God's Word and expect God to
keep his promise to you.

Prayer: Father, we are glad you are a great Giver. We want to
give you our best as a family, so help us live godly lives. In Jesus'
name, Amen.

THE SPIRIT OF SONSHIP

*'Because those who are led by the Spirit of God are sons of
God. For you did not receive a spirit that makes you a slave*

*again to fear, but you received the Spirit of sonship. And by
him we cry, "Abba, Father". The Spirit himself testifies
with our spirit that we are God's children. Now if we are
children, then we are heirs — heirs of God and co-heirs with
Christ, if indeed we share in his sufferings in order that we
may also share in his glory'.*

Jean: These verses should make slumped-over saints stand up
and shout! Let the defeated take a deep breath of the Spirit of
sonship and say, 'Abba, Father!'.

A small boy in a children's home was overheard telling
another orphan, 'Shucks, I ain't nobody's nothin.'

Christians often reflect an orphan's self-image, rather than a
son's. The Holy Spirit does not drive us, but leads us into sonship. If we submit to his leading, he will lead us away from self-
destructive attitudes which enslave and impoverish. We will act
like sons of God. We will develop a fearless affection for God,
free of guilt, condemnation and unworthiness. Once in harmony with the Spirit of sonship, we will not be afraid to testify
for Christ or even to suffer with others for Christ. Such freedom
to love, live or die is the glory of Christ within us.

Build each other up: Turn to one another and say, 'You're
special to God and to me'. Now hug one another.

Prayer: Abba, Father, we love you. We are not afraid to say so.
Help us to show our love to one another. In Jesus' name, Amen.

MAY 6   **JOHN 5:24**

CROSS OVER FROM DEATH TO LIFE

*'I tell you the truth, whoever hears my word and believes him
who sent me has eternal life and will not be condemned; he has
crossed over from death to life'.*

Jean: Often we are told of someone's death in the gentle terms
'They crossed over . . .' It means they have passed from life into
death. Our text refers to the reverse. It is the cross-over from
death to life which transpires when anyone believes in Jesus, the

Son of God, as their Saviour. Until one believes in Jesus Christ in such a manner, one is spiritually dead. This means an unbeliever is as separated from eternal life as a dead person is from earthly life. When we believe in God's Son, we cross over from spiritual death into spiritual life. Not only are we spared the death sentence, but we are free. We are pardoned.

Some people, even though they have accepted Christ as Saviour, still live with the fear of punishment for their sins. They punish themselves with self-condemnation. God has forgiven them, but they do not forgive themselves. They are prisoners who have had the death sentence lifted, but stay in jail for life. If guilt is killing your joy and peace each day, cross over from daily dying into daily living. Enjoy your eternal life now. It started when you believed in Jesus.

Act it out: One of you be the 'prisoner'. Sit in a corner (prison cell). Another be the governor who comes with the parson. Read it to the prisoner. 'You have been pardoned. Your death sentence is removed. You will not die, but live'. The prisoner thanks the governor, who goes away. The guard comes: 'What are you doing here?' Prisoner: 'I know I wont die for my crime – but I am guilty'. Guard: 'No, you are pardoned. You are free to leave this prison. You can go'. The prisoner gets up and goes out.

Prayer: Sing a song of freedom to the Lord.

MAY 7   **1 JOHN 3:14**

LOVE FREELY

'We know that we have passed from death to life, because we love our brothers. Anyone who does not love remains in death'.

Elmer: Brotherly love is the evidence of Christian discipleship. Jesus said, 'By this shall all men know that you are my disciples, if you have love one to another'. Our love for one another as brothers in Christ indicates we have passed from death to life. Here lies a strong two-fold assurance of salvation: we sense the inward life of God and a spontaneous affection towards one another in Christ.

'It follows naturally that any man who has genuine contact with Christ has this life'. But, 'The man without love for his brother is living in death already' (Phillips translation). Jesus expressed varying degrees of love for different individuals at different times. Let us follow his example and allow voluntary love towards members of the body of Christ to flow freely and naturally.

Remember: Satan may try to rob you of great joy and strength with his lie that you can stand alone in Christ. Refute that lie by saying: 'I really do need others, especially . . .' (insert the name of someone you care for very much.)

Prayer: Dear Father in heaven. I need you. I need my Christian friends, too. I know they need me. Help me to serve in loving devotion for as I help and love others, I help and love you. Amen.

MAY 8   **EPHESIANS 2:1-5**

LET'S GET OUR THINKING RESHAPED

'As for you, you were dead in your transgressions and sins, in which you used to live when you followed the ways of this world and of the ruler of the kingdom of the air, the spirit who is now at work in those who are disobedient. All of us also lived among them at one time, gratifying the cravings of our sinful nature and following its desires and thoughts. Like the rest, we were by nature objects of wrath. But because of his great love for us, God, who is rich in mercy, made us alive with Christ even when we were dead in transgressions − it is by grace you have been saved'.

LaDonna: Reona, a member of our Youth With A Mission team, slowly swung open the door of the hotel room in Kabul,

112

Afghanistan. Through the smokey haze she saw a young man slumped in a corner. As she moved towards him he said, 'If you can, help me'.

Reona went to her mission team and after prayer, returned to find the man a raving lunatic. He could not coordinate his limbs or speak coherently. (Acquaintances related that having destroyed his mind on LSD a year before, he had not been sane since. They were astonished to hear he had requested help).

We took him in and began a constant vigil of prayer and reading scripture aloud to him, sometimes we had to follow him as he staggered around our quarters. In two weeks our friend could talk coherently. In four weeks he could read simple scriptures and was witnessing to astounded friends. Jesus had miraculously restored his mind.

Thought: Verse two says that our thinking has been shaped by this darkened world. We have all followed the desires of our mind, becoming children of wrath. Let Jesus wash your mind. When you read scripture allow it to reshape your thinking.

Prayer: Lord, show me the thoughts and attitudes which are shaped by this darkened world. I yield them to you and ask for the wisdom which comes from heaven. Amen.

MAY 9   **JOHN 10:10**

THE TRANSITION FROM DEATH TO LIFE

'The thief comes only to steal and kill and destroy; I have come that they may have life, and have it to the full'.

Alan: There are many religious thieves who roam about this world, seeking whom they may devour. They offer inner peace through meditation, drugs, self-realisation or some god-figure who is meant to be worshipped. These false shepherds lead their flocks over the cliff edge of life into the crevasse of eternal damnation.

The True Shepherd brings new life. It isn't a patch-up job on

113

the old life but a new creation. This new life is not centred on our 'enlightened' selves, drug-induced experiences or fallible human beings, but on God whom we come to know through Jesus Christ. Abundant life is released as the Holy Spirit within us develops our personal relationship with God. He leads us to the restful pastures of eternal life and peace.

Comment: The only things Jesus takes away are those things that are harmful and destructive. He adds much more to our lives than he takes away.

Prayer: Help me today, Lord Jesus, to live more abundantly as I deepen my relationship with you. Amen.

MAY 10   GALATIANS 2:20

PAUL'S PERSONAL TESTIMONY

'I have been crucified with Christ and I no longer live, but Christ lives in me'.

Jean: Paul taught that Christ died not to make the Jews more Jewish, nor the Gentiles more Gentile, nor Jews Gentiles, nor Gentiles Jews! He said Christ died to make them new men. He saw the cross as the great leveller . . . where all are saved, not by works but by grace.

Peter had a problem with that. He wanted to be identified with the Jewish brethren, who insisted that all converts adhere to the Jewish Law and ceremonies. he also wanted to be identified with the Gentiles who were released from all such rules and enjoyed their freedom in Christ. Peter found himself switching sides. Paul challenged Peter to make up his mind where he stood.

This verse is Paul's personal declaration. He had no identity problem. He fastened his eyes on the crucified Saviour and said, 'Here is where I stand'!

Question: Where do you stand? Are you afraid to be identified as a Christian before your non-Christian friends?

114

Prayer: Father, we are not ashamed to take our stand today. Amen.

ALL MY DEBTS ARE CANCELLED

'When you were dead in your sins and in the uncircumcision of your sinful nature, God made you alive with Christ. he forgave us all our sins, having cancelled the written code, with its regulations, that was against us and that stood opposed to us; he took it away, nailing it to the cross. And having disarmed the powers and authorities, he made a public spectacle of them, triumphing over them by the cross'.

Jean: In Paul's day 'the written code' could mean two things. It could refer to the record of debts or crimes which stood against an offender's name. It could also refer to the IOU's or promissory notes unpaid by an offender. These codes under certain circumstances could be annulled or cancelled. To indicate this the record was either sponged away, blotted out, or a nail was driven through them to indicate that power to condemn had been cancelled.

In Paul's day the executed criminal who paid for his offences by death was buried with all the records of his debts and crimes. Nothing remained to perpetuate the charge against his name. Death cancelled all. St Paul saw more on the cross than the inscription, 'Jesus, the King of the Jews'. He saw the accounts and records of every guilty sinner, Jew or Gentile, nailed to the cross. The blood of Jesus had blotted out the whole record of broken law, so that it could never be brought up against the offender again. When Satan brings counterfeit charges against a Christian, the forgiven sinner can laugh in his face and shout, 'It's all settled. Jesus paid it all'.

Project: Write on a piece of paper, 'All my sins'. Take a drawing pin and pin it up in the doorway where you can see it today. Remember, the nails on the cross have cancelled your debt.

Prayer: Thank you, Father, that I am pardoned and forgiven. What a good feeling that is. I know it is true. Amen.

THAT'S WHAT IT'S ALL ABOUT!

'For God so loved the world that he gave his one and only Son, that whoever believes in him shall not perish but have eternal life'.

Jean: Our golden verse today is the heart of our Christian faith. Deep in the verse is a word which stands for any and every body. It is 'Whoever'. God loved our whole world of people so much he gave his Son to save them from perishing in their sins. Whoever believes in the Son will have eternal life. That's what the gospel is all about.

This text is for everybody. Not everyone could have paid or made a pilgrimage, or been good enough in order to be saved, but everybody can believe. If that sounds too cheap or easy, take another look at the cost. God . . . gave his one and only Son.

Tell someone today about the gospel. Share the 'whoever' of John 3:16. The cross has convinced many, it could convince your friends of God's love to them. Everyone should know this verse by heart.

Prayer: Father, thank you for giving us your son. We see the extent of your love as we see Jesus on the cross. Help us to get others to see such love and their need of your eternal life. In Jesus' name, Amen.

LOST CHILDREN

'We all, like sheep have gone astray, each of us has turned to his own way; and the Lord has laid on him the iniquity of us all'.

Jean: In a gloomy bazaar off a narrow street in Kabul, Afghanistan, I saw something I shall never forget. Tacked up on the wall and around the door posts were slips of paper and cards.

Each one was advertising a lost child. Not little children, but teenagers who had made their pilgrimage to Kabul in search of drugs and Eastern religions. Mothers and fathers from many countries, mostly English speaking, were describing their children and offering rewards for any information concerning their lost ones. My eyes filled with tears as I read the sad words. There were loving pleas . . .'Come home. All is forgiven'. Many of those children were sick in Kabul's hospital and jails. Many had lost their identity in the drug culture or were lost in the confusion of many religions. Some were dead. A missionary told me of a 'hippie's graveyard'. The only markers on their unnamed graves were piles of rocks.

Think: The waywardness of these lost ones began in the heart. Is there something in your heart drawing you away from present relationships? Jesus the Good Shepherd knows your heart's deceitful ways. Ask for his arm of salvation. He knows the dangers. Ask him to save you from your own ways. He will lead you in the right path.

Prayer: Father, we thank you for our Good Shepherd, Jesus. We thank you for our family. May we never hurt one another, ourselves, nor you by willful, selfish decisions. In Jesus' name, Amen.

MAY 14   **LUKE 19:10; 15:24**

SURPRISED BY LOVE

'For the Son of Man came to seek and to save what was lost'.
'For this son of mine was dead and is alive again; he was lost, and is found'.

Elmer: Our daughter, LaDonna, accidentally broke a prize possession on her wedding day. It was a fine porcelain horse and rider her mother had given to her. LaDonna cried a little, but soon forgot about the incident on that happy day in Los Angeles. However, Jean remembered other times when I had restored broken articles with a special glue. After LaDonna's

117

wedding, Jean carefully picked every fragment of the shattered statue out of the carpet, tucked them into an envelope and brought the pieces back to London. A couple of years later I surprised LaDonna on her birthday. I worked several evenings putting together the little statue. I bought special enamels, carefully mixed and matched colours and applied multiple coats. At last, the little rider and her horse stood restored on our dining table. When LaDonna entered the room she was overjoyed to see her precious treasure. That which she thought was lost for ever . . . was once more her very own.

Project: Is there something broken in your house? I hope you have some glue. Most of all, I hope you have someone patient enough to put it together again. As he works on it, think of God's patient love as he works on you.

Prayer: Dear God, when we break you know how to put us together and make us beautiful and new for your glory. Thank you Jesus. Pick me up and make me whole. Amen.

MAY 15   **1 PETER 2:25**

THE ONE WHO SEEKS

'For you were like sheep going astray, but now you have returned to the Shepherd and Overseer of your souls'.

LaDonna: We often say of someone who is thinking deeply, heedless of those around, 'He is lost in thought'. Yet we can also be lost in grief, self-pity, over-work, ambition, pain, bitterness or disappointment. We can be lost in a world of music, art, study, even love. When we are lost like that we are deaf to other voices giving warning, comfort, or advice whether it be friends or family.

Praise God, his voice is able to pierce through our preoccupation. If only momentarily, we can detect God's love to us. Thousands over the centuries have been reached by the compassion of Christ when they were lost in grief, disappointment or other things. Christ once wept over the crowds who grew faint, like scattered sheep. He has not changed. He still yearns over lost men and women.

Thought: Have you heard the Lord's voice recently? Perhaps you have become lost in the exhausting busyness of life with its toils and trials, even Christian duties. Take a moment. Lift your head and listen. Christ is calling you. Let him draw you close to his heart like a good shepherd rescuing and restoring a beloved lost sheep.

Prayer: Lord, so often I get lost in daily worries and demanding duties. Right now I am still before you listening for the Shepherd's voice. I will follow you. Amen.

MAY 16   JOHN 3:3

BLINDNESS TO SIGHT

'In reply Jesus declared, "I tell you the truth, unless a man is born again, he cannot see the kingdom of God"'

Alan: When Nicodemus approached our Lord he caught sight of the kingdom as if 'through a glass darkly'. A glow of truth penetrated his darkness and stirred in him a sincere desire for it. Jesus explained how the born-again man can see the kingdom. Praise God.

Although in the kingdom, born again believers at times can come into a narrow place deep in shadows. In those times God's children must remember they are in the Kingdom of God. The question is, 'Is the Kingdom in us?' Is it so viable a part of our living that we illuminate the world around us?

Today, let us be a source of light to those around us who have a darkened understanding of our Saviour's kingdom of light.

Say to yourself: I am God's child. I am a child of the kingdom. I can see his glory, even in the shadows. I am in the kingdom of God and the kingdom of God is in me.

Prayer: Lord, help me in the shadows of my life to see your light penetrate all darkness. Amen.

WE REFLECT THE LORD'S GLORY

'But their minds were made dull, for to this day the same veil remains when the old covenant is read. It has not been removed, because only in Christ is it taken away. Even to this day when Moses is read, a veil covers their hearts. But whenever anyone turns to the Lord, the veil is taken away. Now the Lord is the Spirit, and where the Spirit of the Lord is, there is freedom. And we, who with unveiled faces all reflect the Lord's glory, are being transformed into his likeness with ever-increasing glory, which comes from the Lord, who is the Spirit'.

Jean: The Jewish nation has given the world both the scriptures and the Saviour, yet their minds are blinded to both. Even today, these brilliant people who excel in art, science, literature and the arts often lack understanding of their own prophets' words. There is a veil upon their hearts.

The remedy for spiritual blindness is to turn to the Lord. Then the veil will be taken away. When Christ is in view the blindness goes. When blindness goes, there is liberty. The spiritually blind require outward rules and regulations to live by. The Spiritually sighted have an inner law of the Spirit. Life becomes a free service of love.

Freedom is not a licence to live undisciplined lives. Instead, it is a liberty to desire and to do the very things the law requires, not because we have to, but because we want to, from the heart.

The more we gaze upon him, the more we change. Not the sudden change of salvation, which depends upon how God looks on us, but the gradual change of sanctification, which depends upon our steadfast gaze upon the Lord. If we do the gazing, God will do the changing.

Try this: Take a mirror and look at yourself. Is your nose too long? Do you dislike your freckles? What about your ears? Or is your face dirty? Try to wash your face with the mirror. It won't work, will it? The mirror can show you what you're like, but it can't change you.

120

Prayer: Dear God, help me to look into your mirror more often. Help me to see Jesus, who can change me. Amen.

MAY 18   **1 CORINTHIANS 4:3-4**

LET THE LIGHT SHINE IN

'And even if our gospel is veiled, it is veiled to those who are perishing. The god of this age has blinded the minds of unbelievers, so that they cannot see the light of the gospel of the glory of Christ, who is the image of God'.

Jean: When Muslim women wear veils they identify themselves with their religion. Those who wear the veil of unbelief identify themselves with the god of this age. The unbelief in our scripture reading is not mere doubting. It is an incapacity to understand, created by continuous unbelief. Such habitual unbelief decides the eternal destiny of a soul.

What does the Bible mean by lost? It means to have disappeared . . . out of the possession of its owner. What does the Bible mean to be saved? It means the lost one is recovered and restored to its owner. How we react to the Gospel decides whether we are lost or saved.

The blindness in this scripture was not imposed by Satan, but was self-chosen. The unbelievers were willing subjects to Satan's lies. When unbelievers do not make room for the God of the universe in their hearts, they will make room for the god of this age. Those who reject the light become victims of darkness. In our world are two camps . . . the multitude who are blinded by the god of this world and the multitude who are enlightened by the Gospel of Christ.

Our Saviour is the image of God. We Christians are to become the image of Christ. To be a Christian requires a decision, as it does not to be a Christian. Our decision determines our character and our destiny.

Think about it: Unbelief is like living with your head covered.

Prayer: Father, we welcome the light of the Gospel. We allow it to shine in our hearts – so we can see Jesus. We will not allow

the enemy to blind our minds. We are believers, and servants of
the Lord. Amen.

THE HOUR OF JOY

*'At that time Jesus, full of joy through the Holy Spirit, said,
"I praise you, Father, Lord of heaven and earth, because you
have hidden these things from the wise and learned, and
revealed them to little children. Yes, Father, for this was your
good pleasure"'.*

Jean: Jesus sent the seventy disciples two by two that they
might strengthen and encourage each other. They went into
towns ministering the Gospel in word and in works of power.
They gave a glorious report to Jesus upon their return. One of
the features of their success that thrilled them most was how
demons had been subject to them. Jesus' response is a good
reminder for us that all victories over Satan are obtained by
power derived from Jesus Christ. The Lord must have all the
praise. Beware of pride which is unspiritual and destroys many
ministries.

Notice our Lord's joy. Such hours of joy were few for our
Saviour. In that hour in which he saw Satan fall, and heard of
the good success of his ministers, he rejoiced. Blessed are those
who depend on the teaching, help and power of the Son of God.
The more they listen and obey his words, the more useful they
will be in his service.

Visit someone soon: Don't go alone. Two of you go. First, ask
Jesus to send you to someone who needs you. Second, ask Jesus
to give you a partner who can go with you. You can encourage
each other. Third, when you return, report to Jesus all that happened. Be sure to go in his name and then you will be victorious
over all difficulties Satan may put in your way. Your obedient
and humble service for the Lord can cause Satan's defeat. Who
knows what victories you'll have?

Prayer: Today, Lord God, may you help us to join hearts and hands to serve you. Send us in Jesus' name to those who need to hear the good news of the Kingdom and be delivered from evil. Make us good news people today. Amen.

MAY 20 **PROVERBS 4:18**

THE SHINING WAY

'The path of the righteous is like the first gleam of dawn, shining ever brighter till the full light of day'.

Jean: When I was six years old, my parents took me to visit relatives who lived in the country. I still remember how frightened I was when the evening darkness grew blacker and blacker. I began to cry.

'What's wrong?' my mother asked.

'Where are the street lights? I want to go home where the lights are'. I had lived in the city all my life and lights came on when it grew dark.

My mother took me outside the house. 'Look,' she pointed to the stars. 'God's lights are shining'.

The stars seem a long way off when you're in a dark place. But Jesus, the Light of the world, is always with those who trust in him. When the darkness comes, he shines around us, for he is with us to the ends of the earth. The way of the righteous is light; Christ is their Way and he is the Light.

We will not be perfect until we reach heaven, but there we will shine as the sun. Until then, we walk in the Light of the Way. Our Light will not diminish. We will not end up in darkness, but the light will shine brighter and brighter as we come closer home. We are not going into outer darkness, we are going towards a city, where the Lamb is the Light.

Remember: Next time you ride a motorway, notice how the road gets brighter towards the big cities as the lights come on. Think of the King's Highway and how it will get brighter and brighter as we go towards the heavenly city.

Prayer: Father, I thank you that my walk with Jesus is in light and not in darkness. I thank you Jesus himself is my Way and my Light. He will shed light on any difficult spots I have to travel over today, for he will be right there with me. Jesus, I will look for your Light. In Your name, Amen.

MAY 21   JOHN 1:4-5

THE LIGHT OF LIFE

'In him was life, and that life was the light of men. The Light shines in the darkness, but the darkness has not understood it'.

Elmer: All living things have life in the omnipresent God, but God has life in himself. Life, which is the light of men, comes from Jesus. God made man a living soul. His life was light. Man responded to his environment, not as a mere animal, but as a living soul. His mental capacities distinguished him from the grazing beasts of the field. Man retains the light of reason through Christ the Creator. Self-realisation distinguishes us from the beasts.

We should expect the light of divine revelation from the One who gave us the light of human reasoning. When we see him as creator and sustainer of natural life, we readily see that eternal life radiates from him.

Eternal light shines in man's hopeless, lifeless, spiritual darkness. The darkness cannot put it out. Midnight darkness can be dispelled by a torch but darkness cannot put out the daylight.

Question: Has the light of salvation come to you? To many of us salvation was like a blast of light driving away instantly the darkness of sin. To others the salvation experience has been like the world turning gradually toward the sun until full day dawns. However it came, God's light was not switched on. It was always there. It is always here. It will light our life into eternity.

Prayer: Dear Father in heaven, help me to realise that in you there is light and no darkness. In Christ I live today in your light. I thank you for reason and for faith. Amen.

LIGHT FROM THE KINGDOM OF LIGHT

'. . . to open their eyes and turn them from darkness to light,
and from the power of Satan to God, so that they may receive
forgiveness of sins and a place among those who are sanctified
by faith in me'.

LaDonna: I was taken as a child to see Carlsbad Caverns in
Arizona. As we followed our guide through the series of vast
subterranean caves, we descended into a silent, dim world of
stalagmites and stalactites. At one point our tour-guide paused,
hushed the group and then put out his light. It was utterly black.
Not a ray of light penetrated from the surface. Even when I
lifted my hand directly in front of my face my eyes could see
nothing.

When we finally reached the surface we were totally dazzled.
The sunlight flooded our widely dilated pupils. We lost our
focus. It took a number of minutes for our eyes to adjust. Then
we could see the other things around.

So it is with spiritual life. It takes time to see the new world,
the Kingdom. It takes time to focus, to see things clearly.

Thought: Now that you are in Christ do not expect things to be
the same. There are new laws governing this kingdom of light.
If things aren't working right, adjust to your new perception of
life.

Prayer: Help me, Lord, to be patient with myself as my vision
adjusts to yours. In your name, Amen.

DARKNESS TO LIGHT

'They are darkened in their understanding and separated
from the life of God because of the ignorance that is in them
due to the hardening of their hearts. Having lost all sensitivity, they have given themselves over to sensuality so as to

indulge in every kind of impurity, with a continual lust for more'.

Alan: Spiritual sensitivity is often forsaken for worldly sensuality which increases with indulgence.

From the beginning, man in his need to worship has often forsaken the Lord for the sensual pleasures common in idol worship. What a wonderful freedom we have through Christ to enjoy the good things of this world without becoming slaves to them. Money, sex and power are transient pleasures which can destroy those who worship them.

To overcome, we must look to Jesus, who having suffered temptation, was found perfect. We can be led into spiritual sensitivity and out of worldly sensuality through our relationship with Jesus Christ. Through him we can conquer the deceitful desires of our flesh and be transformed in our attitudes about pleasure.

Think about it: Do you possess things, or do things possess you? One is freedom, the other is bondage. Are you master, or mastered, victor or victim?

Prayer: Lord Jesus, lead me in all truth about the things that I enjoy. I want to avoid idols and keep you first in my life. Amen.

MAY 24   COLOSSIANS 1:12-14

DELIVERED AND TRANSFERRED

'Giving thanks to the Father, who has qualified you to share in the inheritance of the saints in the kingdom of light. For he has rescued us from the dominion of darkness and brought us into the kingdom of the Son he loves, in whom we have redemption, the forgiveness of sins'.

Jean: A Scottish witch sought prayer that she might be released from the powers that used her. I spent some time in prayer with her and saw her set free by the power of the Lord Jesus Christ. 'Thank God,' she exclaimed. 'I'm delivered!' 'You are more than delivered' I said, pointing to this text. 'You are delivered

and transferred'. She had been rescued from the dominion of
darkness and brought into the kingdom of God's dear Son. She
was delivered from one and transferred into the other.

The authority of spiritual darkness, the tyranny of the powers
of the occult world no longer have power over those in Christ's
domain. There is no middle ground mentioned here. We are
either in one or the other. Neither have anything in common
and it is impossible to be in both. The transfer from one to the
other is the result of our choice and God's power. We believe it
and God performs it.

How does he perform it? By redemption . . . through his blood
and the forgiveness of sin. Believers have been rescued by ransom. Jesus' blood paid the price. It was nothing we did or could
have done; it was all grace. We were not only rescued, but
forgiven. Our accumulated guilt was cancelled by the
forgiveness of Jesus Christ. The remission or forgiveness of our
sins covers our past and present. In him we have redemption
now.

Be thankful: Begin now to thank God for your inheritance. It
will enlarge your life. Whatever is his is yours. You are his child
and consequently his heir. Look upward with thanksgiving, forward with praise and backward with joy.

Prayer: Let your prayer time be praise time.

MAY 25   **1 PETER 2:9**

GOD'S OWN PEOPLE

*'But you are a chosen people, a royal priesthood, a holy
nation, a people belonging to God, that you may declare the
praises of him who called you out of darkness into his wonderful light'.*

Jean: In case we feel this verse for today must apply to the Jews
or to the apostles, I want you to see that we are included. If
you've ever felt like a stranger in this world, just passing
through like some pilgrim, take heart, for God has chosen you
for some special task. The world may see you as a heavenly

hobo. You may feel out of place here sometimes, but here is how God sees you. You are part of something great . . . a whole new race of people who are called and chosen. You are in a royal priesthood, you are part of a holy nation. You belong to God so you may declare the praises of him who called you out of darkness into his wonderful light.

You are in the King's service, along with a multitude of others who have been called out of darkness. Today as his servant you can declare the praises of God. Priests bring men to God, and God to men. They intercede. They serve under the one mediator, Christ Jesus. They offer praise to him who has offered himself as the Lamb of God. They intercede, they praise and they represent another nation and another kingdom. They are light-bearers, showing the way to God.

Parents: Serve God as a priest in your home today. Intercede for your family in prayer. Outside the home, praise God before men, declare his goodness and salvation. Be a good representative of God to your family and a good intercessor for your family to God.

Prayer: I thank you, Father, that you have called me out of darkness into light. Now I have something to do and to say in this world. I am a stranger here, but I'm known to you. I am one of your very own people. Amen.

MAY 26   **2 CORINTHIANS 4:6**

SHINING HEARTS

'For God, who said, "Let light shine out of darkness", made his light shine in our hearts to give us the light of the knowledge of the glory of God in the face of Christ'.

Jean: God drove back the darkness at creation's dawn by his Word. In the same way, he drives back the darkness of sin and unbelief in our hearts. The Creator of the Old Testament is the Re-Creator of the New Testament. His Word in Genesis produced natural light. In the Gospel, his Word produced Jesus,

128

the Light of the world. So in Jesus' face we see the likeness of God. His glory can shine deep into human hearts.

The heart is the control centre of our moral, intellectual and spiritual being. The converted heart is a shining heart. The glory of Jesus dwelling in us produces accurate revelation knowledge of God, his ways, and his word. One day in the future we will know God perfectly in full glory. Until then, everyday, more and more, the shining heart enlightens our behaviour, our thinking and our service to Christ.

For the children: Make a shining heart. Draw a heart and colour it yellow or paste silver or gold paper paper on it. Now paste a picture of Jesus in the middle. It is Jesus who makes our heart shine.

Prayer: Father, we need your light everyday. Jesus, keep our hearts alight. The entrance of your word gives light, so we thank you for your word today. Amen.

MAY 27   **ROMANS 3:23-24**

FALLING SHORT

'For all have sinned and fall short of the glory of God and are justified freely by his grace through the redemption that came by Christ Jesus'.

Jean: The words 'fall short' are in the present continuous tense. That means man sinned and man is still falling short of God's glory, which is the perfection of God's character.

I once saw a man who could not walk or even stand long without staggering about and falling down. I was told he had injured a very small part of his inner ear when he fell from some scaffolding. He suffered from a loss of equilibrium. I don't know what became of the poor man, but I do know God has provided a Saviour for the fallen man who keeps falling.

Jesus did not fall short of God's requirement of a sinless, perfect character but he identified himself with fallen man. He

129

took our sins in his sinless person and our punishment upon the cross. We who keep falling can put our faith in him and be healed of our sin-sickness. One day we shall reach the fulness of the stature of Christ and stand complete in him before Father God.

Feel like you are falling? Lean hard on Jesus. He is able to keep you standing.

For the children: Stand in front of your father or mother or older sister or brother . . . Take a step forward. One of you play the Tempter who tries to make us fall. Try to shove the child standing in front the older person backwards. When the child starts to fall, father, mother, brother or sister catches them and pushes them back up. That's how Jesus catches us and puts us on our feet . . . if we are close to him.

Prayer: Father, thank you for Jesus who has made us his very own by his blood. Thank you he is near us today to keep us on our feet, even though we are prone to falling into temptation. Help us to lift up others, in Jesus' name, who are being shoved around by the devil. Amen.

MAY 28   **ROMANS 8:1-2**

'Therefore, there is now no condemnation for those who are in Christ Jesus, because through Christ Jesus the law of the Spirit of life set me free from the law of sin and death'.

Elmer: When Jean and I visited our friends, Jimmy and Carol Owens, in Hawaii, we enjoyed the panoramic view from their mountain home, especially the sunsets. Jimmy pointed out landmarks. 'Far to our left is a restored Polynesian City of Refuge. In ancient times if an islander committed a capital crime he was safe if he could get to a city of refuge. They are found on each island in the chain'.

Later we saw the city of refuge and were reminded of those spoken of in the Bible in ancient Israel (Joshua 20:1-6). If an Israelite accidentally killed someone he could flee to one of the six cities of refuge. There the Levites would protect him. He would be safe, not because he was innocent but because he was in the city.

Comment: You and I, who have put our trust in Christ Jesus, have found a City of refuge. Satan may come with condemnation to the gate but we are safe inside. We are not prisoners in a cell, but are safe in Christ.

Prayer: Father, help me to realise that I am safe and free in Christ. I live and move and have my being in him. Amen.

MAY 29   **ROMANS 5:8-11**

LIFE ABIDING WITHIN

'But God demonstrates his own love for us in this: While we were still sinners, Christ died for us. Since we have now been justified by his blood, how much more shall we be saved from God's wrath through him! For if, when we were God's enemies, we were reconciled to him through the death of his Son, how much more, having been reconciled, shall we be saved through his life! Not only is this so, but we also rejoice in God through our Lord Jesus Christ, through whom we have now received reconciliation'.

LaDonna: For many of us the concept of being accepted by God is pure theory. We believe that having been cleared of guilt we will eventually be allowed into Heaven, but we carry on our daily lives nursing self-rejection.

Usually we manage to cope from day to day without failing in our duties. But sometimes our dissatisfaction with ourselves becomes too burdensome. We either descend into depression or take on increased activity to compensate. There is only one solution. Abiding in Christ.

Jesus' death bought release from judgement. But he rose again so we might live in the power of his life. His life is available to us if we abide in him. Cease endless activity and self-criticism. Centre your whole existence in the living Christ. Relax!

Take a moment: Tilt your head back − inhale − as you do, receive Christ's life. Straighten your head − exhale − as you do release your feelings to Him. Then wait silently thinking of him, until Jesus sends you forth in the power of his life. Make this your prayer.

MAY 30   **ROMANS 8:33-34**

FROM CONDEMNATION TO JUSTIFICATION

'Who will bring any charge against those whom God has chosen? It is God who justifies. Who is he that condemns? Christ Jesus, who died − more than that, who was raised to life − is at the right hand of God and is also interceding for us'.

Alan: We must realise this is not a just world in which we live. We know we're not always fair with others, nor they with us.

In everything we must look to our example, Christ Jesus, who suffered reproach and died to remove our condemnation. Who accuses you? Whom do you accuse? Has condemnation rolled in like a high tide, separating you from others? It cannot separate you from God. Jesus Christ has risen from the dead to bridge that gap between you and the Father. All unfairness, all bitterness and condemnation break upon the Rock Christ Jesus, like waves from a wild sea. Hide yourself in him.

Act it out: One of you be 'Christian'. Another 'Condemnation', and another 'The Rock'. Let 'Condemnation' chase 'Christian'. 'The Rock' stands still. 'Christian' must get behind 'The Rock' to escape 'Condemnation'. If 'Condemnation' touches 'The Rock' he is out. If 'Christian' is caught by 'Condemnation' he is out.

Prayer: Intercede for me, Lord, that your fairness will rule in my heart. The Rock, Jesus Christ is forever unmoved by the waves of injustice and condemnation that would attempt to flood my life. I hide in you. Amen.

DON'T RUN AWAY AND HIDE

*'Whoever believes in him is not condemned, but whoever does
not believe stands condemned already because he has not believed in the name of God's one and only Son'.*

Jean: People have often said to me after I've preached, 'I felt
like you were talking to me, tonight'. Or, 'You hit on everything
that troubles me'. One man accused me of reading his mail!
Another was certain his wife had told me all about him! They
were not condemned by me, they were condemned by their own
selves. The Father sent Jesus to save us, not to condemn us. Yet,
everywhere he went, he divided people. Those who wanted
truth were attracted to him; those who did not want truth either
withdrew or attacked him.

I recall some lines of an old gospel song. '. . . Just take him at
his promise, don't run away and hide' (From, 'It Is No Secret
What God Can Do'). Sin always makes us hide from God. But
you don't need to. God is on your side. Believe it, and you won't
condemn yourself.

Think on this: Be quiet and with closed eyes think about your
Saviour. Imagine him walking towards you. Do you want to
hide from him or do you go towards him?

Prayer: Father, let us come close to Jesus until we can hear him
say, 'I forgive'. Then we will say, 'I accept'. In Jesus' name,
Amen.

JUNE 1   **1 CORINTHIANS 6:9-11**

YOU ARE DIFFERENT

*'Do you not know that the wicked will not inherit the
kingdom of God? Do not be deceived: Neither the sexually im-
moral nor idolaters nor adulterers nor male prostitutes nor
homosexual offenders nor thieves nor the greedy nor
drunkards nor slanderers nor swindlers will inherit the
kingdom of God. And that is what some of you were. But you*

were washed, you were sanctified, you were justified in the name of the Lord Jesus Christ and by the Spirit of our God'.

Jean: St Paul reminded the Corinthians that they were in the Kingdom of God, heirs together of the grace which had made them different from the pagan world they lived in. The new life they possessed would outlive the city of Corinth. Paul listed the wicked in Corinth. They were people who sinned against each other, against their own bodies, who cheated, stole and lied. There was no way for them to think of being in the kingdom of God as long as they continued to live that way.

Paul reminded church members in Corinth that some of them had been just like those wicked people. But now they were different. What happened? They were washed, they were sanctified, they were justified. How? 'In the Name of the Lord Jesus Christ and by the Spirit of our God'. Jesus chose to save them, they accepted his salvation, were baptised and made new people by the Spirit of God. Father God had accepted them on the grounds of his Son's name. In short, they were different because God had picked them up, cleaned them up and filled them up!

Think of it! Take a few minutes to remember how you once lived before Jesus changed your life. Is he sanctifying you? Have you been baptised? Are you full of the Holy Spirit?

Prayer: We thank you Father that we are heirs of the kingdom. We want to live today so that people can see we are different than we used to be. In Jesus' name, Amen.

JUNE 2   **LUKE 6:37**

THREE BOOMERANGS

'Do not judge, and you will not be judged. Do not condemn, and you will not be condemned. Forgive, and you will be forgiven'.

Jean: Have you heard about the Australian aborigine who was given a new boomerang for his birthday, but had a nervous breakdown trying to throw his old one away? The three sentences in our verse for today are boomerangs. Throw them out and they will come back to you. Judge someone and it will come back on you. Condemn someone and you'll be condemned. Forgive and you'll be forgiven.

Condemnation follows hard on the heels of judgement. How much sorrow and pain would be eliminated if we would not set ourselves up as judges in the first place. Those who judge are expected to pass sentence. Once the judgement and condemnation is hurled it rebounds back on the one who threw it. How strongly we defend ourselves. If we defended others as zealously as we defend ourselves we would find a new role . . . the defender, rather than the judge. Of course, if we forgive, rather than judge or condemn, there is no case. All is forgiven by both parties. The case is thrown out of court . . . upon the cross, where it stays, where the Saviour prayed, 'Father, forgive them for they know not what they do'. Each of us should humbly whisper, 'Neither do we'.

Pause to think: Which boomerang would you like to have come back? Judgement? Condemnation? Forgiveness? It's according to which one you throw.

Prayer: Today, dear God, let me throw forgiveness out to all who offend me or others. You know how much I need it to come back to me. In Jesus' name, Amen.

JUNE 3   **1 CORINTHIANS 2:10-13**

THE SEARCHER AND REVEALER

'But God has revealed it to us by his Spirit. The Spirit searches all things, even the deep things of God. For who among men knows the thoughts of a man except the man's spirit within him? In the same way no-one knows the thoughts of God except the Spirit of God. We have not received the spirit of the world but the Spirit who is from God, that we may understand what God has freely given us. This is what we speak, not in words taught us by human wisdom

but in words taught us by the Spirit, expressing spiritual truths in spiritual words'.

Jean: Before being born again our experiences in life are limited to our natural faculties. Afterwards, we have spiritual vision and hearing. We develop new tastes and sensitivity. Awareness is heightened to comprehend spiritual realities. We begin to respond to our daily experiences in the light of what we have seen in the Bible, what we know by faith and what we sense in our spirit. We begin to discern by the power inside us. Spiritual discernment is wisdom revealed by the Holy Spirit. He unveils, explores, examines. He opens our minds to recognise what is against us as well as what is for us. We discern the significance of the world, the flesh and the devil.

For the children: Can you name the five senses? By them you recognise and respond to your world. You can have a sixth sense. The Holy Spirit can give you faith. By faith you can recognise and respond to God.

Prayer: Father, we ask that the Holy Spirit will give us discernment today to recognise what is right and wrong, evil and good. May he also give us power to choose that which is good and reject that which is evil and do right, not wrong. In Jesus' name, Amen.

JUNE 4   **COLOSSIANS 1:16-18**

GOD'S VERDICT ON MAN

'For by him all things were created: things in heaven and on earth, visible and invisible, whether thrones or powers or rulers or authorities; all things were created by him and for him. He is before all things, and in him all things hold together. And he is the head of the body, the church; he is the beginning and the firstborn from among the dead, so that in everything he might have the supremacy'.

Elmer: In Genesis we read that after each stage of creation God pronounced his work 'good'. However, when God created man in his own image, he said all he made was 'very good'.

It is not difficult to agree that God's creation of the heavens and the earth is good. The cosmos is the apex of mathematical perfection, tuned to perfect rhythm. The heavens all in harmony declare the glory of God and are sustained by his presence. In Psalm 139:14, David declared 'I am fearfully and wonderfully made. Your works are wonderful. I know that full well'.

It is hard for some of us to see ourselves as very good.

Think about this: Is it hard for you to believe that you are worthwhile? Of all God's creation you are the best. Even at our worst, dead in sin, God saw us as worthwhile. To judge our worth, we must realise Jesus died for us. The cross is our sign of value.

Prayer: Dear God, help me to see the good you see in me. Take away the evil you see. Create a new heart within me and multiply the good. In Jesus' name, Amen.

JUNE 5   **JOHN 17:15-18**

'PEOPLED-OUT'

'My prayer is not that you take them out of the world but that you protect them from the evil one. They are not of the world, even as I am not of it. Sanctify them by the truth; your word is truth. As you sent me into the world, I have sent them into the world'.

LaDonna: Over the years I have learned what it means to become 'Peopled-out' – burned out and exhausted by the problems and needs of people.

Christ seemed to have vast reservoirs of strength for people. He was sent to a world of people. The incarnation was only the first step in his mission. When exhausted Jesus did not soldier on doggedly under obligation. He renewed his 'sent-status' by taking time with the Father to receive a specific direction to specific people.

Christ said we are sent to the world, the world of people. But there are other worlds we are not to be part of – the evil spiritual world and its worldly system. When we become 'burned-out' we are either under attack spiritually or have taken on the cares of this world. We've lost our 'sent-status' and have become 'members of the madness'.

Take a moment: Remember, heaven is your home. Listen for God's new commission and be sent with power.

Prayer: Lord, help me to see things through your eyes. Don't let me get so absorbed with business that I overlook the people for whom you died. Amen.

JUNE 6   **1 JOHN 2:15-17**

DISCERNMENT OF THE WORLD OF THINGS

'Do not love the world or anything in the world. If anyone loves the world, the love of the Father is not in him. For everything in the world – the cravings of sinful man, the lust of his eyes and the boasting of what he has and does – comes not from the Father but from the world. The world and its desires pass away, but the man who does the will of God lives for ever'.

Alan: The word of God commands us to love Him and not this world. Why? Loving the world brings anguish. Riches can be gone instantly through disaster or bankruptcy. A person too fond of food or drink is in danger of a real bondage to gluttony and alcoholism. Lust of the eyes can stir up passions which remain demanding, unfulfilled desires all one's life. That which is our greatest pleasure often leads to our worst misery. Such a life is like the fantasy of a thirsty man who 'sees' a glass of water in the desert. He watches, uncomprehending as it evaporates and he is left empty.

To love God more than the world releases faith which overcomes the evil of this world.

Make a bold statement: Lord, we will love you and overcome the world!

Prayer: You are our satisfying portion, dear Lord. We drink of the water of life and thirst for more, but we are not empty. We feed upon your Word and hunger for more, but we are not starved. We love you and long to love you more, and we are loved. Amen.

JUNE 7   JOHN 14:30-31

THE HOSTILE INVISIBLE WORLD

'I will not speak with you much longer, for the prince of this world is coming. He has no hold on me, but the world must learn that I love the Father and that I do exactly what my Father has commanded me. Come now; let us leave'.

Jean: The inexplicable hostility, the unreasonable rebellion, the irrational hate that lashes out in violence, man against man and man against God, has a central source. It is the lying mouth of the ancient destroyer, Satan. His rebellion is re-enacted in every individual. Rebellion has developed an organised system called 'this world'. It is the present world order of human existence, without the knowledge of God.

Jesus came into this world, the obedient Son of God. Satan advanced towards him, but there was nothing in Christ the devil could claim as belonging to his realm of rebellion. Satan found in sinners that which was part of his own nature and gave them their due . . . death. But Christ took that spiritual death for us. He overcame the prince of this world. Now every believer can go out to meet the advancing enemy unafraid. Jesus said to his disciples, 'The ruler of this world is coming. He has no claim upon me, but to show the world I love the Father, I do exactly as he commands. Up, let us march to meet him!'

Heart search: Rebellion and disobedience gives the devil a right to condemn us. Obedience gives us the right to condemn the devil. The ruler of the rebellious still comes towards us. We shall rise in the name of Jesus and show the world we love the Father and do exactly as he commands. Up, let us march to meet him!

Prayer: Father, we accept the Lord Jesus' death for us as our shield of faith against the enemy who would accuse us. We advance behind his cross. We want to be your obedient soldiers. Amen.

JUNE 8   ROMANS 8:5-8

MAKE YOUR MIND UP

'Those who live according to the sinful nature have their minds set on what that nature desires; but those who live in accordance with the Spirit have their minds set on what the Spirit desires. The mind of sinful man is death, but the mind controlled by the Spirit is life and peace, because the sinful mind is hostile to God. It does not submit to God's law, nor can it do so. Those controlled by the sinful nature cannot please God'.

Jean: (Excerpt from 'Life In The Overlap' pp. 93-94) When conflict comes between the willingness of the spirit and weakness of the flesh, recognise that you are a human being with two choices. You are the one who can decide whether you will be carnal or spiritual. In your mind are the habits of the body and the soul, most of them developed when you knew nothing of the power of the Spirit. By your choice to obey the Spirit you are able to partake of the divine nature of Jesus and renew your mind. By the knowledge of the Word of God you learn what is the will of God. Obedience to the word and the will of God develops a new life-style and you recognise that more and more you have the mind of Christ . . .

Think on this: Choose this day whom you will serve . . . the flesh or the Spirit.

140

Prayer: Father, I thank you I have the freedom to choose to be a spiritual person rather than a sinful one. Help me by the Holy Spirit to make my mind up. In Jesus' name, Amen.

JUNE 9   **MARK 4:15**

SATAN STEALS THE SEED

'Some people are like seed along the path, where the word is sown. As soon as they hear it, Satan comes and takes away the word that was sown in them'.

Jean: I remember a vacant piece of ground in our neighbourhood. It was an eye-sore. Everybody who wanted to take a short cut bisected it with well-worn paths. Stray dogs and vagrants used it and slowly it became a dumping place for rubbish. Not far away was one of the nicest gardens in the area. It was full of lowers, fruit trees and vegetables. The ground had been cleared and ploughed before it was planted. A fence and gates were put up, not to keep everything out nor everything in, but to allow the owner to control what he wanted in or out.

Those two pieces of ground illustrate the difference between a mind that is unprepared for the word of God and one which is prepared. Jesus describes how the word, like seed, can be sown. If left untended in the mind, it won't stay there for long. Satan, like a bird of prey, will swoop down and take it away. I wonder where he takes it? Perhaps he drops it among those who argue over scripture. Let us have minds ready for the word of God, cleared, ploughed and protected. Let the Holy Spirit renew our minds. Let us plough up the soil by repentance . . . breaking up the hard ground. Let us fence our minds and set up our gates by decision and commitment to serve the Lord.

Question: Last month I suggested you plant some seeds in the garden or window box or even in a flower pot. How does your garden grow? Does it need some care? How about your mind . . . Is it ready for the word of God?

Prayer: Father, clear my mind, break up hardened ground. I will build my fences and gates. I decide now to commit my mind to study your word and to serve you. In Jesus' name, Amen.

JUNE 10   JOHN 17:16-19

HE SANCTIFIED HIMSELF

'They are not of the world, even as I am not of it. Sanctify them by the truth; your word is truth. As you have sent me into the world, I have sent them into the world. For them I sanctify myself, that they too may be truly sanctified'.

Jean: Our grandson Ian Illiott was born with cataracts on both eyes. My heart was broken for my daughter and son-in-law, LaDonna and Alan. Crazy questions poured through my tears and prayers. 'What can we do? What have I done to have this sadness? Is God trying to show us something, say something to us?' 'What's wrong?' After the shock as I waited before the Lord, verse nineteen came to me. 'For them I sanctify myself, that they too may be truly sanctified'.

This is part of the high priestly prayer of our Lord for all who would believe in him. He does not pray for believers to escape from the world, for that would frustrate divine purpose. He does not ask that they be immune from the world's sadness nor hatred, for that would be inevitable, since they were identified with the One most hated by the evil one. No, he prayed they would be sanctified by the truth he had taught them. He prayed that nothing which would happen to them in this world would cause them to give up their task.

Each day we observe God at work in Ian. He has had the cataracts removed. Doctors have given him contact lenses. God has given him sight.

Family: Give yourselves to him who can keep you in this world. Do this for each other and for Jesus' sake.

Prayer: Father, you give us the strength to cope with trials and to praise you in the midst of them. May we glorify you as we sanctify ourselves. In Jesus' name, Amen.

JUNE 11   **TITUS 3:5-7**

HEIRS OF GOD

'He saved us, not because of righteous things we had done, but because of his mercy. He saved us through the washing of rebirth and renewal by the Holy Spirit, whom he poured out on us generously through Jesus Christ our Saviour, so that, having been justified by his grace, we might become heirs having the hope of eternal life'.

Elmer: Peter Aleksin, a young Christian Life College graduate, refers to what he calls 'The worm in the dust concept'. It's the idea that as individuals full of sin and prone to sin, we are not worthy to take very much from God's infinite provisions. However, Peter points out that God has a far different view concerning those who own his son Jesus Christ as Saviour and Lord. Peter believes strongly that according to St Paul, 'God has raised us up with Christ and ". . . seated us together in the heavenly realms in Christ Jesus" ' (Ephesians 2:6). He teaches we have been justified by grace that we might ' . . . approach the throne of grace with confidence so that we may receive mercy and find grace to help us in our time of need' (Hebrews 4:16).

Through the grace and mercy of our Lord and Saviour, we become sons and heirs. Our pardon is complete, and we have been loosed from Satan's bondage. Our record before God is spotless because he sees us, now, in Christ. We are told by St Paul to claim the riches of heaven as our inheritance.

Meditate on this: We have a wonderful hope before us as heirs of God − eternal life.

Prayer: Help me to realise, dear Father, all you have given me freely through Christ. I approach the throne of grace to receive your grace. In Jesus' name, Amen.

SANCTIFICATION – SOMETHING WE
PARTICIPATE IN

*'But thanks be to God that, though you used to be slaves to
sin, you wholeheartedly obeyed the form of teaching to which
you were entrusted. You have been set free from sin and have
become slaves to righteousness. I put this in human terms
because you are weak in your natural selves. Just as you used
to offer the parts of your body in slavery to impurity and to
ever-increasing wickedness, so now offer them in slavery to
righteousness leading to holiness . . . For the wages of sin is
death, but the gift of God is eternal life in Christ Jesus our
Lord'.*

LaDonna: Recently, I watched a television report about airline
pilots who fall asleep at the controls of their fully automated
craft. One man was reported to have been asleep for twenty
minutes during an intercontinental flight before the cabin crew
awakened him. The problem is that once off the ground the air-
craft virtually flies itself, leaving the pilot only as a monitor for
emergencies and with the difficult task of landing.

Becoming part of God's family can seem an automatic pro-
cedure. Christ has provided a complete package of redemption
that only requires our acceptance.

But our sanctification is not so. To grow into the likeness of
Christ requires our active daily participation. Holiness happens
as we do it. Because we don't want to appear hypocritical we
sometimes avoid righteous actions. But Paul says that just as
our participation in sinful deeds corrupted and enslaved us, so
righteous behaviour will lead to being like Christ.

Sanctification is not on 'automatic pilot'.

Thought: What are you doing today? Righteousness or old sinful patterns? Choose to live more like Christ today.

Prayer: Lord, I want to become more like you, today. So today
I'll choose those things that are pure and peaceful. Amen.

RECOGNITION OF OUR TOTAL SELVES

'It is because of him that you are in Christ Jesus, who has become for us wisdom from God — that is, our righteousness, holiness and redemption. Therefore, as it is written, "Let him who boasts boast in the Lord" '.

Alan: Our personalities are like pools that start off reasonably clear but are soon polluted. The years dam up our pools with pain. Our personalities become stagnant. We try to hide our unsightly blockages. However, their odious presence often breaks out through our altered behaviour. Of what, then, can we boast?

We can boast of a new life in Jesus Christ that opens up the channels of the inner self. The sweet water of the Holy Spirit creates a powerful whirlpool. It fills as it whirls to the depths of our souls loosening the filth and corruption, cleansing us until at last He overflows the banks of our personalities and flows through our behaviour. New streams of ever-increasing righteous thought, holy speech and redeemed behaviour pour forth. These are the streams of new life in Christ.

Today: Boast about the Lord to someone.

Prayer: Flood me with your Spirit, Lord, and cleanse me of inner decay. Help me to open up today to the cleansing of my soul. In Jesus' name, Amen.

WHOLLY HOLY

'May God himself, the God of peace, sanctify you through and through. May your whole spirit, soul and body be kept blameless at the coming of our Lord Jesus Christ. The one who calls you is faithful and he will do it'.

Jean: God is a Caller and a Doer. He calls each of us to be totally holy, not by our own doing, but by his. He is the Doer.

We make yielding ourselves to God so difficult. Either we fight the call to a holy life with a flat refusal, or we give ourselves bit by bit in piece-meal offerings, rather than full surrender. We find it hard to let God do it. We would rather do it ourselves, or not at all. Often we act holy outwardly but within are unholy thoughts and desires running free. We may succeed in disciplining the body, but not in harnessing our passions.

The fact is, God has called all of us to live a holy life. It is inherent in our obedience to the gospel. What is the holy life? It is the offering of ourselves totally to live a pure life for his glory. If you feel you could never make it, good! Join the human race. None of us could.

Then what are we to do? First, answer the call. Say yes to God's love. Second, offer ourselves as we are, to live wholly for God's glory. Remember, if we try to live partially committed to God, we will be in conflict. Our Christian experience will be a war that never ends. Third, let God do it . . . that is, trust God to sanctify us through and through. Jesus and the Holy Spirit will unite within to purify our total living. Let go and let God.

Consider this: If you want peace within and without, yield yourself wholly to God and he will pour great spiritual prosperity all through your being.

Prayer: Dear God, I yield my spiritual, emotional and physical self to you. I trust the Son and the Spirit to sanctify me continuously. In Jesus' name, Amen.

JUNE 15   **2 THESSALONIANS 2:13**

GOD HAS PLANNED YOUR SURVIVAL

But we ought always to thank God for you, brothers loved by the Lord, because from the beginning God chose you to be saved through the sanctifying work of the Spirit and through belief in the truth'.

Jean: Against his prediction of dark days ahead when a counterfeit Christ, the Lawless One, would appear with the power of Satan, Paul holds up a bright promise to the humble brethren of Thessalonica, 'God has chosen you to be saved . . .'

We live much closer than they to the revelation of Satan's 'Lawless One'. Our world is being conditioned to believe his counterfeit miracles and every sort of evil. He comes to deceive those who love lies rather than truth.

However, we are chosen as believers, to be sanctified by the Holy Spirit in these last days. We shall be kept holy in a corrupt society. We need not fear evil, for the Lord who loves us is greater than the Lawless One who hates us. It is good news for the youth and for the children of this generation to know God has chosen them to be saved.

Are you intimidated by some corruption which spreads out to rot your soul? Don't fear, God will preserve you by the power of the Holy Spirit. He who is within you is there to constantly purify your life. But you must believe it! Believe God plans for you to be delivered out of the mess you see in lives all around you, for you have chosen to love the truth . . . and the truth sets you free continually.

Question: Are you allowing yourself to be conditioned to believe a lie or are you conditioned by the love of the Lord and the sanctifying power of the Spirit?

Prayer: Father, you have planned for me to be saved, even from the things I see destroying others around me. May the Spirit of truth help me to believe your love will save me. I choose to believe the truth. Thank you Jesus. Amen.

JUNE 16   **HEBREWS 2:11-13**

THE SANCTIFIER AND THE SANCTIFIED

'Both the one who makes men holy and those who are made holy are of the same family. So Jesus is not ashamed to call them brothers. He says, "I will declare your name to my brothers; in the presence of the congregation I will sing your praises". And again, "I will put my trust in him". And again he says, "Here am I, and the children God has given me"'.

Jean: The Sanctifier and the sanctified are all one. Our lives, united with his, become holy as he is holy. What a privilege to bear his name, to be his family. He has delivered and brought into his kingdom former slaves. Has he made us servants? Oh, we would serve him forever! But he has made us more than servants. Friends? Oh yes, what a friend we have! What fellowship. We are even more than friends. We are family. We are his brothers and sisters. We slaves are now sons of God! Is it any wonder we exalt him, our Lord? We praise his name. We are not ashamed to call him our Brother.

Quiet. Listen and bow your head. There is a far greater mystery than the union which transforms sinner-slaves into brothers of Jesus. It is the mystery of love which unites holy Jesus to us so perfectly, he is not ashamed to call us brothers!

God's Son accepts us, God the Father accepts us in the Beloved. Let us accept ourselves as the sanctified. Moreoever, since the One who makes men holy and those who are made holy are of the same family, should we not accept one another?

Family: Take a moment to look at one another. You are a beautiful family. Your lives are entwined. What each of you are, you all are. Let each one assure the other that you are not ashamed to be related to them. You are more than servants, more than friends, you are family.

Prayer: Father, our hearts overflow with praise and joy when we realise you have fully accepted us as brothers and sisters to your Son. Thank you. Help us to bear his likeness more and more. In Jesus' name, Amen.

JUNE 17   **JOHN 12:31-32**

JESUS IS VICTOR

'Now is the time for judgement on this world; now the prince of this world will be driven out. But I, when I am lifted up from the earth, will draw all men to myself'.

Jean: In our text today, Jesus is nearing the time of the great reversal within the invisible realms. In the garden Father God was disobeyed, man was defeated and Satan was victor. Soon it will all change. The Father will be obeyed by the Son, man will be rescued by redemption and Satan will be defeated by the cross.

God the Father and all heaven are near with anticipation. God speaks like thunder to the Son, assuring Jesus that his death will glorify the Father. Jesus feels the nearness of the hour of judgement on this world. He senses the clash of the kingdom of darkness against his kingdom, the struggle and driving out of Satan from his unlawful authority over man. Then he describes how he will die. He sees it clearly; not only the trial, the scourging, the crown of thorns, the nails in his hand and feet, the sword in his heart. He sees more. His death will be a death which will glorify his Father; it will be a death which will judge the world and defeat the prince of this world. Most of all, it will release a magnetic power which will draw all men to himself.

Think of it: The power of the cross drives Satan out and draws sinners in. Let us shout, JESUS IS VICTOR!

Prayer: Son of God, we thank you for drawing us to yourself, and to your Father. May your magnetic love keep us near you this day, and always. Amen.

JUNE 18   **1 CORINTHIANS 15:24-26**

DEATH A CAPTIVE

'Then the end will come, when he hands over the kingdom to God the Father after he has destroyed all dominion, authority and power. For he must reign until he has put all his enemies under his feet. The last enemy to be destroyed is death'.

Elmer: I like the European Easter greeting. 'Christ is risen!' The response is, 'Christ is risen indeed'.

I have known of three people who have been raised from the dead by prayer. But they, like Lazarus in the Bible, died sooner or later. Christ is not only risen from the dead. He is risen INDEED.

Christ's grave seemed a cave of despair to his friends. But they were wrong. Jesus was launched by the power of the Holy Spirit from hell itself into the heavenlies, victoriously. He has not only conquered death for us but continues from victory to victory. He has put all of his enemies and all of our enemies under his feet. He is our victorious champion. We are winning because he has won. On that final day when Jesus hands a redeemed world over to the Father, we will be there.

Let us realise our place in Christ. Let us live victoriously now.

Prayer: Lord, I accept the Holy Spirit who raised Jesus from the dead to quicken my mortal body and make me really alive, now. Amen.

JUNE 19   PHILLIPIANS 2:9-11

POWER OF A NAME

'Therefore God exalted him to the highest place and gave him the name that is above every name, that at the name of Jesus every knee should bow, in heaven and on earth and under the earth, and every tongue confess that Jesus Christ is Lord, to the glory of God the Father'.

LaDonna: As I came zipping off the hectic scramble of Knightsbridge Roundabout, I was cautioned to halt by a policeman. I drove over to one side as a black Daimler slipped through the grand iron gates of the archway to my left. What gave that driver the right to go through prohibited gateways and halt traffic? The name. A royal name. The name of Queen Elizabeth opens doors for a special few.

But for those in Christ, his name supreme controls all realms in heaven, earth and under the earth. His authority is no honorary investiture, but a hard-fought victory. Hell must bow to his authority won at the cross, where he humiliated and defeated evil. What a name!

Thought: The way to complete victory is to allow Christ complete authority in your life. Declare aloud the Lordship of

Christ to situations of unease and confusion. Then watch conflict dissolve into peace.

Prayer: Lord, I submit to your authority in the situations that trouble me today. Bring your reign of peace to my life as I obey your will. Amen.

JUNE 20   **HEBREWS 2:14-15**

FREED FROM THE FEAR OF DEATH

'Since the children have flesh and blood, he too shared in their humanity so that by his death he might destroy him who holds the power of death, that is, the devil — and free those who all their lives were held in slavery by their fear of death'.

Alan: I know what it is to fear death. I had cancer. It wasn't the moment of passing, but the not knowing what I would pass to, that frightened me. 'What's out there' I wondered, as I recalled Sunday-School lessons of years past. Such uncertainty is fear indeed.

Soon after my ordeal with cancer, I was born again. One of the things that took place in me at that precious moment, was the disappearing of that fear. Deep within me I met with a God that had been a man on this earth, who shared both life and death. And now he is doing it all over again, living my life with me.

Action: Through prayer and the reading of the Word, let's start today to understand the mysteries of death that our friend Jesus Christ has unfolded and conquered. If you met a man who had come back from the dead, what would you ask him?

Prayer: Help me, dear friend Jesus, to understand death and your victory over it. Help me to see it through your eyes. Amen.

JUNE 21   **2 PETER 2:4-9**

THE LORD KNOWS

'For if God did not spare angels when they sinned, but sent them to hell putting them into gloomy dungeons to be held for

judgement; if he did not spare the ancient world when he brought the flood on its ungodly people, but protected Noah, a preacher of righteousness, and seven others; if he condemned the cities of Sodom and Gomorrah by burning them to ashes, and made them an example of what is going to happen to the ungodly; and if he rescued Lot, a righteous man, who was distressed by the filthy lives of lawless men (for that righteous man, living among them day after day, was tormented in his righteous soul by the lawless deeds he saw and heard) — if this is so, then the Lord knows how to rescue godly men from trials and to hold the unrighteous for the day of judgement, while continuing their punishment'.

Jean: Often when faced with some perplexing problem in life for which there seems no answer, a Christian can be heard to say, 'The Lord knows'. Sometimes it is a statement of faith, sometimes it is fatalistic. In the midst of all the gloom, doom, flood and fire of our reading, Lot's name appears. He was distressed and tormented by the lawlessness and the filthy lives of his contemporaries. The Bible kindly omits the fact that it was Lot's own decision to live there. He was trapped, and God rescued him.

Don't miss this wonderful truth. Yes, God judges sin, whether it be angels or cities, men of ancient times or modern times. No plans or politics can keep judgement from a sinful people. God also knows how to deliver godly men from trials. He has plans to judge and plans to rescue. How we live determines which plan will work for us. Are you one of the faithful, or one of the fatalists?

Question: Are you trapped in some distressing situation? Anxious? Have you lost the desire and motivation to live? Sit quietly. Think of the words of Jesus, 'Peace, be still'. Begin to say them slowly and lovingly, like he would. Let his rest fill your troubled mind. The Lord knows.

Prayer: Father, we look to you and to your plans to save us. We will not look back in fear nor forward with dread. In Jesus' name, Amen.

FOLLOWERS OF THE WARRIOR

'They will make war against the Lamb, but the Lamb will
overcome them because he is Lord of lords and King of kings
– and with him will be his called, chosen and faithful
followers'.

Jean: There are many interpretations of the mysterious visions
of Revelation. We are not going to try to sort them out. Rising
above the blood, fire and smoke of war against the Lamb comes
the final shout of victory. 'The Lamb will overcome them
because he is Lord of lords and King of kings!' He is Lord and
King because he is the Lamb. There would be no victory, no
throne without the cross. Whose Lamb is he? God's Lamb, but
not his only. He did not die for God, he died for us. God, the
Father gave him to take our sins away. He is ours. He drew us
to him and we will follow him.

   'The King of kings and Lord of lords' title will cause all things
in heaven, on earth and under the earth to bow the knee and
acknowledge him. But it is to the Lamb upon the cross that his
followers first bowed their knee and confessed with their
mouth. When he comes into his glory, his called, his chosen, his
faithful followers will share his victory forever and ever. It will
not be unusual for them to see him victor, for they have known
his victory and claimed it by faith from the cross to the throne.
What joy when faith will turn to sight!

Remember: No matter how hot the battle is right now, you are
on the winning side. Have faith in the victory of the cross. Don't
give up. You don't want to miss V Day, do you?

Prayer: Why not sing, 'He is Lord, He is Lord. He is risen
from the dead and he is Lord, Every knee shall bow, every
tongue confess that Jesus Christ is Lord'. Now add in unison
your Amen . . . 'Jesus is Lord!'

THAT'S WHY JESUS CAME!

*'He who does what is sinful is of the devil, because the devil
has been sinning from the beginning. The reason the Son of
God appeared was to destroy the devil's work'.*

Jean: The epistle of 1 John is a letter about God's righteous
love. As we read it we wonder why he should love us so. Why did
Jesus come to live in our cruel, unjust world? Why did he suffer
and die upon the cross? To save us from the judgement of God?

To be forgiven and cleansed is more than we could ever have
asked for, except by the grace of God. Yet such blessing would
have been short term had not Jesus come to deliver us from our
ancient foe, the Devil. No one knows more about all the trickery
and treachery of sin than the Devil. He's worked it into every
part of the world, whether primitive or civilised, ancient or
modern. Sin is no respecter of persons, times or cultures. He
works with individuals and with nations, in the open and in
secret.

Now for the good news. Jesus came to destroy the works of the
devil. He comes into all the places and to all the people where
the devil has done his destructive work. The devil is strong, but
Jesus is stronger. The devil has been sinning from the beginning, but Jesus was before the beginning and still will be after
Satan has been cast into hell. He will finally destroy the
Destroyer himself.

Just think of it: Our enemy is a defeated foe. He is the terrorist,
who with all his organisation, is under house-arrest, awaiting
the final sentence that will imprison him forever.

Prayer: Today, dear Father, we rejoice in the victory of our
Lord over Satan. We will not let him destroy the love we have
for each other nor our faith in Jesus Christ. We ask the Holy
Spirit to help us resist the devil. Amen.

OUR VICTORY IS IN JESUS

*'I tell you the truth, anyone who has faith in me will do what
I have been doing. He will do even greater things than these,
because I am going to the Father. And I will do whatever you
ask in my name, so that the Son may bring glory to the
Father. You may ask me for anything in my name, and I will
do it'.*

Jean: When we recognise that daily victory in the Christian life
is not in ourselves, but in our Saviour Jesus Christ, waiting
upon the Lord becomes an important use of time. Christians
under stress need to steady their minds many times a day.

If a compass is placed upon a rickety table, the slightest move-
ment will shake the table and swing the needle, making the
compass point untrue. Steady the table, let the compass settle
and it will point aright. Quietness guides us towards victory.

Do it now: To get a faith sense of victory, be perfectly silent for
a few moments. Think of Jesus, the Victor. Drop your worries.
Let frustration fall limp. Relax. Now ask, believing he will do it.

Whisper: Jesus, I ask in your name for peace, for quietness
within. There are things I cannot do, nor know how to do. I'm
listening to hear you say to me, 'I will do it'. Amen.

CALLED TO FREEDOM

*'It is for freedom that Christ has set us free. Stand firm, then,
and do not let yourselves be burdened again by a yoke of
slavery'.*

Elmer: We must constantly and faithfully adhere to the gospel
of Liberty. In chapter four the apostle pointed out that the
Galatians must be careful not to allow themselves to be drawn
back into bondages insisted upon by false teachers.

Jesus, too, taught freedom from the bondage that teachers

would place upon others. He often started teaching by using the phrase, 'You have heard it said by men of old time . . .' These teachings to which he referred were not truly Moses' Law. They exaggerated the law. For instance, Moses' Law said that people should not work on the Sabbath. When a poor cripple whom Jesus had healed on the Sabbath carried his bed roll home, they criticised it as work.

There are other bondages people would force upon us. Be sure and check that your religious prohibitions are found in God's word. Remember Satan is the accuser of the brethren. Although you may 'feel' that you must or must not do something, do not live by feelings, but by faith. Test your feelings by God's word. Realise that it is for freedom that Christ has set you free.

Check it out: Can you say that you are free? Do 'feelings' rule where faith should rule?

Prayer: Lord, help me live free from cultural bondage and religious slave-drivers. In Jesus' name, Amen.

JUNE 26   **COLOSSIANS 2:10; 13-15**

DEATH TO LIFE

'And you have been given fulness in Christ, who is the head over all power and authority . . . When you were dead in your sins and in the uncircumcision of your sinful nature, God made you alive with Christ. He forgave us all our sins, having cancelled the written code, with its regulations, that was against us and that stood opposed to us; he took it away, nailing it to the cross. And having disarmed the powers and authorities, he made a public spectacle of them, triumphing over them by the cross'.

LaDonna: We are complete in Christ! The words sear across the parade of failures peppering my life. Is there something wrong with the statement? Of course not. Then how am I complete? Scripture says we are complete when we are in Christ. In other words when we have passed from death to life into the power of Jesus Christ.

The exalted Christ is complete. He is completely victorious, fully invested with power and authority. He is perfectly fitted with the armour of victory. When we leave our former, futile way of life, and pass into Christ's life, he equips us for victory.

Then why do I fail so often? It is because I choose to wrestle with my problems, instead of lifting high the perfect, shining shield of faith.

Comment: How will you cope with your life today? If you have passed from death to life, you are fully equipped to triumph. Choose to place your faith in Christ's power, instead of struggling to overcome with empty hands of flesh.

Prayer: Dear Lord, I do not want to rely on my flesh. I put my trust in your power and provision. Thank you for helping me use your spiritual weapons for the challenges of this day. Amen.

JUNE 27   **2 TIMOTHY 1:7**

OUR VICTORY IN HIM

'For God has not given us a spirit of timidity, but of power, love and discipline'.

Alan: If God has given us a spirit of power, love and discipline, why do I still experience timidity? Looking back to a particular incident, I noticed several things.

It was one of those days when I was muddling through in my own strength rather than living in God's grace. Was I conscious of the power of the Holy Spirit within? No. I recall being intimidated by the rather pompous and proud attitude of the man I was dealing with. Instead of the love of God in my heart, I was fearful. In fact, I was unprepared for the situation that arose. Why? Total undiscipline in my life. Lack of discipline in a soldier can cost him his life! I was secure in the Lord; what about that man who should have heard the Word of life? I was too timid to say anything. Where was the victory? Was I walking in the Spirit? **THAT** was the problem. The Holy Spirit is the spirit of love, power and discipline — and He is the secret of victory.

Action: Today, let us look for a situation in which we can be bold, not in our own strength and self-confidence but in God's strength which is peace and love.

Prayer: Lord Jesus, today I pray your forgiveness for not walking in the Spirit. Thank you for the One who strengthens and empowers me to do your will. Amen.

JUNE 28   HEBREWS 2:14-15

VICTORY OVER DEATH

'Since the children have flesh and blood, he too shared in their humanity so that by his death he might destroy him who holds the power of death — that is, the devil — and free those who all their lives were held in slavery by their fear of death'.

Jean: The reality of death cannot be counter-balanced by a mere guess, hope or longing, but only by another reality as solid as itself. The resurrection of Jesus Christ is a rock-solid fact. This fact gives us an entrance into life after death.

I talked to a London Taxi driver today about life after death. he said, 'You know, I died once and came back!' 'That happened to my mother, too!' I told him. As he described his experience I was excited by how similar it was to my mother's. My mother recognised her mother in heaven. He recognised his father. 'My mother saw Jesus — did you?' I asked. 'I'm not sure, because all I saw was a great light. A voice told me I had to come back'. We talked of Jesus, the Way, the Truth and the Life. Then we prayed. Afterwards the taxi driver said, 'I feel I'll know him next time. I'm not afraid to die'.

A life and death matter: Prepare for the whole of life — here and hereafter.

Prayer: Father, I am coming home. Let me live today for tomorrow and for eternity by your grace. Amen.

HE GIVES US OVERCOMING FAITH

*'You, dear children, are from God and have overcome them,
because the one who is in you is greater than the one who is in
the world'.*
*'For everyone born of God has overcome the world. This is the
victory that has overcome the world, even our faith'.*

Jean: No matter how strong may be the Christian's inherent
tendancies towards evil, or the habits he may have formed by
successive acts of sin – God is able to deliver. He keeps us from
being overcome. It is possible for a believer to abstain from
fleshly appetites which have been subjugating his soul. New life
in Jesus carries a promise of victory. He undertakes to make us
conquerors.

Take heart! It is possible for you to put your foot on fleshly
desires and reign where you once groaned in slavery.

Question: Who's 'The greatest'? The one who is in the world,
or the One who is in you?

Prayer: Father, I believe Jesus is your Son. My faith in him
gives me confidence to face my world today. Amen.

JESUS REWARDS OVERCOMERS

*'He who overcomes will, like them, be dressed in white. I will
never erase his name from the book of life, but will acknowledge his name before my Father and his angels'.*
*'Him who overcomes I will make a pillar in the temple of my
God. Never again will he leave it. I will write on him the
name of my God and the name of the new Jerusalem, which
is coming down out of heaven from my God; and I will also
write on him my new name'.*

Jean: Those who overcome evil here will see evil overcome
eternally by the Victor, Jesus Christ. Those who confess Jesus'

name here will be named by Jesus before the throne of heaven. Those who have refused to bend, burn or break under life's trials will be made indestructible pillars in the temple of God. Those kept clean by the blood of Jesus will walk with him clothed in eternal purity. Those who lived as pilgrims here will be citizens of the New Jerusalem.

Help for today: Neither depression nor disaster should cause you to give up your faith. Don't let anyone or anything rob you of the Victor's reward. No battle, no victory. No cross, no crown.

Prayer: Father, let me live today so Jesus can put his name on my life and say 'Well done'. Amen.

JULY 1   **JOHN 17:8**

THE WORD IS OUR WEAPON

'For I gave them the words you gave me and they accepted them. They knew with certainty that I came from you, and they believed that you sent me'.

Jean: When challenged by the prince of darkness, Jesus relied on the written Word of God. He made full use of it, and it was an effective weapon in his hands for he was a man of prayer, well acquainted with the scriptures, fully submitted to God and filled with the Spirit. His teaching of the written Word and the spoken, revealed will of the Father were his gift to his disciples. If they were to make as good a use of the Word as Jesus did, they would also need to be men of prayer, well acquainted with the scriptures, fully submitted to God and filled with the Spirit.

Remember: Jesus has given you the Word to use as an effective weapon against the enemy. Use it today.

Prayer: Father, give me words today which will be effective against the enemy. In Jesus' name, Amen.

THE WORD THAT HEALS

'You are already clean because of the word I have spoken to you'.
'When the Counsellor comes, whom I will send to you from the Father, the Spirit of truth who goes out from the Father, he will testify about me'.

Elmer: God spoke at the beginning of Creation, and order appeared out of chaos. We read in the Psalms God sent his Word and healed the Israelites. In the New Testament, Jesus Christ, the Word made flesh, came and healed the sick and forgave sin.

God speaks to men of every generation. If we allow him, the Holy Spirit will speak into our minds, bringing order out of chaos and light into darkness. Our whole outlook will change and we will begin to see the Kingdom of God with a new perception and grasp of things. Revelation will come to us through the written Word, and revelation will come as God speaks words of peace to our hearts. Not only this, the Holy Spirit will help us to speak God's words of faith for ourselves and others.

Receive his word to you now: 'I forgive you by my blood. I heal you by my wounds. I empower you by my Spirit'.

Prayer: Dear Jesus, I receive your words for my healing. Help me to speak words of faith which will inspire and help others. Amen.

SPIRITUAL WEAPONS – THE WORD OF GOD

'The word of God is living and active. Sharper than any double-edged sword, it penetrates even to dividing soul and spirit, joints and marrow; it judges the thoughts and attitudes of the heart'.

LaDonna: At one point in my life I huddled depressed in the middle of a large, darkened room. Everything in my life seemed dark, especially my thoughts. An onslaught of criticism, fear, self-hate and confusion weighed heavily upon my mind. Until that point I had defended myself with reasonable arguments. I thought I knew what was true about myself. Then I spiralled downwards into confusion and self-doubt.

There, alone in my room, I reached for my Bible. Putting aside all human opinion, I began to read aloud. Truth cut through the darkness, severing the lies one by one. After a long time, deception was shattered. I could think clearly. The Word had done its work.

Comment: We are not strong enough to fight the accusations of man and Satan. But the power of the Word severs lies from truth. Speak God's Word aloud into things that confuse you and wait for God's gift of heavenly wisdom.

Prayer: Lord, I submit to you my futile thoughts. Show me the wisdom from heaven in Scripture and help me to confess it with my lips until I see your victory. In Jesus' name, Amen.

JULY 4   **EPHESIANS 6:17**

THE LIFE-GIVING WORD

'Take the helmet of salvation and the sword of the Spirit, which is the Word of God'.

Alan: The power of the Word of God is indisputable. It is both the soothing balm of healing for tortured souls and the fire that burns out impurity. In his word, God expressed his great love for man and provided him a manual for redemption. He commands us to love his word and keep it ever on our lips.

This mighty weapon is best wielded by a disciplined arm. Discipline in daily reading of the scriptures and regular Bible study builds faith and love in the heart, and releases the Holy Spirit to work powerfully in our lives and daily circumstances.

Action: Prayerfully find a Bible verse for a particularly difficult situation in your life and claim its promise. Read it aloud several times and declare God's power through his Word in your life.

Prayer: Lord Jesus, help me today to find that special verse and see your power released in it. As your first disciples said, we pray 'Lord increase our faith!' Amen.

JULY 5   **ISAIAH 49:2**

A SWORD IN MY MOUTH

'He made my mouth like a sharpened sword, in the shadow of his hand he hid me; he made me into a polished arrow and concealed me in his quiver'.

Jean: A sharp tongue wounds. There is a difference between the mouth made like a sharpened sword by the Lord, and a mouth made so by ourselves. The mouth the Lord makes effective is the one that speaks the word of God, is controlled by the Spirit of God and disciplined by prayer. The mouth we make sharp speaks words of self, is controlled by the flesh and undisciplined through prayerlessness.

I have experienced the keen, searching, cutting power of the scriptures. They have pierced my heart more than once. They disturb, uncover and cleanse. Through repeated use, they have become a weapon keener than a sword.

A word to adults: God keeps us hidden in his shadow until the chosen moment comes for his word to be thrust with greatest effect to deliver others from the enemies' power. Let's allow the Lord to 'sharpen' us.

Prayer: Conceal me from my enemies, Lord, until your time comes to release your word in this situation. Amen.

163

THE SWORD IN HIS MOUTH

*'In his right hand he held seven stars, and out of his mouth
came a sharp double-edged sword. His face was like the sun
shining in all its brilliance'.*

Jean: This doubly effective, two-edged sword cuts both ways.
When Jesus spoke to the churches in Revelation his Word
struck sinners, and searched saints. Powerful, two-edged truth
came out of a face shining with glory brighter than the sun. That
glory was both wonderful and terrible. The Victor held the
churches, like stars, in his right hand and in the other the keys
of death and Hades (verse 18).

Those who feel the striking power of the word of God, must
also look into the face of the Word. John knew that fact as he
wrote, 'The Word was made flesh and lived a while among us.
We have seen his glory, the glory of the one and only Son, who
came from the Father, full of grace of truth'. It is the wonder of
grace and the power of truth that we see and touch in the Word.

Let's respond: The truth hurts us, but grace heals us. Shall we
allow the Sword of the Spirit to touch the things God wants to
heal in our lives?

Prayer: Jesus, let me hear your word and see your face. The
sword cuts, but your grace blesses. Thank you, Father, for your
son. Amen.

JULY 7   MATTHEW 4:4

VICTORY IN TIME OF TESTING

*'Jesus answered, "It is written: Man does not live on bread
alone, but on every word that comes from the mouth of
God"'.*

Jean: Jesus was tempted at every level. In the area of physical
desires, he was tempted to use power given for ministry to
others in self-gratification. In the area of the mind, he was

pushed towards self-destruction as proof that his power was God-given. In the area of the spirit he was urged to gain world dominion by winning world approval, doing as Satan commanded, bowing down instead of winning the world to God by self-abnegation.

The victory came by the Word in his mouth. Satan's perversion of scripture was met by 'It is written'. Truth was thrust with accuracy against the lie. This was no self-assertion, but strong dependance upon the Word of God. Angels came and ministered to Jesus, giving evidence that he had been tempted to seek for help.

Remember: All of heaven is on your side when you deny self, declare truth, and depend upon it.

Prayer: Father, Jesus' temptations were as real as my own are right now. Help me to resist the enemy successfully. I have your word hidden in my heart. May your Spirit help me. Amen.

JULY 8   **ZECHARIAH 9:11-12**

A PLEDGE OF DELIVERANCE

'As for you, because of the blood of my covenant with you, I will free your prisoners from the waterless pit. Return to your fortress, O prisoners of hope; even now I announce that I will restore twice as much to you'.

Jean: Historical facts illustrate spiritual realities. The prophet could see Israel, the daughter of Zion, conquered and divided, exiled into Egypt and Greece. His prophecy is all the more amazing, for he foresaw the rise of the Medo-Persian dynasty and the struggles between Jews and Syro-Grecian power in Maccabean times.

The good news to the covenant people is the message of coming deliverance. The blood covenant which was made at Sinai, sealed and attested by the blood (Exodus 24:4-8) still held good and was a pledge to the nation of deliverance and help. Their covenant was a token of the everlasting covenant sealed with the blood of Christ. By his blood shed upon the cross, God's people

165

are delivered from the bondage of sin.

Today's message is to all those who belong to the Lord who are still oppressed and captive to the powers of this world, and to any who are in the pit of despair. Hear his promise: 'I will return twice as much to you'. There is a double measure of blessing for all your suffering.

Say to each other: Get out of the pit, prisoner of hope. You are a blood covenant person.

Prayer: Thank you, Jesus, for your blood shed for me. I do not wallow in a waterless pit. I am redeemed, and restored. Amen.

JULY 9   ACTS 20:28

REDEEMED, AND CARED FOR

'Guard yourselves and all the flock of which the Holy Spirit has made you overseers. Be shepherds of the church of God, which he bought with his own blood'.

Elmer: The church of God was redeemed by the blood of his only son. As redeemed individuals then, you and I are of great worth. We are without price in God's eyes. It is not enough for the church to be redeemed. Every individual member of the flock must be cared for.

In Australia there are wild horses which run very fast, but are worthless for the purpose of racing. They are not cared for, and are untrained. The Queen could spend a mint of money for a fast, well-bred race horse. But if he were not properly cared for, fed, groomed and trained he could not win races.

It is not enough that we are 'bought with a price'. We must be willing to receive care and provision from God's 'Stable hands', the pastors, teachers and evangelists he has placed over us. We can't run the race without their help. We need good teaching and care.

Think about it: How well do you accept the care and training that is given you?

Prayer: Lord, give our leaders wisdom and faith to care for us, and help us to respond to their attention. Amen.

POWER IN THE BLOOD

'But only the high priest entered the inner room, and that only once a year, and never without blood, which he offered for himself and for the sins the people had committed in ignorance . . . How much more, then, will the blood of Christ, who through the eternal Spirit offered himself unblemished to God, cleanse our consciences from acts that lead to death, so that we may serve the living God!'

LaDonna: Monster films and horror stories are full of frantic images of people brandishing crosses to ward off vampires, ghouls and spirits. Consequently, the cross seems as fictional as Frankenstein.

There is a real monster each one of us wrestles with. It's grip is more deadly than any Hollywood fantasy. It is a guilty conscience.

Guilt steals your joy, shadows every smile, and pursues you from failure to failure. But through Christ we can be released from the strangle-hold of guilt. God himself gives us complete pardon through the shed blood of Christ. The enemy now has no right to accuse us.

Thought: Victory is not pretending you never fail, but rather living in divine forgiveness. Have you failed to keep Christ's commands? Have you hurt someone lately? Confess it to Christ, be reconciled. Remind the enemy that your sin is under the blood and then take hold of victory with joy.

Prayer: Father, I acknowledge my weakness and failure to live as you desire. Thank you for giving me complete pardon in Christ and give me the power to obey your will with joy. In Jesus' name, Amen.

THE CLEANSING FLOW

'To Jesus the mediator of a new covenant, and to the sprink-led blood that speaks a better word than the blood of Abel'.

Alan: As Abel's blood flowed out upon the ground, it cried out for restitution. When the blood of Jesus Christ flowed from the cross, it was the heart response of God to called-for restitution. It remains active, cleansing us from the world, making all things new again. Its power is in its absolute purity. Nothing from the world can stain too deeply for its cleansing, nor can the enemy grasp hold of what the Lord washes clean in his blood. Its power is the basis of our new life in Jesus Christ. Its victory is eternal.

Action: Christ's blood was shed for you. Claim and appropriate its power for yourself.

Prayer: I praise you, Lord Jesus, for the sacrifice of your blood shed for me. Help me to understand the purifying power of your blood. Amen.

FELLOWSHIP WITH THE FORGIVEN

'But if we walk in the light, as he is in the light, we have fellowship with one another, and the blood of Jesus, his Son, purifies us from every sin'.

Jean: When we ask forgiveness of our sins, we should intend to forsake the sins we confess. That is, we walk in the light. The promise of forgiveness and cleansing from sin is to those who sincerely endeavour, even imperfectly, to walk in the light as he is in the light. When we walk with him we share his enmity for sin. We also share the efficacy of his cure for sinfulness. The power of his blood keeps cleansing. Let us confess and forsake the sins which nailed Jesus to the cross. When we forsake sin, we have fellowship with the forgiven. We find our brothers and sisters who also walk in the light of Jesus, our Redeemer. The forgiven forgive as freely as they have been forgiven. The same blood purifies us from every sin. Let us not forsake our brothers and sisters.

For today: Be sure that you're in fellowship with the Lord, and with his family.

Prayer: Father, let no dark shadows of unforgiveness mar my fellowship with Jesus and my family. In Jesus' name, Amen.

JULY 13   REVELATIONS 5:9-10
WORTHY IS THE LAMB

'And they sang a new song: You are worthy to take the scroll and to open the seals because you were slain, and with your blood you purchased men for God from every tribe and language and people and nation. You have made them to be a kingdom and priests to serve our God, and they will reign on the earth'.

Jean: Sometimes it seems good goes unrewarded and evil goes on forever unjudged. One wonders if there is any justice. Who will vindicate the faithful believers who have prayed and waited in hope of God's justice? Jesus will! The prayers of saints of all ages will release the judicial power of the Lamb of God. They will break the sad silence in heaven which follows the angel's question, 'Who is worthy to break the seals and to open the scroll?'

The saints, purchased by the blood, have known all along who is worthy. They prayed, and his blood cleansed them from all sin, delivered them from Satan's power, removed all condemnation from their souls and sent evil spirits scattering in fear. Through all the ages, from Calvary to the Day of Judgment, the saints have rejoiced over the power of the blood of the Lamb. Now in John's vision, they break the sad silence of heaven with a love song to the Lamb who stands in the throne room of heaven. He who stood in the midst of the church delivering them from Satan's power now stands to judge all those who have rejected his atoning sacrifice. He is worthy! Worthy is the Lamb!

For the family: Sing a song about the worthiness of the Lord, or the power of his blood.

Prayer: Lord, we accept the power of your blood to protect us from evil today and to save us from the future judgment of the wicked. In your name, Amen.

JULY 14   HEBREWS 11:28

HAVE FAITH IN GOD'S PROVISION

'By faith he kept the Passover and the sprinkling of blood, so that the destroyer of the first-born would not touch the first-born of Israel'.

Jean: The Passover, one of the Jewish festivals, was a perpetual witness of Israel's mighty deliverance out of Egypt. By faith the Israelites sprinkled the blood of a slain Lamb upon the lintel and doorposts of their houses. They were identifiable by the blood. They revealed themselves to be God's people and under his protection. Where there was no faith, no blood was sprinkled and the judgment of God fell upon their firstborn. Our greatest need in life is to have constant faith in God's provision for our salvation. He has chosen a Lamb for us. His sinless blood was shed upon the altar of the cross. Active faith appropriates the blood of the Lamb to the door of our hearts continuously.

Do it today, as you should have yesterday and shall do tomorrow. For daily appropriation identifies you as one who has placed his faith in God for his salvation. Let the enemy, the neighbours and your family know whom you trust to save you from judgment.

Parents: The Israelites made provision for their children's deliverance by selection of a lamb for the household. Today, lay hands on your children and claim the power of the Lamb of God for them. There is power in his blood.

170

Prayer: Father, we thank you for providing the Lamb who offered himself as the perfect sacrifice for our sins. We accept the power of his shed blood. Help us to be clearly identified as your people in this world. In Jesus' name, Amen.

JULY 15   **LUKE 24:49**

HE WILL GIVE YOU POWER TO DO HIS WILL

'I am going to send you what my Father has promised; but stay in the city until you have been clothed with power from on high'.

Jean: The promise was fast approaching; the power of the Holy Spirit was practically upon them. Once he came, they would start moving from Jerusalem farther and farther away towards unknown people in the unknown world. But not before they were empowered. Jesus said they must wait, THEN they could go. They must wait to be clothed with power from heaven.

They knew they needed it. On the night of Jesus' arrest they had been stripped of their own self-confidence and boasted courage. Shaken, fearful and in hiding, these would-be followers of Christ knew they did not naturally have what it would take to do the things Jesus expected of them. So they waited for the promise of power from on high.

It rests with us, as with them. Will we wait for the promise of power? When we feel God is asking us to do something we are not naturally equipped to do, we must wait until he gives us divine power.

The pause that refreshes: Each of you, before you rush out into your world today, wait a moment. Say to yourself, 'I am sent by Jesus into my world. He has promised me power to bring Good News to others. I wait now until I realise the power of the Holy Spirit within me'. Quietly wait until you sense the presence of the Holy Spirit all around you like a long coat, warming you within.

Prayer: Father, we go in the power of your Spirit into our world today. In Jesus' name, Amen.

OUR WONDERFUL TEACHER

'For the Holy Spirit will teach you at that time what you should say'.

Elmer: Think of the best teacher you've ever had. Perhaps it was in primary school or at college. It seemed that your teacher understood you. Complicated things were made simple. You were encouraged to work hard at your lessons, and you wanted to learn because you loved your special teacher-friend. You wished you could always have your inspiring, caring, loving teacher with you.

Jesus said that our teacher, the Holy Spirit, will be with us forever, night and day. He teaches us how to live for Jesus, for others and how to think in a Christian way. As we learn our lessons well, the Holy Spirit's thought-patterns become ours.

Sometimes we are faced with the need to make quick decisions. If we are already acquainted with the Holy Spirit as a constant, personal guide in decision-making, he will help us as our unseen advisor. We will speak correctly because he has taught us how to think. He is our unseen guide whispering from within.

Prayer: Lord, help me to develop patterns of thought that will enable me to respond as a real Christian in times of stress. Amen.

Parents and children: Talk together about your teachers and pray for them.

FIRST RESPONSES

'But the Counsellor, the Holy Spirit, whom the Father will send in my name, will teach you all things and will remind you of everything I have said to you'.

LaDonna: What is your first response when things don't go according to plan? The common occurences of daily life often prove to be the hidden battle-fields providing many subtle victories for the enemy.

The Lord graciously provided Alan, Ian and I with a house. While waiting for the transaction to be finalised, we stayed with friends for about six weeks. Two weeks before we were due to move, we were notified that it had been delayed for another month. Alan and I were deeply disappointed. It meant more moves for our little family during that extra month, and we began to think very negatively regarding the house-holders.

Then the Holy Spirit spoke to my heart. He showed me that we were not expressing God's love to them in the aloof, abrupt business-like attitude we were taking. So we arranged a meeting. We found them open and approachable. But more importantly, we shared how God cared for and directed our lives.

The Lord won a victory in this situation by the way we responded to our circumstance.

Thought: Think of the little challenges of your day. These are potential triumphs for the Lord, or the devil. The Holy Spirit knows what course of action will glorify God. Pause and let him show you how to triumph.

Prayer: Lord, you say that you will give wisdom to those who ask. Come Holy Spirit, and show me how to glorify God in the situations which challenge me today. Amen.

JULY 18   **ACTS 1:8**

POWER FOR SERVICE

'But you will receive power when the Holy Spirit comes on you; and you will be my witnesses in Jerusalem, and in Judea and Samaria, and to the ends of the earth'.

Alan: The disciples received a mighty empowering for service through the gift of the Holy Spirit. It was a new covenant promise which is for us today. If you have not received the gift of the Holy Spirit – seek it! If you have already – use it! There are no 'inferior gifts' as some would call them. All are an empowering for service. If you pray in tongues, pray often for it edifies and strengthens you to serve. If words of knowledge come to you, then be in a place where you can reach people. If gifts of healing become evident, then pray for the sick even if you are not in their presence. All of the gifts are for the equipping of the saints. Use them in your service to the Lord and for his kingdom. They are powerful weapons to aid us in winning the lost, healing the sick, strengthening our brothers and sisters and driving back the enemy.

Respond to the Lord: The Word says God will give us the desires of our hearts. Let's make it our greatest desire to be empowered by God in every way and to not limit the power of God in us in any way.

Prayer: Lord, I pray for the right gifts for me in my situation. I ask that they will flow according to the need and that you will work deeply in me, perfecting me by the Holy Spirit all my life. Amen.

JULY 19   EPHESIANS 3:16

INSIDE POWER AGAINST OUTSIDE PRESSURE

'I pray that out of his glorious riches he may strengthen you with power through his Spirit in your inner being'.

Jean: When Christians are under pressure they need more strength. More of God's strength. The strength of God is personified in the Holy Spirit. Believers can do anything required of them within God's will by the Spirit. Spiritual strength does not come from the outside, but from the inside. It is deep in the believers's inner being; within the core of their real self. Outer conflict should not diminish the inner strength of the Christian, but develop it. The harder the pressure from outside, the stronger the dependance upon the One inside. Have faith and surrender at the deepest level within yourself to the presence of the Spirit. Be filled with the fulness of God. Be strong.

Today: When outside pressures create tension ask the Holy Spirit to strengthen you within. Stop and rest in the Lord until you sense the strength flowing from him all through you. Let tension be the signal of your need of his strength.

Prayer: Father, let me be alert to the signals my mind and body give me when I'm running out of natural life-force to withstand pressure. Teach me to draw upon the Spirit's power in my inner being. Help me to not deal outwardly with my problems so that I'm exhausted, but to deal with them immediately by the Spirit's indwelling power. In Jesus' name, Amen.

JULY 20   **1 CORINTHIANS 2:4-5**

PLACE PEOPLE'S FAITH IN GOD, NOT IN YOURSELF!

'My message and my preaching were not with wise and persuasive words, but with a demonstration of the Spirit's power, so that your faith might not rest on men's wisdom, but on God's power'.

Jean: How foolish we are to try and persuade people to believe in God by argument or eloquence. We are sure to find ourselves embarrassed failures. We are not wise enough in wordly terms to answer the hard questions unbelievers ask.

I was asked some hard questions at a dinner party in Paris. 'Why does God allow war? Why do the innocent die? Is it fair when the good have to suffer?' I answered again and again, 'I don't know. I don't know' until the questions ceased. Then I said, 'I've told you what I don't know, now may I tell you what I do know about God's ways?' My host encouraged me to say more. I told them of God's grace in my life, of miracles of healing in our family. I told how he heals broken hearts, homes and minds. When I finished, the dinner party turned into a prayer meeting. Several guests came to know the Lord and others were healed that night.

The demonstration of the Spirit's miraculous power is the most amazing proof of the reality of Christ. He gives an internal witness and external evidence. Only he can do that.

Discuss: Have you seen God's power demonstrated? Tell each other briefly about it. Your message is your experience of God's power. Try to share that message today with someone outside your family.

Prayer: Father, as I share my testimony today may the Holy Spirit cause that person to place their faith in Jesus. In his name, Amen.

JULY 21   LUKE 11:13

DON'T BE AFRAID, TRUST GOD

'If you then, though you are evil, know how to give good gifts to your children, how much more will your Father in heaven give the Holy Spirit to those who ask him!'

Jean: Some people fear the Holy Spirit. They shrink back from him as one would from a striking snake or slung stone. They consider the Holy Spirit dangerous. Such fear is based upon a misunderstanding of the Father's heart. He provides good gifts for us which are useful, protective and necessary. The gift of the Holy Spirit is not optional. He is the distributor of all the countless good things God has for us. Never doubt that God will give you the best. The Holy Spirit is the Father's answer to your insufficiency, your weakness, your inability to cope, your lack of faith. He is heaven's best answer to any hungry heart. Don't starve yourself to death spiritually because you are afraid of what God will give you if you let him know you are hungry.

Just for fun: Children, ask your father for bread. What does he give you? (Fathers, you may offer inedible things instead of bread. Now give them bread). Lesson: Why did you keep asking for bread, even when you didn't get it? Because you know your father cares about you and because he knows you need bread. Trust God. He cares about you and knows you need the Holy Spirit. He will not play games with you.

176

Prayer: Father, forgive me for not trusting you to give me your best when I hunger and thirst. Thank you for the Holy Spirit. Take away my fear, increase my faith. In Jesus' name, Amen.

JULY 22   **JOHN 14:13**

PRAY PRAYERS THAT GLORIFY GOD

'And I will do whatever you ask in my name, so that the Son may bring glory to the Father'.

Jean: If we're going to receive anything from God, apart from the general blessings which fall on the just and unjust, we must ask for them. Special blessings come from special praying. The Christian's special kind of praying is to ask in Jesus' name. Jesus came to us in his Father's name, now we come before the Father in Jesus' name. Because we belong to Jesus we are authorised to approach his Father. We ask not on the basis of our own merit, but as identified with the Son of God. The Father always hears and answers him whom he calls his Beloved, and we are accepted in the Beloved. Jesus will do for us whatever will glorify his Father. In his mission on earth and in his ministry in heaven, his desire remains to glorify the Father. We may be sure of receiving anything from Jesus which will give glory to the One who sent him. This is a key to effectual prayer.

Question: What do I want Jesus to do for me? Will the answer to my prayer bring glory to God? Discuss this together before you pray.

Prayer: Father, I believe Jesus can bring glory to you by answering this prayer . . . (you add your Father-glorifying request in Jesus' name). Amen.

JULY 23   **ACTS 16:18**

WE REPRESENT THE CROWN

' . . . Finally Paul became so troubled that he turned round and said to the spirit, "In the name of Jesus Christ I com-

mand you to come out of her!" At that moment the spirit left her'.

Elmer: A man in a dark blue suit and helmet may raise his hand and say, 'In the name of the Queen – Stop'. He has the right to give such a command because he is a policeman with authority from the Queen. I might make a similar statement – and would go unheeded because I do not represent the crown.

Jesus said to his disciples, 'All power is given unto me . . . Go ye therefore' (Matthew 28.20). Again he said, 'These signs shall follow them that believe. In my name . . . ' By contrast in another incident in Acts 19 we see that power does not rest in saying the words 'Lord Jesus', but in believing in his name. The word 'therefore' in the 'Go ye therefore' of Matthew 28:19 is very important. It is because HE has all power that we may speak words of faith representing him.

Question: Did you believe in Jesus for salvation? Are you believing him now to complete what he began in you? Continue to believe – and 'signs will follow'!

Prayer: Lord, I believe. Increase my faith. Amen.

JULY 24   **PHILLIPIANS 2:9-11**

THE AUTHORITY OF HIS NAME

'Therefore God exalted him to the highest place and gave him the name that is above every name, that at the name of Jesus every knee should bow, in heaven and on earth and under the earth, and every tongue confess that Jesus Christ is Lord, to the glory of God the Father'.

LaDonna: I've heard many styles of preaching and praying. I remember sermons delivered in tremendously loud, authoritative voices. Sometimes they made my spirit soar with joy. Other times they seemed hollow and abrasive. I've heard people pray with frantic shouts and wailings which seemed effortless, while others spoke a quiet word of authority and the problem fled.

Why is it that sometimes strong, loud praying seems to be effective and other times not? Unconsciously, trust can shift from the power of Christ to a certain authoritative technique. Remember that victory comes from the presence of the exalted Christ. When Christ rules, blessing and power will flow from within.

Think about it: Are you concerned about someone's need or your inner conflict? Put your faith and confidence in Christ's authority. Cease striving and watch the power of his presence work miracles.

Prayer: Lord, I realise your work does not rely on technique and methods but on the power of your presence. I submit to you my ambitions and desires and ask that you fill my life with your glory so that my life might bless others. Amen.

JULY 25   REVELATION 19:16

THE NAME – OUR STANDARD

'On his robe and on his thigh he has this name written: King of Kings and Lord of Lords'.

Alan: A common complaint among Christians today concerns the difficulty of maintaining the 'standard'. 'It's just too hard' we say, or 'I'm not strong enough yet'. The standard has become no more than mere words devoid of power.

Our vision of Jesus Christ is so limited. While being the Shepherd and the Lamb, he is also the coming King, the very breath of whose mouth will slay the enemy. He is the mighty King who conquered hell and death, the Lord of Lords who bruised Satan's head, the King of Kings who is given all power and authority and has shared them with his servants.

Is your standard a mere word, or The Word? Are you his servant? Or just his sheep?

Think about it: In whatever circumstance we may be in, let's make the conscious decision to let the strength of our stand be on that name: Jesus Christ, King of Kings and Lord of Lords. My Lord.

Prayer: I ask today that your name, Lord Jesus Christ, will sur-round me like a cloak with your powerful presence. Thank you for the power of your name. Amen.

JULY 26   **ISAIAH 9:6**

WE NEED A BORN LEADER

'For to us a child is born, to us a son is given, and the govern-ment will be on his shoulders. And he will be called Wonder-ful, Counsellor, Mighty God, Everlasting Father, Prince of Peace'.

Jean: The Prince-Of-The-Four-Names was promised to Israel when the kingdom was slipping into the hands of foreign con-spirators. Leadership was needed; a leader who was aware of the needs of the people and had power to meet those needs. They needed someone to call Wonderful, for they needed wonders; someone to call Counsellor, for they needed a righteous ad-vocate to plead their cause; someone to call Mighty God, for they needed divine protection; someone to call Everlasting Father, for they required a dependable provider and head of the nation; someone to call Prince of Peace, for they were afraid of war. They needed God.

In our times so much we had expected to go on forever in our culture is slipping from us. Strong conspiracies between in-visible and visible forces are pulling our social fabric apart. Someday, perhaps we will recognise our need of the Child who was born, the Son who was given to be all we need. Let us accept the born leader who has identified with us in our need. Name him according to your greatest need. He is your all in all. Do you need a miracle? He is Wonderful. Do you need someone to stand up for you? He is Counsellor. Do you need someone you can count on to care for you? He is the Everlasting Father. Do you need divine intervention? He is the Mighty God. Do you need an end to fighting? He is the Prince of Peace.

Question: Can the children remember the four names of the Promised One in our scripture today? How many more names do you know him by?

Prayer: Jesus, Son of God, I accept you as my all in all. You are everything to me. I love you, Prince-Of-The-Four-Names. Amen.

JULY 27   JOHN 15:16

YOU HAVE BEEN CHOSEN TO BE FRUITFUL

'You did not choose me, but I chose you to go and bear fruit – fruit that will last. Then the Father will give you whatever you ask in my name'.

Jean: We have a built-in resistance to God's will. It is a sin-streak running through our whole make-up; a warp in our personalities; a fixed thought pattern in our brains; a poison in our blood stream. If left to our own choices, we go hell-bent from the cradle to the grave. But a love force repeatedly interrupts and interferes with our own ways. With annoying persistence, it strikes like sunshine in the eyes. God's love speaks words which won't go away; whispers convictions which disturb our inner beings. Love pulls, pleads and persuades until we realise we are not unwanted, but chosen by our Saviour to be loved for ever. Love draws us towards the eternal purpose, until we see that what we are and what we do for him has eternal value.

The only answer to love is to say, 'Father, I choose the Son who chose to die for me. I choose to live the life he has chosen for me to live. I say yes to love'. The Father will answer back, 'Since you've chosen my Son, I've chosen to give you whatever you ask in his name'. Is there any out-giving God?

Question: What kind of fruit can last indefinitely? Two kinds. The artificial kind, or the real fruit which carries seeds for reproduction. Which kind of fruit do you think the Saviour had in mind for those he chose?

Prayer: Father, let your life-giving love flow in and through me to cultivate a fruitful life. In Jesus' name, Amen.

RELATE AND RELEASE

*'Then Peter said, "Silver and gold I do not have, but what I
have I give you. In the name of Jesus Christ of Nazareth,
walk."'*
*'By faith in the name of Jesus, this man whom you see and
know was made strong. It is Jesus' name and the faith that
comes through him that has given this complete healing to
him, as you can all see'.*

Jean: The beggar-man was healed by faith. His own faith. He
looked at Peter and John, heard Peter's words and accepted his
offer of healing in Jesus' name. A few days earlier the name,
'Jesus of Nazareth' had been nailed on a cross above a condemned man's head. The lame beggar may not have seen the
cross himself, but he had certainly heard of it as men passed by
his begging post at the Gate Beautiful. Also he had no doubt
heard rumours of the resurrection of Jesus. But it took meeting
two men who knew Jesus was alive to release his faith in the
name of Jesus of Nazareth.

Today we can reach out and speak to people in a way that will
inspire them to have faith in Jesus Christ. More people are
waiting and able to receive miracles than we realise. They have
heard pros and cons about Jesus. They need to meet someone
who really knows he is alive. Someone who knows his name and
the power of it. Someone like you!

Remember: Here's how to relate to people in a way that will
release their faith. 1. First touch Jesus personally by prayer.
2. Keep filled with the Spirit. 3. Deeply feel the needs of others
and desire them to have faith in Jesus' name. If you know the
chorus, 'Silver and gold have I none', sing it with the actions.

Prayer: Father, today I will relate to people in a way which will
release their faith in Jesus. I trust your Spirit to lead me. In
Jesus' name, Amen.

HOW TO HANDLE AFFLICTION

'We are hard pressed on every side, but not crushed; perplexed, but not in despair; persecuted, but not abandoned; struck down, but not destroyed. Therefore we do not lose heart . . . for our light and momentary troubles are achieving for us an eternal glory that far outweighs them all'.

Jean: All believers are at times hemmed in and cast down with a succession of indignities and sufferings. Paul was troubled, perplexed and persecuted in every way. Yet affliction did not destroy his faith. Why? Paul accepted suffering as part of the Christ-life in him (vv.10-12). Trouble identified him with the One who had been neglected, defamed and despised. For Jesus, he died daily and was 'killed all day long', so that the life of Jesus would be obvious to all who looked on. His perseverance and preservation was proof of God's life in him. Affliction improved his efficiency. His astonishing success in the face of his enemies was proof that the power he had was not of himself, but was the power of Christ. Besides, Paul had a long-range view of affliction. He saw it in the light of eternity where God's glory transforms tears into pearls, brokenness into mortality, pain into songs of victory.

Look at trouble as part of your Christian life. Expect and extract the blessings hidden in it. Take hold of affliction and use it to make you Christlike rather than letting affliction take hold of you and make you devilish. Be a consternation to the enemy and a constant wonder to your friends.

Question: Do you know someone who is going through a prolonged time of affliction? Let them know today you understand and do not judge them. Help them to hold on. PRAY FOR THEM NOW.

Prayer: Father, we join in prayer for . . . .

THE RULES OF THE RACE

*'No one serving as a soldier gets involved in civilian affairs
– he wants to please his commanding officer. Similarly, if
anyone competes as an athlete, he does not receive the victor's
crown unless he competes according to the rules. The hard-
working farmer should be the first to receive a share of the
crops'.*

Elmer: In writing to his young friend Timothy about the
Christian life, St Paul uses the terminology of soldiers and
athletes. 'No soldier gets involved in civilian affairs'. So we
must be careful not to involve ourselves in the affairs of Satan.
An athlete does not receive the gold medal unless he competes
according to the rules. What are the rules?

A young man came to Jesus asking about the rules. Jesus
answered that all of God's rules hung on this one law: 'Love
God with all your heart, mind and soul and love your neighbour
as yourself' (Matthew 22:37-40).

With Jesus in our hearts we can truly love God. We must love
ourselves for Christ is in us. Then we can love and help others.
That's how we'll win the race.

Think about it: I must serve God by his rules . . . not my own.

Prayer: Dear God, may the rule of love be the rule of my life.
In Jesus' name, Amen.

THE THIEF

*'Timothy, my son, I give you this instruction in keeping with
the prophecies once made about you, so that by following them
you may fight the good fight, holding on to faith and a good
conscience. Some have rejected these and so have shipwrecked
their faith. Among them are Hymenaeus and Alexander,
whom I have handed over to Satan to be taught not to
blaspheme'.*

LaDonna: Not long ago, my dad had his wallet stolen. Not thinking, he had slipped his wallet along with a bundle into a carrier bag. Somebody was watching. Seconds later, the carrier bag was whisked from his hand. The thief disappeared.

Scripture says the Devil comes to steal, kill and destroy (John 10:10). In much the same way as an ordinary thief, the enemy lurks hidden, waiting for us to neglect, even momentarily, the powerful gifts God has given us. One such gift is faith.

How can faith be stolen from us? By neglect. Paul exhorted Timothy not to forget the promises of God and to keep a clear conscience. Absorption in complex controversies and doctrines can cause us to neglect pure, powerful faith.

Thought: Pursue faith pure and simple. Make a conscious effort today to avoid hectic activity and controversy. Cling to the simple truth of the promises of God.

Prayer: Lord, you have given me your word and special promises. Today I lay aside those things that misplace my faith. I put my trust in what you have told me. Amen.

AUGUST 1   **1 TIMOTHY 6:9-11**

FILLED WITH THE OBJECT LOVED

'People who want to get rich fall into temptation and a trap and into many foolish and harmful desires that plunge men into ruin and destruction. For the love of money is a root of all kinds of evil. Some people, eager for money, have wandered from the faith and pierced themselves with many griefs. But you, man of God, flee from all this, and pursue righteousness, godliness, faith, love, endurance and gentleness'.

Alan: I suppose love could partly be described as a longing to possess the object loved. If, as in this scripture, the object is money, what would be the fruit of such a love-affair? Greed, selfishness, stinginess, taking and not giving, theft, perhaps even murder for gain.

If the object loved is Jesus, what can we expect the fruit of such a relationship to be? The very attributes of his divine nature – righteousness, godliness, faith, love, perseverance and gentleness! Which love-object do you choose?

Action: Throughout our relationship with Jesus we will find objects that draw some part of our affections away from the Lord. Today, let us locate one such object in our lives and bring it under submission to God's perfect will.

Prayer: Lord, help me to bring into submission anything that detracts from my relationship with you. Lead me into whatever change may be necessary as I learn to trust your love for me. Amen.

AUGUST 2   **2 CORINTHIANS 1:8,9,10**

COPING WITH PRESSURE

'... *We were under great pressure, far beyond our ability to endure ... Indeed, in our hearts we felt the sentence of death. But this happened that we might not rely on ourselves but on God ... He has delivered us ... he will deliver us. On him we have set our hope that he will continue to deliver us'.*

Jean: God always sees us when we have gone beyond our ability to endure some great pressure. He will deliver us. Has he not done it before, and will he not do it again? His faithfulness is our hope.

Sometimes God's servants, even the strongest, break down under burdens beyond their strength and sink into despair. Excessive afflictions can wear them down to the point where the only escape seems to be death.

If you are under severe pressure of affliction or danger, don't let fear make you forget the One who has delivered and still delivers those who put their trust in his faithfulness.

Note: St Paul adds a P.S. in verse 11. 'As you help us in your prayers'. Intercessory prayer is a mighty force against the enemy who strikes God's servants when they are down. If God has persistently reminded you of someone recently, perhaps he wants you to pray for them. Intercessory prayer works both ways; if you are presently under severe pressure beyond your strength, you can be sure God is speaking to someone to pray for you. Don't give up.

Prayer: Dear Father, help me to learn not to rely upon myself, but upon you. I have set my hope upon you. In Jesus' name, Amen.

AUGUST 3   2 CORINTHIANS 2:8,11

REAFFIRM YOUR LOVE

'Reaffirm your love for him . . . in order that Satan might not outwit us. For we are not unaware of his schemes'.

Jean: Satan scores if either an individual is driven to despair or the peace of a church is destroyed. He hates both individuals and the church and uses every scheme he can devise to wreck either one or the other. When a family commit themselves to the family of the Lord Jesus Christ, it won't be long before they will see a Satanic scheme in action to break up their unity.

Satan is a powerful, personal being. He extends great influence over the minds of men everywhere. His intelligence and organisation is beyond our conception. He seeks to pull down every work of God in man and community alike.

What is our mightiest weapon against such destructive power? Love which cares enough to discipline and to forgive. Such love outwits the enemy. Let us take a lesson from Paul's letters to the Corinthian church. Spot the devil's schemes. Discipline the sinner according to the sin. Then, forgive, affirm and re-affirm your love.

For the family: If someone in your family has needed discipline recently, they may still feel insecure. Even if you've said you have forgiven him, he may not have accepted it. It takes a long time to forgive oneself. So, strengthen him by saying it again, 'I forgive you. I love you'.

Prayer: Thank you, Father, for the mighty weapon of forgiving love. We use it today to fight off any attempt of Satan to mar our family unity. Amen.

AUGUST 4   JOHN 16:33

FAITH PRODUCES PEACE

'I have told you these things, so that in me you may have peace. In this world you will have trouble. But take heart! I have overcome the world'.

Jean: In the days of the Early Church, it is said that the Christian greeting often was, 'How's your faith?'

A genuine faith is an overcoming faith. We can't calculate exactly the degree of faith we have, but there are ways to make a good estimate. Can we visualize the things that are invisible? Can we retain our vision under discouraging circumstances? Are we able to keep going under stress?

Jesus knew that between the apostles and the fulfilment of their mission was a world of hostile forces. But he had overcome that world. Their faith in his victory would produce a peace through it all.

Discuss: How do you measure your faith? Try by checking how far you have come towards the goals God has given you as a family or personally.

Prayer: Today, dear Lord, I will take heart. Whatever lies ahead, you have already overcome. I have your peace. Amen.

AUGUST 5   ROMANS 8:15

A SLAVE AGAIN TO FEAR

'For you did not receive a spirit that makes you a slave again to fear, but you received the Spirit of sonship. And by him we cry, Abba, Father'.

Jean: After the American Civil War, many liberated slaves crawled back to their former masters begging to be slaves again!

188

They were unable to cope with liberty, for they were slaves to fear. Fear drove them back into bondage. The fear of a new life. They lacked identity. They didn't belong to anyone. They had such a low self-image that no matter where they were they were still slaves. Under their old masters they knew who they were and where they belonged.

When Jesus died upon the cross he emancipated every slave to sin. Are you living free? Unless you have let the Holy Spirit imprint the truth upon your heart and mind, you may still be living in fear and driven into bondage. Realise that the spirit of fear is no longer your master. Your Lord has given you the Holy Spirit and he is the Spirit of love and power and a sound mind.

Parents: Are you fearful of what shall become of you or your children? Your Father is the Owner of all things. His kingdom and power are boundless. Do you lack wisdom concerning your affairs and family? Let the spirit of Sonship be strong within you and claim the gifts of the Holy Spirit. You have power, use it. Get used to a new way of living as a child of God.

Prayer: Father, you have not given me a spirit of fear, but of Sonship. I say to my fear, 'Go, in Jesus' name. I am God's child. I will not fear'.

AUGUST 6   **JOHN 8:34-36**

LIVING IN FREEDOM

'Jesus replied, "I tell you the truth, everyone who sins is a slave to sin. Now a slave has no permanent place in the family, but a son belongs to it for ever. So if the Son sets you free, you will be free indeed"'.

Elmer: This is our declaration of emancipation: 'IF THE SON SHALL MAKE YOU FREE, YOU SHALL BE FREE INDEED'. Yet we notice from verses 31 and 32 that a single 'believing experience' is not in itself sufficient. As Christ's disciples we must continue to walk in the truth of his word. As we continue in the truth, we are continually set free.

Those who continue in the word are set free from the grievous burdens and traditions of ceremonial law. We are freed to serve God and his church as privileged sons. We are freed from prejudices, mistakes, false notions and cultural bondage. We no longer serve sin together with its enslaving lusts and passions. Though we may fall into sin, we need not be its slaves; the Son has released us from bondage.

Remember this: You are a SON of God and not a SLAVE to sin. Live in your sonship!

Prayer: Lord, I accept your forgiveness and freedom. Help me to walk freely using your word as a guide for my life. Amen.

AUGUST 7   **GALATIANS 4:6-9**

'WHO DO YOU THINK YOU ARE'

'Because you are sons, God sent the Spirit of his Son into our hearts, the Spirit who calls out, 'Abba, Father'. So you are no longer a slave, but a son; and since you are a son, God has made you also an heir. Formerly, when you did not know God, you were slaves to those who by nature are not gods. But now that you know God — how is it that you are turning back to those weak and miserable principles? Do you wish to be enslaved by them all over again?'

LaDonna: 'Who do you think you are?' Such a phrase has been levelled at me by Christian friends whose values differed from my own. As a teenager my friends' choices sometimes made me feel distinctly uncomfortable. My family had helped me to discern the difference between things that were clearly sinful and the things which were unprofitable to spiritual growth. As I grew up I felt inner conflicts because I tried to conform to my friends' standards. Some would say, 'You're super-spiritual', 'Too good', 'Let yourself be human'. Such words would make me feel hurt and alienated.

It was a great day of liberation when I realised I was too good.

Not because of who I thought I was, but who He thought I was. I was his child. His Spirit was in me. Because of the cross, for Jesus' sake, I would not allow myself to fall into the unproductivity of worldly behaviour.

Thought: Productive Christian living comes when you know who you are: a child of the King. You can do better than wallow in the world's ways. You are too good because of Christ.

Prayer: Father, thank you for giving me your goodness. Please show me the traps of the world that would impede your work in my life today. In Jesus' name, Amen.

AUGUST 8   JOHN 1:12
'IN CHRIST'

'Yet to all who received him, to those who believed in his name, he gave the right to become children of God'.

Alan: John Collins, Vicar of Holy Trinity Brompton recently made a statement worthy to be carved in stone. He said, I would rather we consider ourselves as In Christ than Christians. It is a more accurate description of our position.

To me his words remove from us what has become a nondescript label to a positive and clear declaration. It states where we stand both in this life and for eternity.

All too often I find myself acting like a slave in the Kingdom of God, rather than a son of the King. What is my position? Where do I stand? Simple. 'In Christ'. Hallelujah!

Action: Look for an opportunity to tell someone you are in Christ and what it means to you to be a child of God.

Prayer: O Lord my God, King and Saviour, help me to fully understand with all humility the awesome honour you have given me. May I stand firm on the unshakeable knowledge that I am in Christ. Amen.

191

AUGUST 9   PHILIPPIANS 2:14-16a

BE A STAR!

*'Do everything without complaining and arguing, so that you
may become blameless and pure, children of God, without
fault in a crooked and depraved generation, in which you
shine like stars in the universe as you hold out the word of
life'.*

Jean: 'Everything, Lord?' we ask. 'Everything', he replies.
Isn't it hard to do everything without complaining and arguing!
In fact, for some of us it isn't easy to do ANYTHING without
questioning and grumbling. God our Father wants contentment to become a good habit in our lives. That habit is acquired
by doing everything with a pleasant frame of mind. A person
with an unpleasant disposition is like a threatening thunder
cloud.

Often Christians don't appear to look nor act much different
from non-Christians, when asked to do something they don't
want to do. What a testimony it is when others are complaining
if we do the task without argument. It testifies to inner peace
and contentment with our place in this world. It is the radiance
of a soul which is in the centre of God's will. Against the
darkness of a world reeling with discontent and insecurity, such
Christians shine like stars in the universe; they hold out to us
the word of life . . . a life of inner peace and contentment.

Remember: It isn't always what you say, but what you don't
say that says the most. In other words, actions speak louder than
words.

Prayer: Father, let me develop today the habit of doing
everything without complaining and arguing. Make me a star
witness. In Jesus' name, Amen.

AUGUST 10   2 PETER 1:3-4

A BETTER QUALITY OF LIFE

*'His divine power has given us everything we need for life and
godliness through our knowledge of him who called us by his*

own glory and goodness. Through these he has given us his very great and precious promises, so that through them you may participate in the divine nature and escape the corruption in the world caused by evil desires'.

Jean: Within every blessing God gives to believers is the promise of a better quality of life. The blessing of salvation holds the promise of eternal life. The blessing of the Spirit gives promise of a Spirit-filled and Spirit-led life. His name, his blood, his Word all contain promises of a victorious life. Healing promises us an overcoming life of faith. Why is this so? Because every spiritual blessing contains his divine nature! God pours into our lives the very life of Jesus.

It is as though God is saying, 'Look, I have put within your reach a divine quality of life. You saw my goodness and glory in my Son's life, now take hold of it and make that same goodness and glory your very own. Participate in the divine nature!'

Participating in his glory and goodness does not make us little gods, nor does it make us less than human, but it does give us a divine quality of life which depends upon our faith and his faithfulness. Let us develop an accountable faith.

Today: Believe your life can be more glorious than it was yesterday. Believe you can show more goodness towards people than before. Take a heart full of his divine nature into your day.

Prayer: Father, it's all here, within me . . . Your glory, your goodness. Thank you for the promises of a better quality of life. You have set me free from a corrupt life caused by evil desires. I have escaped into a new way of living. Hallelujah! Thank you, Jesus. Amen.

AUGUST 11   **1 JOHN 3:1**

AND THAT'S WHAT WE ARE!

'How great is the love the Father has lavished on us, that we should be called the children of God! And that is what we are! The reason the world does not know us is that it did not know him'.

Jean: I overheard an angry woman shout at her husband, 'Know what's wrong with you? You've got such a low-down opinion of yourself, you let everybody walk all over you. You don't know who you are. That's what's wrong!'

When you don't know who you are you're not likely to stand up for yourself. I suppose because of sin-consciousness and self-consciousness, many Christians do have a low self-esteem. They have an 'I am unworthy' complex towards God and an 'I don't belong' complex towards the world. Many only see themselves as sinners and strangers.

We need to see ourselves as our heavenly Father sees us. We are his dearly beloved children. That's what we really are! It doesn't matter that the world can't see who we really are; it is so and God knows it.

Do you? It really matters that you see yourself a child of God. There are plenty of evil forces in this world who will walk right over you unless you live like someone who is important to your loving, heavenly Father.

Question: Ask yourself, 'How do I see myself?' Ask a close friend or relative, 'How do you see me?' Above all ask God, 'Who am I?'

Prayer: Father, I need affirmation today about my personal identity. You know how I feel about myself. You know the things that make me feel this way. I need to feel your loving approval. For Jesus' sake, Amen.

AUGUST 12   **PSALM 44:5**

TRAMPLED OR TRIUMPHANT?

'Through you we push back our enemies; through your name we trample our foes'.

Jean: A Christian's victory over the enemy does not come through trust in his own strength, but trust in the strength of the Lord.

Sometimes believers strut about like boys dressed as soldiers, shouting commands at the devil. It is often called, 'Using the believer's authority'. A soldier in God's army is given authority, but he does not use it as he wishes, anywhere or anytime, but under the Lord's orders. I have seen the demon-possessed literally fall back at the name of Jesus when the authority has been released under the guidance of the Holy Spirit. At other times, I have seen the evil spirits attack those who shouted, 'In the name of Jesus', because the command was spoken in the frustration of anger at the devil.

The Psalmist knew that it was not Israel's own might which won their victory. It was through the strength and the name of the Lord. Until we learn this, we're likely to find ourselves under the enemy's feet, rather than the enemy under our feet. We will be trampled rather than triumphant.

Consider this: Perhaps you have been endeavouring to oppose some evil attack upon yourself, your family or others . . . and your effort has seemed ineffective. Wait patiently upon the Lord before your next move. Wait for orders!

Prayer: Dear God, the enemy of our souls pushes very hard against us at times. We dare not push back unless we are strengthened by you. May the Holy Spirit quicken us. Give us faith to wait for that quickening. We know that you, our King, decree victories. In Jesus' name, Amen.

AUGUST 13   **2 CORINTHIANS 10:3-5**

THE WEAPON OF LOVE

'For though we live in the world, we do not wage war as the world does. The weapons we fight with are not the weapons of the world. On the contrary, they have divine power to demolish strongholds. We demolish arguments and every pretention that sets itself up against the knowledge of God, and we take captive every thought to make it obedient to Christ'.

Elmer: We do not wage war as the world does. It is true that we are in a battle. Jesus said that he did not come to bring peace but a sword. Yet he said, 'My peace I give unto you'.

Our weapons are not guns and tanks. Hatred and malice cannot prevail against Satan. His fortresses are the hearts of the unsaved. The sword of the Spirit, the Word of God, wielded in the love of God, breaks down even strong walls of fear.

God sent Jesus to love an unlovely people. Jesus sends us in like manner.

Today: Let us use the weapons of truth and love to destroy the works of the enemy.

Prayer: Lord, help me to remember that the most powerful weapon in Christian warfare is love. May your great love for me, and my love for your world break into people's lives today. In your name, Amen.

AUGUST 14   **EPHESIANS 3:10-11; 6:10-12**

WARFARE, NOT DETENTE

'His intent was that now, through the church, the manifold wisdom of God should be made known to the rulers and authorities in the heavenly realms, according to his eternal purpose which he accomplished in Christ Jesus our Lord'.
'Finally, be strong in the Lord and in his mighty power. Put on the full armour of God so that you can take your stand against the devil's schemes. For our struggle is not against flesh and blood, but against the rulers, against the authorities, against the powers of this dark world and against the spiritual forces of evil in the heavenly realms'.

LaDonna: Not long ago, my husband and I visited the Chelsea Barracks. A young soldier approached as we stood in the parade grounds talking to an officer. He saluted and stomped his feet with incredible force. There was no doubt in my mind that the man was strong and disciplined, a trustworthy man for the battlefield.

Military strength is not so fashionable in our society today. Similarly, today's church often teaches fellowship and worship to the expense of spiritual warfare. The scriptures urge us to recognise our enemies in spiritual realms. If we are to survive

the attacks of evil forces and be victors, we must be strong,
dressed in battle gear, equipped to fight that which opposes the
will of God.

Think about it: Your strength comes from the Lord's mighty
power. Remember your enemy is not a human being, but a
spiritual power. Your battle gear is truth, righteousness, peace,
faith, the Word of God and Spirit-directed prayer. These are
our spiritual weapons.

Prayer: Lord, help me not to see things according to my
natural sight and understanding. I ask for your strength. Show
me how to take advantage of my spiritual weapons today. Amen.

AUGUST 15   1 THESSALONIANS 5:8

EQUIPPED FOR SERVICE

*'But since we belong to the day, let us be self-controlled,
putting on faith and love as a breastplate, and the hope of
salvation as a helmet'.*

Alan: Before Jesus Christ came into my life, the word 'sober'
was a bad word and a condition to be remedied at the earliest
possible convenience. The Lord has helped me to conquer that
problem area of my life to the point where I no longer have the
desire to be anything but sober.

However, I didn't give up drinking just for the sake of fitting
into the expected Christian mould. I deliberately put it aside.
Drink would have hindered the work God wanted to do in and
through me.

I want everyone to see that our helmet, the hope of salvation,
is solid, protecting our minds from temptation, and idle
thoughts of a lazy afternoon in some beer garden. Be ready at all
times to serve the Lord. No longer desire to take your ease in
life. Aim to help others into eternal life.

Action: Today, think of the protection you receive from the
helmet of salvation and the breastplate of faith and love. What
more do you need?

Prayer: Teach me, Lord, the meaning of sobriety. Show me if there if anything in my life causing me not to think clearly. I thank you, Lord, that you have the solution. Amen.

AUGUST 16   HEBREWS 4:12

THE LIVING SWORD OF LIGHT

The word of God is living and active. Sharper than any double-edged sword, it penetrates even to dividing soul and spirit, joints and marrow; it judges the thoughts and attitudes of the heart'.

Jean: The Bible you hold is the word of God. Hold it carefully, for it is alive! It is God speaking now. It is not a dead letter, but a living message. It is also a sword, a sword of light. It penetrates and reaches the parts of the heart other books can't reach. It dissects and separates the basic animal drives in our nature from our high spiritual aspirations. It removes deep inner infection in our souls. It judges. It throws light upon the secret parts of our hearts and judges us accordingly.

When you look into the word of God, remember, the word of God is looking into you! Praying with the Bible open before you is the best way of seeing what God sees in your heart. It is also a good way to see what is in his heart.

Family: Pass the Bible around from one to another. As each one of you takes it, say what the word of God means to you.

Prayer: Lord, we open our hearts to your word. May your sword of light search out what needs to be cleansed away. May it also reveal how deep our desire is to glorify you in our lives. In Jesus' name, Amen.

AUGUST 17   JAMES 4:7

SUBMIT AND RESIST

'Submit yourselves, then, to God. Resist the devil and he will flee from you'.

Jean: Painful memories of the past which trigger off negative moods often trouble people even after conversion. This manoeuvre is a ruse of the accuser of our souls. Persistent effort is required on our part to dislodge those thoughts and subsequent reactions. Our verse today suggests a two-directional act of faith.

First, have a humble, dependent attitude of faith towards God. Second, take a position of faith against the anemy. Resist him.

This two-directional attitude of faith is not easily adopted, but it can be developed. It is a way to win victory over depression.

Believers should refrain from being arrogant when resisting the enemy. Don't attempt to show off your spirituality before the devil. He's no fool. He knows your weak spots and will aim at them with deadly accuracy. However, nothing baffles the devil like the power released when a believer humbles himself before the Lord and pleads the merits of the shed blood of Christ. The devil knows God stands behind the one who kneels before the cross.

Submission to God is not passivity. Rather the submission of the believer towards God is like that of a soldier to his commander. He is under authority and when he acts the enemy is pressed back. Resist and restrain.

Act it out: Two of you stand back to back, like siamese twins. One strike a pose of submission to the Lord. The other, a pose of resistance against the enemy. This pictures the two-directional attitude of mind we must have when dark thoughts and painful memories disturb our peace.

Prayer: Today, dear Lord, we go to do your will with peace of mind. We submit to you and refuse to let the devil misuse our memories. Amen.

AUGUST 18   **2 PETER 5:8,9a**

BE ALERT!

'Be self-controlled and alert. Your enemy the devil prowls around like a roaring lion looking for someone to devour. Resist him, standing firm in the faith . . . '

Jean: Peter had experienced the awful peril of falling asleep when he should have been on guard. Gethsemane was still a painful memory. On that same unforgettable night Peter had been caught off guard by the maidservant and had denied his Lord. He warns all who read his letter 'Be alert'!

Why? Because the same adversary Peter had still stalks about to devour us. We dare not act silly or fool around with our enemy. He is no myth. Jesus warned Peter, 'Satan has asked to sift you like wheat . . .' Lion, reaper, whatever the disguise, Satan desires to chew us up or shake us down.

We need a steadfast, strong faith in Jesus who said, 'I have prayed for you that your faith may not fail'. Believe Satan is defeated and Jesus is victor. Stand up to the responsibilities before you and resist the enemy who would put you to sleep when the Lord needs you. Control yourself and let God control the devil. Use your faith in the name of the Lord. Resist the devil. You're not alone. 'Your brothers throughout the world are doing the same'.

Think about it: Am I in danger of being a 'sluggard' by ignoring the attacks of Satan? Am I failing in my Christian duty by avoiding spiritual warfare? Am I dealing with people whose problems are due to demonic powers, without first resisting the enemy?

Prayer: Dear Lord, grant me diligence in my prayer life. Develop my discerning of spirits so I may know what is of you, myself or the enemy. Make me alert to the danger of the Devil and sensitive to the desires of the Holy Spirit. In Jesus' name, Amen.

AUGUST 19   **MATTHEW 16:19**

I GIVE YOU THE KEYS

'I will give you the keys of the kingdom of heaven; whatever you bind on earth will be bound in heaven, and whatever you loose on earth will be loosed in heaven'.

Jean: There is only one entrance to the kingdom of heaven –

Jesus the Door of Life. That door is never locked; it is open to whoever will believe. Then why keys to the kingdom of heaven? Why did Jesus promise them to Peter?

Peter was a man with revelation knowledge. By the gift of God, he knew Jesus was not mere man but the Son of God. He not only knew it, he believed it. He not only believed it, he confessed it before others. Jesus offered the keys of the kingdom of heaven to the believer who witnessed to revealed truth. Jesus said that this kind of faith was of such strong stuff, he would build his church with it and even hell wouldn't destroy it.

Inside, the kingdom of heaven is like a great mansion full of many rooms with many doors. Doors of opportunity, doors of ministry, revelation and all the things God has prepared for us.

The keys are words. Not just talk, but words spoken by faith out of the revelation God gives us. It only takes a small key to open a big door. Peter found that out when he opened the door of the gospel to the Jews at Pentecost and the Gentiles in Caesarea (Acts 2 & 10).

Today: Open the doors of blessing to someone who seems shut out. Use the faith God has given you. Speak what you know by the Spirit about the Lord and his kingdom.

Prayer: Dear Father, as your Spirit reveals more and more to us about your kingdom, let us receive it, believe it and witness to it. Amen.

AUGUST 20   **1 CORINTHIANS 3:5-6**

SERVANTS OF THE LORD

'What, after all, is Apollos? And what is Paul? Only servants, through whom you came to believe — as the Lord has assigned to each his task'.
'I planted the seed, Apollos watered it, but God made it grow'.

Elmer: The word here translated ministers, or servants (v.5) is 'Diakonos'. In other places in the Bible it is translated 'deacon'. The Greeks used it to mean a 'Waiter on table' or a servant in some other menial task. The Early Christian church used it to

201

mean a teacher or pastor. They saw teachers and pastors as deacons and servants of God to the people of God. Paul points out here that he and his colleagues were good and able servants. They had ministered the truth in heart-felt love which gave life to the body of believers.

We are all encouraged to be God's servants ministering the word in life-giving love.

Look out for ways to be a servant of the Lord, today.

Prayer: Lord, help me to speak words of faith, truly caring for those to whom I speak. Amen.

AUGUST 21   HEBREWS 3:1

A HEAVENLY CALL

'Therefore, holy brothers, who share in the heavenly calling, fix your thoughts on Jesus, the apostle and high priest whom we confess'.

LaDonna: In this busy and often stressful modern life of ours, it is easy to consider things such as heavenly callings reserved for saints and recluses. But our verse tells us that all believers are partakers of a divine call.

When I was seventeen, I was stopped by a young man as I made my way towards a marquee where my mother was about to speak. He wanted my mother to pray for him. I was a little exasperated by the request knowing she was preparing to preach.

Suddenly I sensed a deep confidence. Bluntly, I said, 'Why do you need mom? Can't we expect God to answer our prayer?' Stunned, the young man hesitantly prayed with me there and then. I moved on. Two years later we encountered each other and he related that his sister had been freed from the trap of the occult as a result of that prayer. The prayer of two average young people.

Think: On what or whom do you depend? An evangelist, counsellor or a spouse? Consider Jesus. He is your high priest.

Pray in faith and expect a miracle!

Prayer: Lord, I acknowledge that you alone have the power to meet all my needs. And I know that you will hear my prayer because you love me. I give you the things that weigh on my mind and expect your solutions. Amen.

AUGUST 22   **HEBREWS 4:14-16**

A ROYAL PRIESTHOOD

'Therefore, since we have a great high priest who has gone through the heavens, Jesus the Son of God, let us hold firmly to the faith we profess. For we do not have a high priest who is unable to sympathise with our weaknesses, but we have one who has been tempted in every way, just as we are — yet was without sin. Let us then approach the throne of grace with confidence, so that we may receive mercy and find grace to help us in our time of need'.

Alan: Life was not simple for the dedicated priests of the Levitical priesthood. They had to be ceremonially washed, and clothed with new, clean garments. They had to be anointed with oil and an offering made for their sins. A bull's blood had to be sprinkled on the altar and dabbed on the priests. Any priest approaching the mercy seat unprepared would die. The priests of the tabernacle did not go through all this preparation and more to serve themselves. They served the living God and interceded for the people.

Their ministry was only a shadow of the ministry of our Great High Priest, the Lord Jesus Christ. When we draw near to the throne in prayer, let's not forget that he has done everything we could not do. Through his blood we have been washed clean from all sin and now have pure white, heavenly garments. We are anointed by the Holy Spirit and empowered for service. We have access once and for all, into God's presence, as priests set apart for him.

Action: Discover your priesthood and the function in which God intends you to use it. This could be at work, at home or church or in your community. God has a job for each one of us to do.

Prayer: Lord Jesus, please teach me the job of serving you. Help me to listen and be obedient in the work you have for me. Amen.

AUGUST 23   **ISAIAH 61:6**

NAME ME 'SERVANT OF GOD'

'And you will be called priests of the Lord, you will be named ministers of our God'.

Jean: God's plan at Sinai was for the whole nation of Israel to be a kingdom of priests. Such a wonderful prospect was never realised in Israel's history. Although they agreed to covenant with God and to do all he said, the sin in their hearts kept them from it. Instead, the Old Testament priesthood was limited to one family from one tribe; the rest of Israel had lesser rights and responsibilities. The realisation of God's kingdom of priests is with the community of believers, the redeemed people of God, the Church of Jesus Christ. He has, by his sacrifice, made us all kingly priests for God.

Jesus has opened the way for every one of us to draw near to God; to intercede; to offer spiritual sacrifices. His blood cleanses us so constantly we are able to minister. Therefore, we have been named, 'Ministers of our God'.

Question: What would you have people say about you? How do you want to be known? By what you own? By your success?

Prayer for fathers: Lord, I long to give my family the remembrance of our times together in prayer. Make me a faithful priest to my family. Amen.

WHAT IS YOUR ANSWER?

'... *"You will be for me a kingdom of priests and a holy nation". These are the words you are to speak to the Israelites. So Moses went back and summoned the elders and set before them all the Lord had commanded him to speak. The people all responded together, "We will do everything the Lord has said". So Moses brought their answer back to the Lord'.*

Jean: We read yesterday of Israel's failure to fulfill God's purpose. Instead, through our blessed Saviour, we are the fulfillment of God's plan for a royal nation of priests.

But are we living according to our priestly privileges and responsibilities? Perhaps it would benefit us to reflect upon the reasons for Israel's failure.

Their intentions were good, but: first, they had little knowledge of the spirituality of the Law they were to observe. Second, they had little knowledge of their sinful selves which hindered them. Third, they offered lip service with no change of heart.

Would we not function better as believer-priests if we knew more about the Word of God and the Spirit of it? Don't we need to better understand our limitations and dependance upon the Holy Spirit? And would we not serve the Lord more faithfully if we were to commit ourselves whole-heartedly to love him forever?

Remember: Service is never slavery to the one who loves.

Prayer: Lord, let us be earnest and sincere in our response to you. We do you no favour by serving you, instead, you have privileged us by letting us serve you. Amen.

WHO LOVES YOU?

'... *And to him who loves us and has freed us from our sins by his blood and has made up to be a kingdom and priests to serve his God and Father — to him be glory and power forever and ever! Amen'.*

Jean: Who loves you? Jesus loves you. Look at Calvary and you can know for sure. The cross has liberated you from your sin, and so you know he loves you now. His historic act of love on the cross is active in his love for us in the present. We are free because he has made us free. Believe it and it shall be so. Jesus is not only the great Liberator from sin, but also the Great High Priest who opened the way for former slaves into the royal priesthood!

Suddenly we see it! The One who loves us is our Great High Priest. Love made the sacrifice. Love now intercedes. Love blesses. Love calls us to be priests unto him, offering sacrificial service, interceding for others, blessing all in his name, exalting him with praises forever. Love, crowned with everlasting glory will come again. We shall reign with him when he comes forth to bless the nations in his priestly reign of righteousness. Hallelujah! Get the glory of the future in your heart today.

Children: God has put you into a family of priests! Priests in the Old Testament wore crowns. Why not draw a crown with 'Jesus Is Our King' written on the front . . . like a crest. Put it up where you can see it to remind you of who you are and what you will be.

Prayer: Dear Father, in Jesus' name we bless one another today (Lay hands on each other and release the love of Jesus in benediction). Amen!

AUGUST 26   1 PETER 5:4

THE VICTOR'S CROWN

'And when the Chief Shepherd appears, you will receive the crown of glory that will never fade away'.

Jean: The crown usually in the mind of the New Testament writers was not a royal crown like the one to be seen at the Tower of London, but a victory wreath, worn by athletes in contests. Their wreaths would wilt the day they were given. Even crowns lose their prestige. But the Christian's crown of victory will never lose its value nor its beauty.

Who receives this crown? Not those who have run a solo race and outstripped all others. Rather, it is the shepherd who leads his flock, who stays on when others leave, who leads by walking with the sheep. It is the shepherd whose heart is moved with compassion for those who are scattered and lost, who hears the cry of the hungry. It is the shepherd who watches and prays, warding off attack. This shepherd will receive a crown.

If you are one whose heart is bound to a group of very needy people who depend upon you, perhaps demanding more than you can give, remember you are there by divine appointment. The Chief Shepherd has sent you. They are his sheep, not yours. Your faithful service will not be unrewarded. He who is invisible today may appear tomorrow with your unfading crown.

Parents: Jesus said, 'Feed my lambs'. Your parenthood is a sacred shepherding duty God has given you. Don't underestimate the value of what you are doing nor the reward God has for you.

Prayer: Father, help us as a family to stay close to one another, to protect one another, and follow where you lead. In Jesus' name, Amen.

AUGUST 27   PHILIPPIANS 3:20-21

THIS WORLD IS NOT OUR HOME

'But our citizenship is in heaven. And we eagerly await a Saviour from there, the Lord Jesus Christ, who, by the power that enables him to bring everything under his control, will transform our lowly bodies so that they will be like his glorious body'.

Elmer: We have been born from above. Our new home is the City of God, the New Jerusalem. In our Father's house are many mansions and there is a place prepared for each one of us.

We eagerly await the return of our Lord Jesus who will come again, bodily, as he went. He will take us home to be with him forever. Our lowly, weak sick bodies will be transformed to be like his own glorious body. Those who have died, believing in Christ, will be transformed first, rising from the dead as he did on the first Easter morning.

The Lord gave the disciples a glimpse of those new bodies on the Mount of Transfiguration. We know, according to St Paul, that when our Lord shall appear, we shall be like him.

Happy are those who hold this blessed hope.

Thought: This world is not our home. So let's live as if we are just passing through.

Prayer: Help me to live for you, Lord Jesus, so that I will be ready when you come for me. Amen.

AUGUST 28   2 THESSALONIANS 2:13-15
GLORY SHARED

'But we ought always to thank God for you, brothers loved by the Lord, because from the beginning God chose you to be saved through the sanctifying work of the Spirit and through belief in the truth. He called you to this through our gospel, that you might share in the glory of our Lord Jesus Christ. So then, brothers, stand firm and hold to the teachings we passed on to you, whether by word of mouth or by letter'.

LaDonna: Since living in London, Alan and I have become friends with a young Columbian woman who is a student here. She came from a large, loving and supportive family and for the first time she has been separated from them. After her arrival here she became withdrawn, indifferent about herself.

Then, her family arrived to stay for a month. Alan and I were invited to a meal with the reunited family. For the first time we saw our friend as she really is. Surrounded with her precious loved ones, her face glowed with joy. Her actions were lively and youthful. She was a different person. Family love had glorified her.

Christ provides us with his glory — the loving family unity of the Trinity.

Thought: We rob ourselves by not recognising our place in God's love; by trying to avoid being too Christian; by shunning Christian gatherings. Let Christ glorify you by embracing all that is of him.

Prayer: Father, help me to seek all that is of you; your ways, your people, your love, your Word. Amen.

AUGUST 29   **COLOSSIANS 3:1-4**

CLIMB TOWARDS GLORY

'Since, then, you have been raised with Christ, set your hearts on things above, where Christ is seated at the right hand of God. Set your minds on earthly things. For you died, and your life is now hidden with Christ in God. When Christ, who is your life, appears, then you also will appear with him in glory'.

Alan: Imagine yourself a mountain climber. You've lost all your companions, all your gear. You're hungry and weak, about to lose your grasp and fall into the depths below. But you lift yourself over a ledge. Suddenly you're looking at a hidden meadow rich with life. Ample food and water and oxygen-rich air give you a new lease on life. You rest here a long while. But all the time over your shoulder is the shadow of the mountain. It's waiting for you to finish the climb; it's always there, just over your shoulder. Finally you decide to go, to reach out and take the top of that mountain. It's not easy. There are slides and dead ends, cliffs and bad weather. But once at the very top, you look at the clouds below your feet. You're standing on the peaks of God's creation. You've made it!

Action: As we climb our way through life, let's not look back, not stop short. Set our minds on the glory of God that will crown the summit of our earthly experience.

Prayer: Teach me, Lord, how to climb along the right path and help me to keep my eye on your glory just up ahead. Amen.

AUGUST 30   HEBREWS 10:36

YOU WILL RECEIVE WHAT HE HAS PROMISED

'You need to persevere so that when you have done the will of God, you will receive what he has promised'.

Jean: Let all who feel like giving up hear these words, 'You need to persevere'. You need to keep on doing what you're doing, especially if it is the will of God. When one is discouraged one begins to doubt whether he is in the will of the Lord.

The wisest advice I ever had along that line was given to me by a senior employee of a bank where I worked. My job on a book-keeping machine was very hard for me. I wanted to quit. When I reported to her she said, 'I heard you say when you came in here that you felt this job was "God's will" for you'.

I faltered 'Yes, I said that . . . but now I'm not so sure'.

'Well', she said sharply, 'Either it is or it is not. Don't ever decide to stop when you're not sure either way. I have a rule I go by. When I have to make a decision I take as much time as circumstances allow before making it. If I have three months, I take it; three weeks, I take it; three days, I take it. If I have hours, I take three hours. If I have to make a decision on the spot, I try to snatch three minutes before I decide. I recommend this to you'.

I took my three weeks and I was certain I should go. I went assured I was leaving within the will of God, as I had come within the will of God. The timing was perfect. I went from one job to the other on the same day. One I hated, the other I loved . . . hand painting Franciscanware pottery!

Talk it over: If you as a family or individually are considering giving up on something you thought was God's will . . . how much time have you given yourselves to pray about it? How much time do you have? Take it.

Prayer: Father, while I struggle with this present problem, don't let me forget what you have promised me. Above all I want to be in your will. Amen.

AUGUST 31   1 CORINTHIANS 15:57-58

YOU'LL LAST FOREVER!

'But thanks be to God! He gives us the victory through our Lord Jesus Christ. Therefore, my dear brothers, stand firm. Let nothing move you. Always give yourselves fully to the work of the Lord, because you know that your labour in the Lord is not in vain'.

Jean: Do you ever feel that death might just cheat you out of your rewards in life? Does it seem that old age, or sickness, is going to snatch from you the sweet taste of victory. Especially after you have fought such hard battles to reach maturity, keep your health, maintain your marriage, rear your family, develop your talents or expand your influence?

Well, don't believe it. You've got a share in the greatest victory of all. It is Jesus' victory over death and the grave! Even your body will be released from the grave. Everyone who is precious to you and to him is wrapped up in his victory. You shall rise and be gathered together with your loved ones and go on living. You have just begun to live. Death is a little holding of our breath before we take a huge leap upwards into eternal life. We'll live on forever without old age, sickness or senility!

Bring your family and friends to Jesus now, then you'll have them for keeps. So, dear friend, do your best as a husband, wife, parent, or in whatever your special job is for the Lord. Live abundantly, as if you'll last forever, for you will!

Family: Say together our text: 'Thanks be to God! He gives us the victory through our Lord Jesus Christ!'

Join hands and pray: Father, we thank you we belong to you and to each other forever. Amen.

211

SEPTEMBER 1   MATTHEW 25:40

WHAT A SURPRISE!

*'The King will reply, "I tell you the truth, whatever you did
for the least of one of these brothers of mine, you did for me" '.*

Jean: An astonishing joy is in store for the righteous on judgement day. They'll be surprised to see the unexpected
significance of their ordinary kindness to the family of God.

Our Lord is very close to his family. A large reward will come
out of the small acts of love we have done for each other in his
name. Therefore, heaven will be a kingdom full of surprises.

Hear the generosity in his words: 'Come you who are blessed
by my Father; take your inheritance, the kingdom prepared for
you since the creation of the world'. A kingdom for what? For
feeding a hungry brother, taking in a stranger, giving some
neglected saint clothing, looking after a sick child of God,
visiting Christians in prison!

Our works today will be our witnesses tomorrow before the
judgement seat. Everyday unselfishness towards our brothers
and sisters in the Lord has an eternal reward.

Think about it: The humblest servant of God is a child of the
King. Are you able to help one of his royal subjects today? Treat
someone today like royalty. Surprise them now and you will
have a surprise later!

Prayer: Lord, show us today the hungry, the forgotten and
lonely, the sick brother or sister we can reach. Make us faithful
in the simple everyday acts of love. In Jesus' name, Amen.

SEPTEMBER 2   2 CORINTHIANS 5:20

THE KING'S MESSENGERS

*'We are therefore Christ's ambassadors; as though God were
making his appeal through us – we implore you on Christ's
behalf. Be reconciled to God'.*

Jean: We are directly commissioned by the Lord to offer people

212

wherever we go peace with God through our Lord Jesus Christ.

I've had the words hurled at me, 'Why are you here? Aren't there enough heathen in the United States?'

Those critical of missionary effort say, 'Leave the people alone. They have their culture and it is what they want. It's good enough for them. Why disturb them with Christianity?'

We need not apologise for taking our calling and duty seriously. We are under orders to go where he sends us, near or far, as his representatives and messengers. We go not where we are asked, we go where we are sent. We speak not what men want to hear, but what has to be heard. Our message is from our King; our citizenship is with him and our conduct, wherever we are, is to reflect his character. We must give account to him.

Our message is: 'Be reconciled to God'. We are not taking God to men. He has come. We are bringing men to God. Love is always there before us.

Question: Are you being sent to someone who lacks the peace of God? Are there barriers? God has removed the barriers on his side. You can remove them on their side by saying what God gives you to say . . . and by your winsome manner.

Prayer: Father, today we go into a world you love. May we be a message of peace. Give us courage to speak to the ones you particularly send us to. Amen.

SEPTEMBER 3   1 CORINTHIANS 2:1-4

POWER THAT CONVINCES

'When I came to you, brothers, I did not come with eloquence or superior wisdom as I proclaimed to you the testimony about God. For I resolved to know nothing while I was with you except Jesus Christ and him crucified. I came to you in weakness and fear, and with much trembling. My message and my teaching were not with wise and persuasive words, but with a demonstration of the Spirit's power'.

Elmer: Corinth was one of the most evil places in the ancient world. Gross immorality was rampant. Even the pagan people of the day disdained Corinth. Yet, St Paul's powerful message of faith bore fruit quickly. The new church there did not lack in supernatural gifts of the Holy Spirit.

A powerful message of faith meets deep needs. So where sin abounds, grace will much more abound.

Those who are sick need a physician. So we should not be surprised that where there is great sin there is often a great openness and readiness to respond to the Gospel. When it is preached in the power of the Holy Spirit, with signs following, it's a power that convinces. Let's not minimise the need for the 'demonstration of the Spirit's power'.

Comment: God's power shows up best in weak people. So let's not be fooled by outward appearance.

Prayer: Dear Father in heaven, help me today to let my light so shine before men that they will see my good works, and glorify you. May all that I do and say have the mark of the Spirit upon it. Amen.

SEPTEMBER 4   EPHESIANS 2:10

GO BARE-FACED TO GOD

'For we are God's workmanship, created in Christ Jesus to do good works, which God prepared in advance for us to do'.

LaDonna: At the age of eighteen, I went to Afghanistan where I was involved in evangelism to hippies. One day, as I boarded a bus I found the men and the women were segregated. In the women's section I sat among faceless mounds of grey clothing. There was not a bare face, hand, foot, or eyebrow to be seen anywhere. I wondered if I was still on the same planet! I was astonished to think that these were women just like myself who stared at my bare face. Suddenly, I appreciated the freedom of my Christian society which allowed me to go where I wanted and to talk to whomever I chose.

In much the same way those women hid themselves from men, we sinners would have once hidden ourselves from God, to avoid his wrath. Through Christ's sacrifice, which covers our sin, we now can go to the Lord in bare-faced boldness. We know we'll be accepted. We can stop hiding ourselves. We are his workmanship.

Thought: We often wear masks – although masks are not part of our national dress. Let's drop them, so that people can see who we really are. Can you think of some masks people wear to cover up their real selves from others? Are you wearing one?

Prayer: Lord, thank you for your sacrifice which enables me to be fully accepted by you. Help me to walk confidently in this world. For when I'm accepted by the Lord of heaven, there is nothing I need to fear. Amen.

SEPTEMBER 5   COLOSSIANS 1:20

GET YOUR ACT TOGETHER!

'And through him to reconcile to himself all things, whether things on earth or things in heaven, by making peace through his blood, shed on the cross'.

Alan: 'Get your act together' was a popular phrase when I was a teenager. It meant uniting one's energies to cope with life. I spent a lot of time trying to get my act together, but my spirit was dead, my soul in anguish, my mind confused and absorbed with pain and preoccupied with the effort of trying to relieve that pain. Then I was reconciled with God through Jesus Christ.

Reconciliation gets your act together. People come together. Feelings become controlled. Thoughts make sense.

The unity that comes through being reconciled with God and man bridges all conflicts and results in peace. Jesus Christ is the only one who can bring such reconciliation.

Action: Are you 'all together'? Or do you find (as I do) that your soul, your intellect, your emotions, your will, still argues with your spirit? Let's take a good look at ourselves. Appropriate the blood of his cross to our lives and live in peace.

Prayer: Bridge the gaps in me, Lord, and unite my heart, I pray. Amen.

SEPTEMBER 6   ROMANS 10:14-15

HOW? HOW? HOW? HOW? HOW!

'How, then, can they call on the one they have not believed in? And how can they believe in the one of whom they have not heard? And how can they hear without someone preaching to them? And how can they preach unless they are sent? As it is written, "How beautiful are the feet of those who bring good news!"'

Jean: How? How? How? How? Those words hammered upon my heart when I was sixteen years old and they still do! 'How can they call . . . ?' 'How can they believe . . . ?' 'How can they hear without someone preaching . . . ?' 'How can they preach unless they are sent . . . ?'

Through a peculiar twist of English grammar the 'how' becomes part of the answer. How? Why, by messengers who will not be held back but who run over mountains of difficulty. 'How beautiful are the feet . . . '

I was looking over my feet the other day. They were hot and tired. As I looked at them, a bit misshapen by age, I had to admire them. For nearly fifty years they have been carrying me to many countries to tell people about Jesus. I've walked some strange roads in my time. I've climbed a few mountains to get where I've been. I've stood for long hours and ministered. I thank God for good feet and good news!

Feet appreciation day! Take a look at each other's feet. You might even take time today to bathe and massage someone's feet. Have a foot washing! While you're doing it, pray those feet will go where God wants them to go.

Prayer: Father, I hope you think my feet are beautiful because they are following your paths. Give me strength of heart to climb the mountains between here and the places you want me to go. Please help me not to take unnecessary steps. I've a long way to go yet. In Jesus' name, Amen.

SEPTEMBER 7   ROMANS 10:9-10

HOW TO HELP A PERSON ACCEPT CHRIST

'That if you confess with your mouth, "Jesus is Lord", and believe in your heart that God raised him from the dead, you will be saved. For it is with your heart that you believe and are justified, and it is with your mouth that you confess and are saved'.

Jean: I often use what I call the three A's of salvation to help a person who wants to become a Christian. Here they are!

ACKNOWLEDGE Christ died for you, rose from the dead and is alive now. (This involves intellect). ASSENT. Believe Jesus lives to forgive your sins, to change your heart, to give you a brand new life. (This involves emotions). APPROPRIATE the benefits of Christ's death upon the cross, his resurrection, his exaltation. Commit yourself to live for him. (This involves will).

The three A's have helped many to move from head faith to heart faith: Faith without confession is incomplete. If possible, I encourage a person who has just acknowledged, assented and appropriated (or placed their faith in Jesus Christ for their salvation) to tell a friend immediately. Open confession often helps a believer's spiritual life, strengthens his assurance, and deepens the reality of his Christian experience. Moreover, it calls the attention of those who hear to their own belief and confession.

Children: Illustrate the text on a piece of paper. 'That if you confess with your mouth (Draw a mouth), "Jesus is Lord" (Draw a crown), and believe in your heart (Draw a heart) that God raised him from the dead (Draw a cross), you will be saved'.

Prayer: Lord, we believe with our hearts that God raised you from the dead. We confess with our mouths, 'Jesus is Lord'! Hallelujah! Amen.

SEPTEMBER 8   ACTS 5:20

STAND UP FOR JESUS!

'Go, stand in the temple courts, he said, "And tell the people the full message of this new life"'.

Jean: Where is the Lord asking you to stand today?

The angel of the Lord told the apostles to go right back where they had been arrested a few hours earlier. He freed them from jail, but not from witnessing.

It is one thing to talk about Jesus where everyone is on your side. It is another thing to testify in a park, on a street corner, in a coffee shop or an office. But God wants his truth proclaimed where the opposition is the hardest.

The apostles were re-arrested but got off with no less than a beating. That didn't stop them. 'Day after day in the temple courts and from house to house, they never stopped teaching and proclaiming the good news!' (v.42).

Be a good news person day after day. There are those listening who are wondering if you'll change your story or even stop. Don't become a bad news person or a silent one. There's no such thing as a silent witness.

Project: If you have difficulty in witnessing try to find a group of Christians who go out together in street evangelism or door-to-door. Be the praying partner until your courage grows to speak.

Prayer: Father, let me stand where you send me to stand to tell the full message of this new life. Thank you for the Holy Spirit whom you've sent to empower me, just as you did the apostles. Amen.

RECONCILIATION IS A MINISTRY OF LOVE

*'Again Jesus said, "Simon son of John, do you truly love
me?" He answered, "Yes, Lord, you know that I love you".
Jesus said, "Take care of my sheep" '.*

Jean: This intimate conversation of reconciliation reveals how
Jesus reacted to one who had failed him, and how one who had
failed reacted to him. It is a lesson of love.

Peter had denied the Lord three times publicly. He is challenged three times before his fellow-disciples. Was it to embarrass
him? Did he need to be taken down a peg or two? Was it to put
him out of fellowship? NO! It was to reinstate him into his calling before them all.

How did Jesus do it? Did he ask an accusatory question like,
'How could you have done such a thing to me, Peter?' Did he demand, 'Promise me you will never fail me again'. No. He
restored Peter with the compassionate question which went to
the heart of the matter. 'Do you truly love me?'

The Lord looks for love. He knows love produces obedience.
Love also develops humility. He who loves the Lord, loves
others. Humility releases one into a new identity with others.

It is interesting to see the consequence of reconciliation between Peter and his Lord. Repentance released him from self-
reliance and pride in his own efforts. He had a new relationship
with his Master. The big fisherman would no longer be identified with his trade, but with the Great Shepherd and his sheep.

Question: Do you suppose if we were to stop demanding
perfection from those who have failed us and asked for love we
might discover a new identity with each other and a new release
of ministry?

Prayer: Jesus, teach us the ministry of reconciliation. Release
a greater love between us. We long to see the greater works of
which you speak. In your name, Amen.

THE FIRST COMMANDMENT

'"Teacher, which is the greatest commandment in the Law?" Jesus replies: "Love the Lord your God with all your heart and with all your soul and with all your mind. This is the first and greatest commandment. And the second is like it: Love your neighbour as yourself"'.

Elmer: Our Sunday School teachers used to tell us to put God first, others second and ourselves last. Someone recently said to me, 'With four billion people on the earth, if I consider all the others first I will never get to myself'.

Jesus' teaching was not so. Truly, we are to love God first, for God is love. His is the original love. Love flowed in a unified trinity before ever there was creation or the angels, even. From this position of perfect love God first loved us.

Likewise, we must love ourselves. To love others as we should, we must have proper self-realisation. We must see the good that Christ has created within us by his loving presence. Then we can love others from a personal position of self-appreciation. 'Christ IN US the hope of glory'.

Realise today: When we share ourselves with others, we are sharing Christ.

Prayer: Lord, help me to see the good that is within me. It is the good that I can share with others. Work in me that which is well pleasing in your sight. Lord, help me to impart to others the love that you have given me. Amen.

SIMPLY LOVE AND CARE

'My brothers, if one of you should wander from the truth and someone should bring him back, remember this. Whoever turns a sinner away from his error will save him from death and cover over a multitude of sins'.

LaDonna: In our coffee bar at Bournemouth, there was a

young man who had a talent for winning people to Jesus and helping wayward Christians get right with God. There was nothing particularly attractive or outwardly charismatic about him. One might, at first glance, think he was timid. In the midst of the noise and jostling of the coffee bar, Steve would sit quietly talking and listening while people slowly poured out to him all the things that troubled them.

Steve knew sin gave them so much pain. But he never scolded them for it. He simply listened for their point of need and led them to the cross where they could find relief. He wooed many into heaven by simply loving and caring.

Think: Chuck Shoemake once said, 'Personal evangelism should be like running your fingers gently over a person's soul until you find the 'chink in the armour' – their point of need'. When you know someone really cares it's easy to lay down your sins and repent.

Prayer: Lord, give me a heart of compassion for those around me, believers and unbelievers alike. Help me through love and care to make it easy for people to come to you and find relief from the pain of sin. Amen.

SEPTEMBER 12   JOHN 13:3-5

SECURE IN GOD'S LOVE

'Jesus knew that the Father had put all things under his power, and that he had come from God and was returning to God; so he got up from the meal, took off his outer clothing, and wrapped a towel round his waist. After that, he poured water into a basin and began to wash his disciples' feet, drying them with the towel that was wrapped around him'.

Alan: This passage records one of the most beautiful, humble acts of love any man has done. We look on with envy, praying that we too could love as simply, as boldly, as humbly.

St. John has recorded for us also the basis from which Jesus could operate such love. Jesus knew his purpose for being here. He was secure in his relationship with the Father. He recognised the authority he had in his ministry. With that kind of security, Jesus could wash the feet of simple men, or walk on water. He ministered love with purity and simplicity because he had sufficiency of riches and glory in God.

Action: Let's study Jesus' basis for security. See how we can become more confident in ourselves and in our relationship with God. Then we can love others more freely.

Prayer: Help me to build a firm foundation of security in you, Lord Jesus. I want to love others more and follow the example of your humility. Amen.

SEPTEMBER 13   1 CORINTHIANS 16:13-14

SOLDIERS AND LOVERS

'Be on your guard; stand firm in the faith; be men of courage; be strong. Do everything in love'.

Jean: There was a lot of hot debate going on in the early church. There were issues about the use of spiritual gifts, matters of worship, church discipline and what to eat and not to eat. Paul certainly didn't sweep them all under the rug with a statement like, 'It really doesn't matter how you do these things, just as long as you love one another'.

In our homes, as well as in our churches, we as families must face agitating issues. We dare not be weak and wobbly cowards. It is surprising how much help we can get from the scriptures on most things. There are guidelines and clear commands which, if recognised and practised, will maintain a Christian home. But not practised in harsh regimentation.

By all means discipline, but do it in love; make your family decisions, but do it in love; choose your butcher (which kind of meat you'll eat), but do it in love. Parents, like church leaders, have a duty to be on guard, to be firm in the faith, to be courageous and strong. Be soldiers and keep out of your home divisive elements. Also, be lovers and keep your children in the circle of God's love.

Discussion: Are there some hot issues smouldering in your family? Talk about them until there can be a cool, clear family decision made. You need to listen to each other, look in the scriptures and learn together how to do everything in love.

Prayer: Father, help us not to fight each other over things we do not agree about. Let us be on our guard against the enemy who would divide us. Make us soldiers who love one another. In Jesus' name, Amen.

SEPTEMBER 14   EPHESIANS 6:6-8

WHOLE-HEARTED SERVICE

'Obey them not only to win their favour when their eye is on you, but like slaves of Christ, doing the will of God from your heart. Serve whole-heartedly as if you were serving the Lord, not men, because you know that the Lord will reward everyone for whatever good he does, whether he is slave or free'.

Jean: Learning to work and to work well is a very important key to being a happy person in this world. Christians have the best reason of all for being good workers.

Work is the will of God and what Christians do they should do as if they were serving the Lord. The Christian life is not part sacred and part secular. We are sent into the world to live out God's will in whatever we have to do. With the deep conviction of serving God in the whole of life motivating a person, it is possible to stand up under the most difficult situations.

Christians can honour those they work for by obeying orders whole-heartedly. Honest work comes out of honest commitment. Many have found that the Lord honours those who honour him. Promotion comes from the Lord.

Do everything as doing the will of God. He works in what you're doing. Do everything as doing it for Christ. He expects it of you. Do everything from your heart. He sees your heart. Do everything as if the Lord was the paymaster. He is!

Discussion: Talk about the people you work for . . . at school, in business or industry. Can you witness better to them through your work than you are? Do you need better pay; better work conditions? Have you told your Boss?

Prayer: Father, forgive me for half-hearted work because of discontent. Help me to cope as a Christian, not as a wordly employee or student. In Jesus' name, Amen.

SEPTEMBER 15   LUKE 10:27-28

LOVE SEES, STOOPS AND SAVES

'He answered: "Love the Lord your God with all your heart and with all your soul and with all your strength and with all your mind", and "Love your neighbour as yourself" '.

Jean: Mugging is a growing threat on the streets of London. Elmer was left unconscious on an underground station platform after being knocked down by young thugs. It was a case of sheer violence, for although he wore jewellery and had a good sum of cash on him, he was not robbed. To this day, we do not know the people who came along and found them kicking his helpless body from one to the other. They chased them off and phoned for the police. Christians or not, they showed the kind of concern for a person when he's down that Jesus was talking about when he told his Good Samaritan story.

The whole story came out of his answer to an expert in the Law who asked, 'What must I do to inherit eternal life?' and 'Who is my neighbour?' Jesus' answer to both questions came out of the 'expert's' own book on religion, the Old Testament. He knew full well what was required, but it took Jesus' words to make him see what it would mean to him.

First, it meant a fully-fledged, no-holds-barred abandonment of himself in love to God. Second, it meant a no-favourites, unrestricted love for anyone who was in need of help . . . no matter the colour, class or creed.

Question: What would it mean for you to love God with all you've got? What would it mean for you to respond to those left by the road to die? Would you want to know their colour, nationality or religion first?

Prayer: Father, we do love you and want to love you more. We do care about people who are hurt through violence and indifference. We don't have to ask you what to do, we know. Help us in Jesus' name to act. Amen.

SEPTEMBER 16   **LUKE 14:31-33**

SELF-SACRIFICE

'Or suppose a king is about to go to war against another king. Will he not first sit down and consider whether he is able with ten thousand men to oppose the one coming against him with twenty thousand? If he is not able he will send a delegation while the other is still a long way off and will ask for terms of peace. In the same way, any of you who does not give up everything he has cannot be my disciple'.

Jean: Often a person feels outnumbered when he attempts to face up to confrontation. He sees the challenger and his heart grows cold! He'd give anything to avoid a big fight, especially when he isn't sure of winning. So, why not compromise? How about making peace with the enemy?

In war and politics, 'Peace at any price' tactics may be right at times. Not, however, in the kingdom of God.

Jesus addressed a multitude of followers who had come along without much forethought or consideration. Jesus told them to face the facts. They would be in a warfare. They would be outnumbered by their opponents. They would not escape confrontation. If they didn't attack, they'd be pursued. Their enlistment into his forces would affect every part of their lives and those they loved would be affected too. Would they be able to forsake them, if necessary?

It costs to be a true Christian. Perhaps today you are wishing you could avoid the inevitable confrontation caused by your decision to follow Christ. Friend, count the cost if you do, and count the cost if you don't. If it means giving up Christ in order to have peace, are you sure the price of peace isn't too much?

Lesson: Don't undertake what you have neither the strength nor the time to achieve, or anything for which you are not prepared to sacrifice, if need be, your life itself.

Prayer: Lord, I want to be your disciple, at any cost, by your grace. Amen.

SEPTEMBER 17   MATTHEW 19:29

DON'T BE AFRAID TO GIVE

'And everyone who has left houses or brothers or sisters or father or mother or children or fields for my sake will receive a hundred times as much and will inherit eternal life'.

Elmer: There is a memory strongly imprinted on my mind. It is of two diminishing figures, a man and a woman, standing on the very end of the pier in San Pedro harbour near Los Angeles, California. They were my father and mother. They had driven 1,800 miles from Iowa to California to say goodbye to Jean and me and their two grandchildren. We were on our way by ship to Australia. Once again we were answering God's call to go afar with the Gospel.

On the pier, before we left, Mother said to me, 'I would rather that you were on the other side of the world serving God, and me proud of you than for you to be in your own home town and me to be ashamed'.

Who gave the most to God that day? We left mother and father. They gave their children and grandchildren.

In time, the Lord fulfilled his promise. He gave us many more, both young and old, to love. Also, here in England our joy is multiplied by dear people who love us more deeply than we ever thought possible.

Let's reflect a moment: We can never give up anything for God's sake without being blessed in return. Let's not be afraid to obey God in whatever he asks of us.

Prayer: Lord, help me to keep on giving myself to others. I know, then, that others will reciprocate with tender love and care to me. Amen.

226

TRUE GREATNESS

'. . . Not so with you. Instead, whoever wants to become great among you must be your servant, and whoever wants to be first must be slaves of all. For even the Son of Man did not come to be served, but to serve, and to give his life as a ransom for many'.

LaDonna: What is greatness? Perhaps the simplest definition of the word is 'Influence'.

My grandmother, Grace Murphy, influenced many lives. After World War II she was awarded a medal for the encouragement she had given to many of the women on the factory floor who had husbands and sons in battle. Right until her death, Grace supported and encouraged people. She was a real servant to others and her influence still affects us today.

What does it take to be a servant as Christ intended? Time! Grace Murphy was willing to take time to invest herself in the ones Jesus led to her. To serve like that will make you great in God's Kingdom.

Think: Everyone around you may seem self-sufficient and secure. But there is someone who needs YOU and your time. Time is a precious commodity, free yet costly to give. Become that person's servant by taking time to give yourself away.

Prayer: Lord, I know that to grow more like you I need to become a servant of others. Show me who I can serve with my time and myself. Thank you for giving me the courage to give. Amen.

SECURE IN GOD

'Do nothing out of selfish ambition or vain conceit, but in humility consider others better than yourselves. Each of you should look not only to your own interests, but also to the interests of others. Your attitude should be the same as that

of Christ Jesus: Who, being in very nature God, did not con-
sider equality with God something to be grasped, but made
himself nothing, taking the very nature of a servant, being
made in human likeness. And being found in appearance as
a man, he humbled himself and became obedient to death —
even death on a cross!'

Alan: I used to think of humility as a form of self-depreciation
– the 'I am nothing' syndrome. That's not what this scripture
says to me. It says I'm to have the attitude that Jesus had. He
knew perfectly who he was, where he came from, what he was
doing and where he was going. His humility had the strong
foundation of a deep trust in God and a deep relationship with
God. Such security does not lead to an 'I am nothing' complex;
rather, 'I am something special to God', and nothing can change
that fact.

From this foundation of security in one's life, there is no
longer a need for self-centredness or conceit. God fulfills all our
needs if we let him and makes it possible for us to count the
needs of others first.

Action: You may have a social or business rival. Try taking
your security in God by faith and try to serve the needs of that
person, trusting God for his provision for you.

Prayer: Help me, Lord, to rest in the security I have in you. I
want to be a solid platform along which your supply can pass to
others. Amen.

SEPTEMBER 20   **PHILIPPIANS 2:3-4**

ARE YOU INTERESTED IN OTHERS?

'Do nothing out of selfish ambition or vain conceit, but in
humility consider others better than yourselves. Each of you
should look not only to your own interests, but also to the in-
terests of others'.

Jean: Every family has squabbles, and at times, real fights. The
problem, usually, is selfishness. The remedy? Humility

before God and each other!

The ancient world despised the term humility. In their minds it meant cowardliness. It was cringing self-depreciation. Then, Jesus came along and changed all that by his teaching and life. Christianity made a bad word a noble word. Humility became a virtue.

When you're bothered about other people's weaknesses, consider yourself. When you're green with envy over other people's gifts, count your blessings. If you just can't bear someone, pray for them and then take time to write down all the good things you can think of about them. Come on, there must be something! If you admire someone so much that it leaves you feeling like a worm, don't squirm in the dust. Emulate them. Recognise who they are and what they do, but remember they had to start somewhere . . . Worms can turn into butterflies! If you really want to be loved (and who doesn't?) think about others. Don't be so preoccupied with your own concerns that you miss the fun of watching others grow.

Family: If you've got a particular quarrel going on, maybe a little talk around this scripture may help you to sort it out.

Prayer: Father, Jesus has given us the new meaning of humility. Help us to live it out so the world will never again think it is a bad word. Amen.

SEPTEMBER 21   **ROMANS 14:19-21**

DON'T MAKE OTHERS STUMBLE

> *'Let us therefore make every effort to do what leads to peace and to mutual edification. Do not destroy the work of God for the sake of food. All food is clean, but it is wrong for a man to eat anything that causes someone else to stumble. It is better not to eat meat or drink wine or to do anything else that will cause your brother to fall'.*

Jean: Let's not be so preoccupied about what liberties we may take as Christians that we forget to help our fellow believers spiritually. Concentrate on the growth of one another's character. Those who say 'I'll do as I please' are usually not too concerned about the spiritual development of others. It is not right for us to do even 'pure' things which cause offence to other Christians. It is far better not to use our liberty, and spare our brother's feelings, than to insist on exercising liberty and wounding him! This is true self-denial. It is requisite in the ministry of reconciliation.

A strong Christian bears the heavier burden in the matter of 'questionable things'. A Christian's convictions are never merely matters of private opinion or of personal sincerity. They must be based upon intelligent knowledge of God's word and responsibility to his brothers and sisters.

Remember: Every person exerts influence for good or for evil. Forgo practices which you know are stumbling blocks to weaker Christians. On the other hand, don't be so scrupulous about your conduct that you become intolerant and critical of Christians in matters not specifically prohibited by the Word of God.

Prayer: Father, help us to remember our brothers and sisters who are watching us. We want them to grow strong. We love you and them. Amen.

SEPTEMBER 22   **MARK 9:35**

GREATNESS IS SERVICE

'Sitting down, Jesus called the Twelve and said, "If anyone wants to be first, he must be the very last, and the servant of all" '.

Jean: Jesus was the great Illustrator. He taught by taking some familiar object and using it to prove his point. Never did he illustrate better than when he took a child into his teaching − a living visual aid. 'He took a little child and had him stand among them. Taking him in his arms, he said to them, "Whosoever welcomes one of these little children in my name welcomes me; and whoever welcomes me does not welcome me but the one who sent me" '.

Children were considered of little significance in the ancient

230

world. But he made that small boy feel like somebody special that day. Would that child ever forget being picked out and held in the arms of Jesus?

Jesus was preparing his disciples for servanthood which would include caring for the insignificant. It has always remained a characteristic of those who have been great servants of God. They cared when no one else cared. To be great, one must stop wanting to be number one and be ready to be the last, ready to be a slave of all. Greatness is service.

Project: Make somebody, especially a child, feel wanted, needed and special today. Be someones servant today, in Jesus' name.

Prayer: Father, I don't need to be first to know I am important to you. I'm secure enough in your love to step back and let others be first. Use me to serve them. In Jesus' name, Amen.

SEPTEMBER 23   GENESIS 3:9-10

GOD'S LOVE CALL

'But the Lord God called to man, "Where are you?" He answered, "I heard you in the garden, and I was afraid because I was naked; so I hid". So the Lord God made garments of skin for Adam and his wife and clothed them'.

Jean: God's call was a call of love. It was not to locate Adam. God knew where man was. Adam was afraid, naked and uncomfortable in the presence of God. His attempts to cover his nakedness and hide himself were doomed to failure. Man could not conceal from God the effects of his sin.

The great deception is for man to think he can conceal himself or his sin. When the fabric of life starts falling apart; when the heart breaks; when love is torn from marriage . . . what do we do? Do we hide or call on God? Do we accept responsibility for our misery? Or do we blame everyone, including God? We need to turn ourselves over to God, not for a patch-up job, but for a new God-given covering. A new kind of love.

Listen: God is calling you. He knows exactly where you are in your ruined happiness. You can't conceal a broken heart from him, nor the sin which caused it. He has a better way for you to deal with it, than the bitter, painful way you would take.

Prayer: Father, I know nothing is hidden from you. Please give me the courage to say what I've done to offend you. I fear judgement and have no place to hide except I hide in you and accept your covering, through Jesus Christ my Lord. Amen.

SEPTEMBER 24   1 PETER 4:8

A COVERING FOR MY BROTHER'S SIN

'Above all, love each other deeply, because love covers a multitude of sins'.

Elmer: There is a covering for sin which is commended in Scripture. It is to cover the sin which is not my own, but that of another. In love, first of all, I must make every effort to keep the sin of my unfortunate brother from being made public knowledge.

Why should I thus cover the sins of my fellow-mortal? Because God has done this for me, through his Son. I will uncover the sins of others only to the Lord, when ALONE with him. But I must not cover my own sins. 'He that conceals his sins does not prosper' (Proverbs 28:13). 'But whoever confesses and renounces them finds mercy'. If I uncover my sin to the Lord he will blot it out by his precious blood. Only God can blot it out and that is better than concealment.

Thought: Are we as generous and forgiving towards others, as God is towards us?

Prayer: Dear God, forgive me my trespasses. Forgive those who trespass against me. Amen.

CLOTHED WITH RIGHTEOUSNESS

'The son said to him "Father, I have sinned against heaven and against you. I am no longer worthy to be called your son.". But the father said to his servants, "Quick! Bring the best robe and put it on him. Put a ring on his finger and sandals on his feet"'.

LaDonna: Mrs. McPherson, the founder of a Pentecostal denomination in United States, once invited a female opera star to sing in her church. When the woman stepped to the platform the congregation gasped. She had come dressed in the formal attire suited to her occupation – a shimmering gown with a breathtaking, plunging neckline.

Mrs. McPherson responded immediately. She stepped quickly to her side and put her arm around the soloist, allowing the long blue cape of her vestments to drape around the woman's bare shoulders. As she interviewed the lady, people soon forgot about the revealing dress and took interest in this person for whom Christ died.

In just such a way Christ befriended us. In his embrace we are clothed with his righteousness. But do we provide that same grace for others?

Think: Determine today to clothe the weakness and possible failure of another with your understanding and love. Name that person in the following prayer.

Prayer: Lord, I have received such great forgiveness from you. Help me to give that same grace to . . . . (name someone). Amen.

TURNING THE CLOCK BACK

'Blessed are they whose transgressions are forgiven, whose sins are covered. Blessed is the man whose sin the Lord will never count against him'.

Alan: When I was ten years of age I decided one evening to make myself a cup of tea. Full of confidence, I carefully put my mother's antique silver teapot, which had been my grandmother's, on a low heat gas burner. Suddenly I heard a crash. I discovered that silver melts away to nothing under direct heat. My mother, though upset by the loss of her beautiful teapot, was understanding and forgiving. I, on the other hand, was upset at the damage I had caused. To this day I wish I could turn back the clock and undo the sad mistake.

In a sense, God has done this for us. His forgiveness through the death of Jesus, means we don't have to pay for our sins. Forgiveness brings with it a clean beginning, as if all the things we had done had never happened.

I remember being very relieved at the thought of not having to pay for my mistake with the teapot. I am even more grateful that Jesus Christ has paid for my sins.

Action: Let's demonstrate our love and gratitude to God by praising him! Let prayer be praise today.

Prayer: 'I will bless the Lord at all times, his praise shall forever be in my mouth'! Amen.

SEPTEMBER 27 ROMANS 8:1,3,4,34

STOP TRYING TO BE GOOD!

'Therefore, there is now no condemnation for those who are in Christ Jesus'.
'For what the law was powerless to do . . . God did by sending his own Son in the likeness of sinful man to be a sin offering . . . in order that the righteous requirements of the law might be fully met in us, who do not live according to the sinful nature but according to the Spirit. Who is he that condemns? Christ Jesus, who died — more than that, who was raised to life — is at the right hand of God and is also interceding for us'.

Jean: Gross sins like immorality, profanity and dishonesty probably don't trouble most Christian families. There are other sins, weaknesses, which trouble us more, like telling small lies, being unreasonable with each other, a tendency to gossip, to over-eat, the inability to talk to others about Christ, prayerlessness and the like. Victory over such weaknesses is not achieved simply by self-effort or keeping the rules, whether they be God's rules or our own custom made ones. There are too many imperfections in our natural make-up for that to work.

It takes a long time before we realise we can't cope with our sins by ourselves. Before we plead for God's help, we must come to the point of utter helplessness. We must stop trying to be good and trust the Lord's goodness. Let him take over and he will stick up for you when the accuser comes around.

Lesson: Are you rising above the temptation to lie, lose your temper, think impurely, gossip? If not, make certain you have received Christ as your Savious. Then, read Romans 8. Ask to make it your own. Saturate yourself with the Word of God.

Prayer: Lord, I want to prove your power within me to overcome the condemnation I feel. I know it's a lie, for you said 'There is now no condemnation'. Thank you, Lord. Amen.

SEPTEMBER 28   HEBREWS 9:14

HOW MUCH MORE!

'How much more, then, will the blood of Christ, who through the eternal Spirit offered himself unblemished to God, cleanse our consciences from acts that lead to death, so that we may serve the living God?'

Jean: There are lots of external things one can do to conceal a guilty conscience. One can keep busy, play loud music, rationalise, keep company with those who condone our sin and avoid those who condemn it. We can stop reading the Bible, pray less and change churches. Yet, none of these things will drown out the inner voice which troubles the guilty.

Why don't the guilty give up and admit they need an inside job done on the conscience? One problem with such an admission is that it involves confession to God (and probably to others), brokenness and turning away from the thing. That is hard, but worth it.

It is really great to be able to pray without feeling any sin blockage. What a joy it is to wake up with a light heart and sing praises to God. How good it is to feel good and not feel you shouldn't. It's wonderful to do the things a Christian does and not feel like a hyprocrite.

Reflect: Are you living with a cleansed conscience, or with an uncleansed one? The condition of your conscience decides on whether you are happy or miserable. If you're happy, praise God. If not, pray to God.

Prayer: Father, don't let us keep doing things which lead to the death of joy and peace in our lives. Help us each day to live joyfully free from guilt. Guilt keeps me at a distance from you. Forgiveness draws me close. I want to stay close to you. In Jesus' name, Amen.

SEPTEMBER 29   1 JOHN 3:19-20

WE SET OUR HEARTS AT REST

'This then is how we know we belong to the truth and how we set our hearts at rest in his presence whenever our hearts condemn us. For God is greater than our hearts, and he knows everything'.

Jean: We all need reassuring at times, even though we know we are the children of God. Our hearts condemn us and disturb our assurance more often than we wish to admit. Sometimes the accusations are true and sometimes they're not. The accuser of God's children is not slow in hitting us with old memories of past failure. Whether true or false, the accusation must be confronted. But not by ourselves. We must answer in the presence of the Lord . . . that is, through prayer.

As one Christian put it, 'When the accuser comes to my door I send Jesus to answer the knock!'

We can confess our sins before the Lord in prayer if the accusation is true. If it is not, we can refute the accusation and claim the truth. Only the Lord and we ourselves know whether our hearts are condemning us on true or false grounds. If we are con demned and confused, then let us set our hearts at rest in the presence of the Lord. He will sort things out. Don't be your own judge and executioner!

Pause a moment: Be still and wait quietly before you pray until your heart is at rest in the presence of the Lord.

Prayer: Father, I thank you that Jesus has taken all the condemnation for my sin. I don't have to live with a condemned heart, but with a pardoned heart. I go to be a pardoning person today towards others. In Jesus' name, Amen.

SEPTEMBER 30   ISAIAH 53:7

SILENCE UNDER SUFFERING

'He was oppressed and afflicted, yet he opened not his mouth; he was led like a lamb to the slaughter, and as a sheep before her shearers is silent, so he did not open his mouth'.

Jean: The voice of doubt or the voice of guilt usually cries out under the pressure of suffering. Either the afflicted confesses his wrong to God or he claims no wrong and challenges God in argument.

Jesus, the Servant, is unique and solitary in his silence under suffering. He has no guilt of his own, no doubts about his God. He knows there is a purpose, that good will be achieved. He has committed himself to it. He sees his suffering not as punishment, but as service laid upon him by God. He is performing the service of redemption.

Premature suffering and injustice are two afflictions we find hard to bear. When the young are hurt, the honest person cheated, the kind cruelly mistreated, the privacy of the peace-loving invaded, we cry out in defence, 'This should not happen!' Few bear such indignities in silence. That is, unless they are in the path of service pledged to the One they love more than all else. Then, the Spirit of the Servant comes upon them. They are able to suffer in silence. They have redemptive love. They have faith.

Think of it: ' . . . He did not open his mouth'.

Prayer: Father, I have asked you to make me Christ-like. Now, under the pressure of affliction give me the faith to not cry out against you. I await the time of deliverance. You shall have the glory. Amen.

OCTOBER 1   **REVELATION 5:9-10**

ONE IN CHRIST

'And they sang a new song: "You are worthy to take the scroll and to open the seals, because you were slain, and with your blood you purchased men for God from every tribe and language and people and nation. You have made them to be a kingdom and priests to serve our God, and they will reign on the earth"'

Elmer: There is no indication in Scripture that racism will exist in heaven. The terms 'Chinese', 'African' and 'Caucasian' will probably be unknown there.

Even here on earth Jesus makes nationalities and races equal for we are all one in Christ. Colour prejudice must go. By his blood, Jesus purchased a people for God from every tribe, nation and people. He integrates us in one kingdom and we are to work together as believer priests.

Thought: As Christians we are a race apart, a chosen people and a holy nation!

Prayer: Lord, help me to draw near with a pure heart, not only to you but to your people.

OCTOBER 2   **EPHESIANS 5:1-2**

'I LOVE YOU'

'Be imitators of God, therefore, as dearly loved children and live a life of love, just as Christ loved us and gave himself up for us as a fragrant offering and sacrifice to God'.

238

LaDonna: Recently Alan and I led seminars for teenagers at our Family Camp. One morning I was feeling very tired and unable to give to the teenagers in the way I really should. During the coffee break, someone called me out of the tent for a moment to say, 'I love you'. It meant a great deal to me. The rest of the morning I was able to really give myself to others with joy. I had suddenly become more loving.

I think it's fair to say we can only love others when we know we are loved. Yet even when we are loved, we often find it hard to accept it fully.

The greatest manifestation of God's love for us is the cross. But God didn't stop there. He keeps pouring out his love through daily situations, friends, family and material blessings.

Question: How well do you respond to God's love? Do you accept it from those around you? Are you loveable?

Prayer: Lord, help me to see the love you have for me through the cross. Open my eyes daily to the little ways you pour your love upon me. Then help me to give that love to others. Amen.

OCTOBER 3   EPHESIANS 2:14-16

NO MORE BARRIERS

'For he himself is our peace, who has made the two one and has destroyed the barrier, the dividing wall of hostility, by abolishing in his flesh the law with its commandments and regulations. His purpose was to create in himself one new man out of the two, thus making peace, and in this one body to reconcile both of them to God through the cross, by which he put to death their hostility'.

Alan: When I was young, loneliness was a part of my life. Even as a child, I remember spending a lot of my time alone, and that not through choice. As a teenager and young adult I still felt alone very frequently. Sometimes I could relate to a special friend or even a group, but the relationship never lasted.

When I became a Christian, well! What a change! Over and over again I have been joyfully surprised to find myself relating to people from all over the world. Words like 'friendship', 'love' and 'fellowship' took on a new meaning! I began to realise they were realities. Jesus Christ changed things. He changed me and my circumstances.

Action: Someone around you needs to be loved. Maybe it's you. Jesus has given us love to share. He has broken down the barriers between people. It's up to us to reach across the empty spaces and touch them.

Prayer: Lord, help me to love and allow others to love me. Help me to become one with you and your body and to reach out to others. Amen.

OCTOBER 4   1 PETER 1:18-19

RANSOMED!

'For you know that it was not with perishable things such as silver and gold that you were redeemed from the empty way of life handed down to you from your forefathers, but with the precious blood of Christ, a lamb without blemish or defect'.

Jean: There is nothing cheap about our redemption. It is not just a sweet story of a grieving God looking for sinful man. It is not restoration, as in the story of the prodigal son. It is redemption, where holiness confronts sin. It is a conflict. It isn't a pay-off but a struggle, to death itself. It is not God waiting, yearning at home in heaven for his lost family to come to him. It is God on the cross fighting hell for us.

When we remember the Lamb's appalling struggle at such incalculable cost to himself, we fear God lest we insult his love. We fear to foolishly flirt with sin. Our fear of God is not the cringing fear of slaves. It is the fear of one who loves and does not want to damage his relationship with dear Father God.

Think of it: You have been redeemed from an empty life into an abundant life. Think of the ways God has filled your life with meaning.

240

Prayer: Father, thank you for saving me from an empty way of life. I am not worthless. You have given me value. My faith is not an empty traditionalism but an overflowing way of life. Thank you, dear Lamb of God. Amen.

OCTOBER 5   **1 JOHN 3:16**

WHAT WE OUGHT TO DO

'This is how we know what love is: Jesus Christ laid down his life for us. And we ought to lay down our lives for our brothers'.

Jean: Self-sacrifice is the essence of love, human or divine. The self-sacrifice of divine love is the cross. There the Son of God laid aside his own rights and privileges to be our Lamb. His own identity had to be forfeited in order for him to become the recognisable, acceptable substitute for our sins. He who knew no sin became sin for us.

We ought to lay down our rights and privileges to be identified with the people whom God wants us to love as brothers. Not only should we be willing to lay down our well-earned position, privileges and recognition, but we OUGHT to do it. Not upon request, not of necessity, but by our own initiative.

Self-sacrifice is part of our commitment to serve Jesus Christ. The Son of God laid down his life as a Lamb upon the cross. He took it up again as the Lamb upon the throne. If you and I will lay down our lives with humility, then we will take them up again with glory. In so doing we will have discovered what love really is.

Discussion: Ask yourselves how much self-sacrifice is evident in your relationships with each other and with your Christian brothers and sisters. Have you laid aside your rights in order to help another?

Prayer: Father, put more love into my service for you. Pour that love through me to my brothers and sisters. Not because they ask it of me, but because I ask it of myself. For your sake I pray, Amen.

WHAT DOES HE MEAN TO ME?

'The next day John saw Jesus coming towards him and said, "Look, the Lamb of God, who takes away the sins of the world!'

Jean: Have you ever wished you were there the day John pointed out Jesus as the Lamb of God? His words would have been very meaningful to every Jew. They would have thought of God's provision for Abraham's altar on Mount Moriah. Or they may have seen him as the offering of blood for deliverance, as the lamb slain for the exodus from Egypt. Perhaps they might have recalled Isaiah's prophecy of a lamb led to the slaughter, the suffering coming Messiah.

But you and I were not there. So what can John's words mean to us? Notice the last part of his proclamation: ' . . . who takes away the sins of the world!' Ah, every sinner longs to have his burden taken away. Is this Lamb for us?

Yes, he took away the sins of the world . . . not only Abraham's, or Isaiah's or Israel's, but of the world. Not only once and for all, but continuously. He takes away and takes away, as an endless river washes all it passes over. He does it because he lives to make constant intercession on the basis of his sacrifice.

Sing together: Can you think of a hymn or chorus about the Lamb of God and his precious blood shed for you? Sing together before you pray.

Prayer: We praise you, dear God, for the power of Jesus' blood which cleanses and keeps cleansing us every day. Thank you, Jesus. Amen.

RAIN OR SHINE – LOVE

'You have heard that it was said, "Love your neighbour and hate your enemy". But I tell you, "Love your enemies and pray for those who persecute you, that you may be sons of

your Father in heaven". He causes his sun to rise on the evil and the good, and sends rain on the righteous and the un-righteous'.

Jean: Develop a persistent love, even when you are misjudged and mistreated. Turn your enemies into objects of your love. Don't ignore them, pray for them.

How can we have indestructible love? In Jesus. He is the only source of such love. He can pour persistent love into our un-loving hearts. He did it when we were born into his family. It now becomes a characteristic attitude and identifies us to others as children of God.

Everybody needs love – the evil and the good, the righteous and the unrighteous. Shine it. Rain it. Just as God sends rain and sunshine on us all.

Project: Write the names of those who are nice to you and those who are not. Then, alongside their names tick the ones YOU are nice to and the ones you are not. Now pray for those whom you need to love.

Prayer: Father, I want to develop the Christian characteristic of persistent love. Help me to turn an enemy into a friend, today. Amen.

OCTOBER 8   **MATTHEW 6:14-15**

THE SPIRIT OF RECONCILIATION

'For if you forgive men when they sin against you, your heavenly Father will also forgive you. But if you do not forgive me their sins, your Father will not forgive your sins'.

Elmer: Christ came into this world not only to reconcile us to God, but to one another. The spirit of reconciliation evident in our attitude towards others shows we are at peace with God. On the other hand, a lack of forgiveness towards our brothers and sisters in Christ indicates all is not right between us and God. It is not that God refuses to forgive us. Rather, the same barrier which keeps us from the one who has sinned against us is keep-ing us from God.

I remember many years ago as a small boy how my father had been wronged by my grandfather. My father said to my mother one day, 'I've been robbed of my property . . . The way it is now, I'm being robbed of my father, too. So, I'm going home as if nothing had happened'. This action took God's forgiving grace on my father's part. Later, father was vindicated. But it was good that dad went back home before he was proven right. Dad could forgive because his heart was right. He could ask God's forgiveness for the same reason.

Today: Let us respond quickly in forgiving love to those who hurt us.

Prayer: Father in heaven, help me to forgive people who have wronged me, even when they show no remorse. Help me to take the first step towards reconciliation. Amen.

OCTOBER 9   MARK 11:24-25

BLOCKAGES TO POWERFUL PRAYER

'Therefore I tell you, whatever you ask for in prayer, believe that you have received it, and it will be yours. And when you stand praying, if you hold anything against anyone, forgive him, so that your Father in heaven may forgive you your sins'.

LaDonna: A minister friend of ours once confided he had suffered greatly for two years with opposing factions in his fellowship. As accusations increased, finally culminating in public criticism of his leadership, the power of the Spirit waned. The gift ministries declined and a heaviness fell over the fellowship. The minister was blamed for this. Finally the faction group left. The pastor stayed. Suddenly the worship was light, faith became active and people began to progress spiritually. It was not the structure or the minister that had crippled the church, but rather unforgiveness and criticism.

Think about it: Many believers desire to see miracles accomplished today as the Lord described in v.24. Yet as much as

244

we yearn for it and as hard as we try, they still don't happen. It is because so often we separate v.24 from v.25. Jesus did not point at structure or technique as the key to powerful prayer. Rather, we are reminded to pray pure prayers from hearts free from bitterness and unforgiveness.

Prayer: Lord, it's so easy to hide in my heart the things that displease you. Jesus, bring me closer to you so that your loving touch can cleanse away anything unacceptable in your sight. Amen.

OCTOBER 10   LUKE 7:37-38

WE FORGIVE BECAUSE HE FORGAVE

'When a woman who had lived a sinful life in that town learned that Jesus was eating at the Pharisee's house, she brought an alabaster jar of perfume, and as she stood behind him at his feet weeping, she began to wet his feet with her tears. Then she wiped them with her hair, kissed them and poured perfume on them'.

Alan: This story reminds me of Daniel in the lion's den. Those Pharisees seemed to want to devour Jesus. Perhaps they really hated him, or thought him a joke they would enjoy over dinner. They may have been genuinely interested, but found Jesus just too much to take. Instead they became critical and argumentative. Because Jesus was willing to forgive those people, look what we have gained. The testimony of a woman's love for Jesus and wonderful divine acceptance.

It's a beautiful and touching account. See how our Lord responds in the midst of debate, criticism and humiliation. He was ready to love and forgive.

Action: Take this example of love into your work, school or social situation. Choose not to get your own back or to win an argument for the sake of winning. Be ready to love and forgive. Someone may turn to Jesus through your testimony.

Prayer: I thank you for your word, Lord Jesus. In my own strength I am not strong enough for this. But God is at work within me, making me more like the example I seek to follow – YOU. Amen.

OCTOBER 11   EPHESIANS 4:32

NOT COMPETITIVE, BUT COMPASSIONATE

'Be kind and compassionate to one another, forgiving each other, just as in Christ God forgave you'.

Jean: One of the first things we realise after we are born again is that we are part of a family, God's great kingdom-family. As his children, we should all have one aim, to glorify him.

When we do, all kinds of gifts, talents and abilities appear in innumerable combinations, resulting in varieties of ministry. As long as these flow harmoniously towards our main aim, to glorify the Father, all kinds of blessings are enjoyed.

If competitiveness develops instead of mutual edification, there will be mutual destruction. Instead of many enjoying the fruits of labour in the vineyard, only a few will enjoy the fruits of many labourers. This cannot be allowed, for the weakening of a few is the weakening of all.

Family: You as a family have a unity and responsibility to each other none of your neighbours have towards you. As a family, work towards developing your gifts, talents and abilities which will appear. Don't compete with each other, love each other. Be compassionate.

Prayer: Father, make us patient and forgiving with each other so that we as a family will glorify you and help each other to be all you want them to be. Amen.

OCTOBER 12   COLOSSIANS 3:13

LOVE IS A BOUQUET OF ROSES

'Bear with each other and forgive whatever grievances you may have against one another. Forgive as the Lord forgave you'.

Jean: Love is like a large bouquet of roses. It says, 'You are special to me'. It is full of the fragrance of compassion. It is sensitive to others' sorrows. It is ready to act in pity. Such love demands a lowliness in estimating one's own claims. It bears evil without resentment and pours out Christlike forgiveness.

All these attributes could turn our world into Eden if they were the prevailing attitudes of all God's people. But there are many contrary forces hard against the fragile bouquet of love.

All of us together cannot fill the whole world with love today. But each one of us can give a bouquet of compassion, forgiveness and understanding to someone. Often our hands are so full of the problems of self-centredness we are unable to take hold of love and give it to another. The best way to be remembered is to forget oneself and make someone else feel special. They'll appreciate the lasting fragrance of love.

Give a bouquet of love: Roses are out of season, but love is always in season. As you would pick out flowers in a bouquet, choose to love. Think of different ways you can show love to someone you want to make feel special today.

Prayer: Father, we thank you for the Rose of Sharon whose fragrance has filled our hearts. Let us carry your kind of love to others. In Jesus' name, Amen.

OCTOBER 13   1 PETER 3:9

THE LAW OF NON-RETALIATION

'Do not repay evil with evil or insult with insult, but with blessing, because to this you were called so that you may inherit a blessing'.

Jean: I read in the Reader's Digest of a woman who was bitten by a dog. Her doctor advised her to write her last wishes, for she might die of Hydrophobia. She took such a long time writing, he asked if she had a lengthy will.

'My will!' she snapped. 'I'm writing the list of people I'm going to bite!'

Her attitude was certainly not the mood of our text! Peter must have been recalling some of the words Jesus spoke in his Sermon on the Mount: 'Do not resist an evil person . . . Love your enemies . . . Do good'.

Retaliation and revenge can run like poison through families for generations. New birth gives us a new start. We inherit blessing so we can stop the curse of revenge. To this we are called, to bless, not to bite back.

Project: List those who have not done right by you and insulted you. Are you going to bless them or bite them?

Prayer: Father, out of the resources of your blessing in my life I want to bless and not curse. Make me a blessing today. Amen.

OCTOBER 14   ECCLESIASTES 4:9-10

TWO ARE BETTER THAN ONE

'Two are better than one, because they have a good return for their work: if one falls down, his friend can help him up. But pity the man who falls and has no one to help him up!'

Jean: Friendship is indispensable to happiness. Those who do not feel the need of it are sick of mind and starved in their souls.

Two can certainly do more in life than one alone, and they are happier. 'It is not good for man to be alone', God said. If it was not good for man to be alone in Paradise, then how could it be good in our world to be alone?

Togetherness makes our work less like slavery. Togetherness gives us more stamina to outlast our troubles. We have more faith when we pray together. We enjoy life more in the company of each other. Our Lord knew this when he sent forth his labourers two by two. Left alone, we are likely to grow cold and selfish, but the nearness of each other warms our hearts with generosity.

Act it out: One of you play the part of the person who wants to

'Go it alone', without the help of friends. As he starts to walk, another offer to walk with him. The 'loner' shakes him off. As he walks on, he falls down. He calls for help, but no one is near. Then act it out the opposite way. Two walk together, one falls, the other helps him up.

Prayer: Father, today I will let my friends help me, and be thankful. Also, help me to lift up someone else who has fallen down. In Jesus' name, Amen.

OCTOBER 15   MATTHEW 18:15

TALK WITH EACH OTHER

'If your brother sins against you, go and show him his fault, just between the two of us. If he listens to you, you have won your brother over'.

Elmer: 'Those that feared the Lord talked with each other' (Malachi 3:16). So often Christians will allow barriers to come between them. These conditions arise when we have failed to communicate honestly with one another. Small grievances begin to take on large proportions. Jesus taught 'Go, make things right with your brother, then pray and give your gifts to God'.

People readily forget that God is everywhere. But he is present to bless in a special way when people truly meet in his name. To meet in his name, truly representing him, we must meet in harmony.

How good it is for brothers to dwell together in peace. In that peace we will find his blessing and hear his voice.

Take a moment: Stop – forgive – listen! You will hear him.

Prayer: Lord, help me to live in peace with my neighbour. May I learn that the way of forgiveness and reconciliation must be my way of life. Amen.

SAVE YOURSELVES FROM THIS
CORRUPT GENERATION!

*'With many other words he warned them; and he pleaded
with them, "Save yourselves from his corrupt generation".
Those who accepted his message were baptised, and about
three thousand were added to their number that day. They
devoted themselves to the apostles' teaching and to the fellowship, to the breaking of bread and to prayer'.*

LaDonna: Alan and I have friends who work in secular theatre.
A Christian actor will often have to travel from town to town
with his theatrical company for many weeks. During these
times, completely severed from Christian friends, a believer can
lose his bearings and begin to doubt his Christian standards.

One actress found that she was the only female in a small tour-
ing company. When the men found she had high moral and
spiritual standards, they began a campaign of abuse. When she
was in their presence they would behave very crudely and tell
obscene stories. Unable to escape the constant bombardment
she longed for loving Christian fellowship.

For this woman, the battle was obvious. Each one of us,
however, is affected by the darkness of this present generation
in a personal way.

Think: How are you being saved from this corrupt generation?
Are you fighting alone? Alas, it is easy to overlook the times you
compromise and lose sight of Jesus. Through fellowship, you
can find strength to keep growing into the likeness of Christ.
Seek Christian friends.

Prayer: Lord, I thank you for Christian friends who give me
love and support as I fellow your path. Help me in turn to love
and encourage others you send my way. Amen.

OCTOBER 17 COLOSSIANS 3:12-14

BEAUTIFUL ATTITUDES

'Therefore, as God's chosen people, holy and dearly loved, clothe yourselves with compassion, kindness, humility, gentleness and patience. Bear with each other and forgive whatever grievances you may have against one another. Forgive as the Lord forgave you. And over all these virtues put on love, which binds them all together in perfect unity'.

Alan: I recently read about a woman who lives alone in the Alaskan wilderness with her sledge dogs. Her nearest neighbours are miles away,. Perhaps she found people just too much to deal with and could only take them in small doses. Who can blame her? People can be the meanest animals alive! That is why we find such instructions as those above in scripture.

St Paul is speaking to those chosen of God. He shows us the attributes we need to identify with and to love one another. They are attributes hidden in every Christian, although they are often covered up with anger, criticism and the various defence mechanisms which come from deep inner hurts.

Action: Thank God we can receive healing of our hurts, and can put on life-giving, loving attitudes. What kind of attitudes can you ask of God today?

Prayer: Father, please show me what part of my old self I can hand over to you for more of your love, compassion and gentleness. In Jesus' name, Amen.

OCTOBVER 18 PHILIPPIANS 1:3-5

LIGHT UP YOUR MEMORY WITH FRIENDS

'I thank my God every time I remember you. In all my prayers for all of you, I always pray with joy because of your partnership in the Gospel from the first day until now'.

Jean: When Paul wrote these words he was a prisoner of Rome, confined to close quarters, under guard day and night. How he must have missed the liberty of travel and the fellowship of the churches.

But he still had his memories. As he waited year after year for his trial, and probable execution, Paul could have become an embittered, mean, quarrelsome old man. How did he maintain a grateful, joyful personality?

He didn't think about his enemies, he thought about his friends. He prayed until his enemies were the least of his worries and his mind was full of the faces of those who filled him with joy.

Some intercession brings tears, for prayer carries to the throne of grace those who have turned away from God, churches which are dead and desolate and the sick souls of an unrepentant nation. But others in our intercession light up our lives with joy. We are not burdened nor sad, we are full of gladness.

Family: Recollect together the friends with whom you have shared happy times.

Prayer: We thank you, God, for the joy of blessings and victories we have shared with friends. Remembering them strengthens our faith for those who need our prayers today. Our friend ..... needs your help today. We pray with joyous faith. In Jesus' name, Amen.

OCTOBER 19   **1 JOHN 1:7**

YOU'LL NEVER WALK ALONE IN THE LIGHT

'But if we walk in the light, as he is in the light, we have fellowship with one another, and the blood of Jesus his Son, purifies us from every sin'.

Jean: Walking in the light consistently cleanses the whole person. One can become an 'open house'. Such a person has good friends as opposed to acquaintances. He is trustworthy. He can be a close friend and keep confidences. He is not preoccupied with concealing his own problems. He seems to know how to keep his own life uncluttered of old grievances, unsettled problems and broken relationships. Such a person attracts others who need such a friend to give them faith and hope.

The benefit of walking in the light, aside from having good friends, is that one has a good life. The good life for a Christian is an honest and pure life. It is being saved for something special and for someone special. It is to be set apart for God and his glory. He is kept from sin for the Master's use.

Walking in the light happens when one says, 'This is the way I want to go, the life I want to live. Jesus is the One I want to trust. I place myself in his hands and I'll keep walking in his light'. Do this, and you'll never walk alone.

Question: Are you the kind of friend who is undefeated by personal problems so you can bear the burden of others, or are you a burden to others who need your help? Do you inspire fear or faith?

Prayer: Father, unclutter my life and free me from old grievances and unsettled problems. I confess those things I know are sin. Forgive me and make me forgiving. Amen.

OCTOBER 20   GENESIS 50: 19-20

RELEASE YOUR FAMILY INTO LOVE

'But Joseph said to them, "Don't be afraid. Am I in the place of God? You intended to harm me, but God intended it for good to accomplish what is now being done, the saving of many lives. So then, don't be afraid. I will provide for you and your children". And he reassured them and spoke kindly to them'.

Jean: I recommend you read the whole passage (vv.15-21) with your family. It is the happy ending of a family feud. It is love's answer to hate. The fear of retribution is overcome by forgiveness. Sins of arrogant youth are covered by saintly maturity. The evil intentions of man are overthrown by the good intentions of God. The short-sighted, impulsive plans of selfish men are used by God in his long-term plans to use one unselfish man to bless many.

253

'So don't be afraid . . . ' Instead, observe the providence of God, his sovereign grace, his omnipotence, his omniscience and his love. Don't fear your past. It cannot ruin your present, if it is forgiven. Forget it and it won't hurt you. Put it out of your conscious thoughts. Think upon how good God is now. Don't fear the future, either. Don't worry about what will happen to your children. Trust God's love. He has been with you and he will be with them.

Practise love: Release every member of your family as Joseph did his by forgiveness, faith and kind words of reassurance. Release them into future years of rich enjoyment of each other and their children. Leave them with a legacy of faith: 'God will surely come to your aid . . . '

Prayer: Father, give me so much love that I will not only forgive, but forget that I have forgiven. Forgiveness remembered re-infects the wound. I will not nurse old wounds. In Jesus' name, Amen.

OCTOBER 21   **ROMANS 15:5-6**

CHRISTIAN'S CO-OP

'May the God who gives endurance and encouragement give you a spirit of unity among yourselves as you follow Christ Jesus, so that with one heart and mouth you may glorify the God and Father of our Lord Jesus Christ'.

Jean: God's work is done best in a climate of harmony. Friction and discord never contribute to fruitfulness. Co-operation among Christians is God's plan.

One of my earliest school memories is a grade card I received when I was eight years old. My teacher had written 'Jean does not cooperate for the good of the group'. My shame and my mother's shock still make me uncomfortable when I remember it. My feelings change, however, when I recall a later commendation. 'Jean is a good leader. She works well with people and inspires them to work well together'. Only God's grace in my life explains the difference between those two statements.

Like my mother, I felt the main thing our children must learn was how to get along with others. Before I looked for their academic grades, I looked to see their behaviour report.

Our attitudes towards others deeply affect our future destiny. Success or failure depends more upon how we treat others than on how clever we are. Develop the need of others. Appreciate and develop friendships. Have a deep desire for unity and an ability to be interested in other's interests. If you do, you'll have all the resources to endure and be courageous throughout your life.

Discussion: Think about each other's interests . . . your jobs, subjects at school, hobbies, your plans for the future. Show interest in each other and then pray for each other's expectations.

Prayer: Father, we join our hearts to pray for each other . . . Amen.

OCTOBER 22   EPHESIANS 2:4-7

CHRIST'S LOVE OUR LOVE

'But because of his great love for us, God, who is rich in mercy, made us alive with Christ even when we were dead in transgressions — it is by grace you have been saved. And God raised us up with Christ and seated us with him in the heavenly realms in Christ Jesus, in order that in the coming ages he might show the incomparable riches of his grace expressed in his kindness to us in Christ Jesus'.

Elmer: One of the basic factors of human personality is the ability to give and receive love. This is because God who IS love made man in his image. Even spiritual death, the consequence of man's sin, did not stop the flow of the love of God, for to stop God's love would be to destroy God. God goes on loving, for it is his eternal nature to do so.

While we were dead in sin, he loved us. He made us alive in Christ, therefore the life of Christ is our life, and the love of Christ is our love.

Challenge: Let us live in such a manner, that people will see that God's love in us is a life-giving, transforming, constant experience.

Prayer: Thank you, God, for your rich, loving mercy revealed through Jesus Christ to me. May your mercy flow from the well of love within me. In Jesus' name, Amen.

OCTOBER 23   COLOSSIANS 3:1,12

GIVING IT ALL AWAY

'Since then, you have been raised with Christ, set your hearts on things above, where Christ is seated at the right hand of God'.
'Therefore, as God's chosen people, holy and dearly loved, clothe yourselves with compassion, kindness, humility, gentleness and patience'.

LaDonna: A few years ago I, with a team, ran a Christian coffee-house in Bournemouth. Located in an ordinary semi-detached house, it consisted of a pleasant room with a kitchen offering warmth, coffee and ginger nuts. While people took advantage of the warmth and free coffee we talked to them about God.

One man came to see us in action. He found some shabby street people, a few lonely individuals, an old tramp and the team busily serving coffee and chatting. He became concerned. 'They are just having you on', he said. 'They don't want the gospel. They're just pinching your coffee'. 'But that's what we are here for' I replied. 'Can anyone steal what we give away free?'

Think: Have you put demands on someone before you accept and minister God's love to them? Seated with Christ, let us give ourselves in the spirit of Christ, in gentleness and compassion.

Prayer: Lord, I release to you all the demands I put on others. Help me to reach out to them as you do in gentleness and love. Amen.

PRIESTS UNTO GOD

'The point of what we are saying is this: We do have such a high priest, who sat down at the right hand of the throne of the Majesty in heaven . . . '

Alan: Our High Priest in heaven has appointed those who come to him as priests on earth. Not with rules and rituals, but with service and sacrifice. We are to serve the Lord in obedience to his commands and willingly sacrifice that which he asks of us. We serve him by ministering to the needs of others and offering him sacrifices of prayer and praise for lost souls and broken lives.

Action: Let's begin to learn what it means for us as individuals to be priests of the Living God. The Lord has a special task for each one of us today.

Prayer: Lord, I thank you for calling us to be your 'priests'. Help us to serve you today – even if it means sacrifice. Amen.

A CLEANSED CONSCIENCE

'Let us draw near to God with a sincere heart in full assurance of faith, having our hearts sprinkled to cleanse us from a guilty conscience and having our bodies washed in pure water'.

Jean: Guilt often blocks the path to prayer. Fear to draw near to God paralyses faith.

A troubled conscience is not always right, however. It may be feeding back to us feelings of guilt based on wrong information. Conscience is like a navigator. It steers us alongside what we believe is right.

Some are educated to believe that wearing jewellery, make-up or short hair is 'wrong'. Such persons will be troubled with all kinds of negative signals if they walk any other way. The signals try to prevent them from making a mistake.

What your conscience does to you depends upon your own basic beliefs. Check out your conscience. Have you given it man-made rules, accusations or have you given it scriptural guidelines to go by? Perhaps you are feeling unworthy, guilty or undeserving over things which are not wrong at all. Your conscience must be based on truth. 'Know the truth and the truth will set you free'.

Remember: If you are oppressed by excessive guilt: if your mind is malfunctioning because of a constant barrage of condemnation; if your nerves are frayed by fear . . . you need the Holy Spirit to draw you near to God.

Prayer: Jesus, you are my high-priest before God's throne. Please cleanse my conscience from lies. Show me the truth about myself and your will. I want to feel clean and uncondemned. For your glory, Amen.

OCTOBER 26   1 PETER 2:4-5

YOU ARE CHOSEN, NOT REJECTED

'As you come to him, the living stone – rejected by men but chosen by God and precious to him – you also, like living stones, are being built into a spiritual house to be a holy priesthood, offering spiritual sacrifices acceptable to God through Jesus Christ'.

Jean: Once freed from a condemning conscience to a commending one, we become part of something concrete, observable and functional.

It is the believer-priesthood, chosen and precious to God. From the days of Abraham, this one people of God has formed a continuous life of service and sacrifice by faith. Now the whole church is God's special people chosen to offer spiritual sacrifices to God. The priestly service of the Church includes the whole life of each member. When we go to church we demonstrate and celebrate in our worship our offerings to God. But outside the church we are still priests and we give a

258

sacramental meaning to all of our lives. In the home, school, office or factory we serve God. Our whole lives are an offering, not always splendid in themselves, but in Christ acceptable to God.'

Did your mother or father reject you? Did the one who promised to marry you for better or for worse walk out on you? Are you forgotten by your friends or children? Feel ashamed no longer. You now belong to him who was supremely rejected. He was rejected by his own religion. Even his own family at times stood apart from him. But you, like him, are precious to the Father who loves you.

Family: Say to one another, 'I love you and accept you as my .... (whatever the relationship is: husband, wife, parent, child, friend).

Prayer: Father, we thank you for making us prayer-partners together in your priesthood. Amen.

OCTOBER 27   1 JOHN 3:17-18

MINISTRY BEGINS AT HOME

'If anyone has material possessions and sees his brother in need but has no pity on him, how can the love of God be in him? Dear children, let us not love with words or tongue but with actions and truth'.

Jean: True priestly service to God is not only expressed in our worship to God, but in our sacrificial offerings towards others. Sometimes we are so caught up with the big vision of some future, heroic service we will give to God, we overlook our present opportunities to serve now. The missionary vision should start as a home missionary vision. Love is the name of the ministry most needed around us. Love which is willing to surrender what is valuable to us for the good of another. Love which isn't just spread out over everybody, but offered to somebody in particular.

Caring for someone who needs us is dealing with reality rather than fantasy. Practical Christianity produces a great inner peace within. We dare not close our hearts if we claim to have God's love in us. Fear, rather than not caring, often holds us back. We fear becoming involved, we fear that we are inadequate for the task, we fear we may be rejected. But perfect love casts out all fear.

Remember: If you really want to enjoy living, start loving.

Prayer: Dear God, keep me from fantasy and let your love in me lead me into reality. Don't let my vision be so far off I overlook those near me who are in need. In Jesus' name, Amen.

OCTOBER 28   MATTHEW 18:19-20

THE POWER OF UNITED PRAYER

'Again, I tell you that if two of you on earth agree about anything you ask, it will be done for you by my Father in heaven. For when two or three come together in my name, there am I with them'.

Jean: You have come together, therefore he is with you. Because you are together you can pray with the assurance that your prayers will be answered. Why? Because you are his family.

United prayer is powerful use of the believer's faith. That is why the enemy of our souls fights so persistently against family prayers. Families who pray together exercise unique authority. Their unity is one of the most spiritually strong forces in the world.

First, the husband and wife from a unity based on their marital union that is as close as that of Christ to his Church. Then, their children have an understanding of their parents and the parents of their children unlike any other relationship. They have the same mind. Their prayers, based on mutual understanding, can be powerfully effective.

Don't let the enemy tempt you to not use your God-given family unity in prayer. All kinds of excuses will be available, but not very many good reasons can release you from the duty and the privilege you have to ask for the things on which you agree.

Think of it: What a promise! 'It will be done for you by my Father in heaven'.

Prayer: We claim that promise, Father. Thank you for the powerful faith you have given us as a family. We want to use that faith for each other. Amen.

OCTOBER 29   MARK 16:15-20

PUT YOUR FAITH IN ACTION

'He said to them, "Go into all the world and preach the good news to all creation. Whoever believes and is baptised will be saved, but whoever does not believe will be condemned. And these signs will accompany those who believe: In my name they will drive out demons: they will speak in new tongues; they will pick up snakes with their hands; and when they drink deadly poison, it will not hurt them at all; they will place their hands on sick people, and they will get well". After the Lord Jesus had spoken to them, he was taken up into heaven and he sat at the right hand of God. Then the disciples went out and preached everywhere, and the Lord worked with them and confirmed his word by the signs that accompanied it'.

Elmer: If signs following were promised only to preachers (v.15), miracles might have been limited only to preachers. Notice, rather, that signs follow **believers.** Those who hear the wonderful good news of salvation and respond with heartfelt faith become people of faith. Are you a believer? Then believe for signs to accompany your life of faith.

Today: Put your faith in action. God responds to an active faith.

Prayer: Lord, help me to believe for my friends' needs and see signs following in my life. Amen.

NOTHING WILL HARM YOU

'I have given you authority to trample on snakes and scorpions, and to overcome all the power of the enemy; nothing will harm you'.

LaDonna: On reading this scripture, an experience I had at a family camp immediately sprang to mind. After an evening meeting in the big marquee, a number of people stayed behind to pray in the wonderful spiritual atmosphere. Suddenly, a landrover came roaring through the wide entrance, headlights ablaze, engine racing, aiming straight for the people at the front.

Like one man, we leapt to our feet, stretched out our hands and shouted, 'In the name of Jesus STOP!'

The vehicle jolted and stopped as if hitting an invisible wall, while the enraged driver swore and gunned the motor. In frustration, the man climbed on to the bonnet and shouted obscenities over the noise of the motor until someone coaxed him down.

We witnessed how under the authority of God that car could not harm us! What gave us such power that night? It was the powerful unity we had in Christ and with one another.

Think: Christ said, 'I give you authority over all the power of the enemy'. Let's learn how to walk in the power of the Spirit of Christ daily.

Prayer: We thank you, Father, for the authority you give us in your Son's name. Teach us how to walk in unity before you so that your power may be released effectively through us. In Jesus' name, Amen.

THAT'S WHAT HE SAID!

*'I tell you the truth, anyone who has faith in me will do what
I have been doing. He will do even greater things than these,
because I am going to the Father. And I will do whatever you
ask in my name, so that the Son may bring glory to the
Father. You may ask me for anything in my name, and I will
do it'.*

Alan: Is it possible for us to believe we can actually do greater
works than Jesus did when he was here on earth? Well, that's
what The Man said! So, let's believe and trust that it can be so.
Let's pray in his name, according to his will, that God may be
glorified all the more. His power and authority brings glory to
God and salvation to men.

If I take Jesus at his word – and I must – I will have to allow
my ministry to be shaped and re-worked by the Lord so that it
becomes the expression of his will, clothed with his power and
effective in his harvest fields. The great blessing is that his
ministry brings me closer to God.

Something to think about: When one is driving a car, one has
the power and the authority of that vehicle. Likewise, one must
learn how to control the power and authority latent in one's own
ministry and to know the direction in which God wants it to go.
We dare not go beyond our faith, nor short of it.

Prayer: Teach me, Lord, the power and authority you have for
me. Help me to use it for your glory. Amen.

WE ARE A ROYAL FAMILY

'Praise be to the God and Father of our Lord Jesus Christ, who has blessed us in heavenly realms with every spiritual blessing in Christ'.

Jean: According to this world's value systems, the Darnall family is not very important nor worth very much. But in heaven's estimation we are part of a royal family, rich in grace.

Elmer and I implanted in our children's hearts their significance as part of a family who belonged to God. Both of them were converted before the age of six. Through their adolescence and into adulthood the Holy Spirit has maintained their sense of spiritual self-esteem. To this day, their priorities and pleasures are strongly governed by their awareness of who they are. As a family we all feel it matters more who we are in the sight of God than who we are in the sight of men. What we possess in the heavenly places must not be forfeited in our attempts to gain things here.

Every Christian family is a royal family, reinforced by heaven's power to live in this world for the glory of God. We have this strong sense of self-esteem and spiritual values not because we are especially holy but because we, like all of God's children, are chosen to be in him. 'In Christ' is the key to our inheritance. Those two words open the treasury to every spiritual blessing.

Question: What do you think 'In Christ' means?

Prayer: We praise you, Father, for placing us in a royal family. Thank you for an eternal inheritance. We claim today the blessings we need as a family in Christ. In Jesus' name, Amen.

NOVEMBER 2   **PHILIPPIANS 2:9**

HIS GIVEN NAME

'Therefore God exalted him to the highest place and gave him the name that is above every name . . . '

Jean: The humility of Christ brought forth the glory of Christ. The cross was the bottom step of his ascent to the throne. The crown of thorns was cast aside for a crown of victory.

The exaltation of Christ was heaven's greatest expectancy. The Father planned it. Creation groaned for it. Angels yearned for it. Hell trembled because of it.

His name, the Father's gift at his incarnation, becomes the gift of his coronation. The name above all names, Jesus! Heaven sings for joy, the Saviour of the world has come to his throne.

His followers upon earth have been given the power of his name to heal the sick, to forgive sins, to dispel demons, to bless the world. No other name has meant so much to so many for so long.

Sing: Lift up your hearts to praise the enthroned Jesus. Sing of the power of his name.

Prayer: Father, we thank you for the Name you gave your Son. It is precious on earth and in heaven. We praise the name of Jesus. Amen.

NOVEMBER 3   **ACTS 3:12-16**

GO IN HIS NAME

'When Peter saw this, he said to them: "Men of Israel, why do you stare at us as if by our own power or godliness we had made this man walk? By faith in the name of Jesus, this man whom you see and know was made strong. It is Jesus' name and the faith that comes through him that has given this complete healing to him as you can see"'.

Jean: Individuals are tremendously important to God. The same power given Peter by the Holy Spirit to touch thousands touched one helpless, crippled beggar.

While we pray for the spiritual awakening of Britain, we must not lose our concern for the individual in the house across the street. Or for the sick person in the next block. You and I have the power of the Holy Spirit to speak life-changing words of faith. All around us are 'cripples' with injured, broken lives.

The whole world seems to be on crutches of one kind or another. Today, as you go in the name of Jesus, lovingly give what you have to give. Faith flows with the giving. Expect a miracle.

Sing: 'Freely, freely you have received . . . '

Prayer: Father, help us to minister to the physical and temporal needs of others in the name of Jesus. We know that you will meet their spiritual needs as well. Help us to cause helpless, hopeless people to fairly leap into the Kingdom! Amen.

NOVEMBER 4   2 CORINTHIANS 1:10-11

KEEP THE LINES OPEN

'. . . On him we have set our hope that he will continue to deliver us, as you help us by your prayers'.

Jean: Open lines of communication are vital to the effectiveness of intercessory prayer.

I have talked with friends interested in developing a divine healing ministry. My advice has been, 'Ask God for prayer partners. Don't attempt to pray for the sick by yourself. You need others behind the scenes who will pray, as well as those who stand alongside'.

Prayer partners can participate in the spiritual battles. Don't keep one another in ignorance of your needs. Ridiculous spiritual pride can clam one up and block prayer when one needs it most. Such independence robs others of the use of their spiritual weapons in warfare and the joy of victory.

Of course, if one's pride or the enemy prevents the requests from getting through to one another, God hears. 'Headquarters' takes over. The Holy Spirit sends words of knowledge to others who are alert. Through their prayer those under attack later tell how suddenly and mysteriously they were delivered.

Discussion: Are you under some attack which you're keeping to yourself? As a family, keep the lines open, share your requests . . . and the victories.

Prayer: Holy Spirit, keep us alert in case our prayers are needed. We humbly recognise we cannot cope on our own. Teach us to ask for help. In Jesus' name, Amen.

NOVEMBER 5   ROMANS 15:30

JOIN IN MY STRUGGLE

'I urge you, brothers, by our Lord Jesus Christ and by the love of the Spirit, to join me in my struggle by praying to God for me'.

Elmer: Troubles, joys, struggles. As Christians we should never experience these things alone. The love of Christ shed in our hearts and made operative by the Spirit, will cause us to enter deeply into the feelings of those we love in his church.

There are both times of crisis and times of great joy – (loss of loved ones, sickness, home-comings, Christmas) to share. Even more important are the times which come in between, the times of struggle and painstaking growth. Then we must allow our love to be poured out by the Holy Spirit in intercessory prayer for those facing hardship.

God may even send you to join the struggle and share actively in it. As you pray, be willing to lend a helping hand if necessary. Take responsibility for your natural family – and your spiritual family.

Thought: Words are not enough. They need to be accompanied by acts of loving service.

Prayer: Father, show me how to love in the Spirit, so that I can pray with true heartfelt compassion. In Jesus' name, Amen.

NOVEMBER 6   2 CORINTHIANS 7:5-7a

COMFORT FOR THE DEPRESSED

'For when we came into Macedonia, this body of ours had no rest, but we were harassed at every turn – conflicts on the outside, fears within. But God, who comforts the downcast,

*comforted us by the coming of Titus, and not only by his com-
ing but also by the comfort you had given him'.*

LaDonna: Can someone in the Lord's work become depressed? Our verses for today reveal that it is possible. Paul had
suffered great stress in Macedonia: no rest, outward conflicts,
inward fears. That period of extended turmoil, Paul freely
admits, caused depression.

Praise God – Paul acknowledged reality. Our joy is not that
God's servants never get weary and discouraged, but that we
have a God who comforts the despondent.

God sent Titus to cheer Paul up and release him from depression. A good friend of mine once stayed with me for a few days
while she toured London on holiday. She was unaware of how
miserable I felt. As we caught up on news, her conversation was
entirely about the Lord and his work in her. When she left, my
sadness departed, too. Praise the Lord, he is a God who comforts the depressed.

Think: Someone you know may be suffering from discourage-
ment. Ask the Lord to help you bring release and joy like Titus
brought to Paul. Remember, God is a God who comforts the
depressed.

Prayer: Thank you, Father, for your love that understands and
comforts me when I am discouraged. Use me, Father to extend
your comfort and release to others. Amen.

NOVEMBER 7   **PHILIPPIANS 1:19-20**

LOOK BEYOND!

*'For I know that through your prayers and the help given by
the Spirit of Jesus Christ, what has happened to me will turn
out for my deliverance. I eagerly expect and hope that I will
in no way be ashamed, but will have sufficient courage so that
now as always Christ will be exalted in my body, whether by
life or by death'.*

Alan: Look beyond. This is today's message. Look beyond the

268

problems you face, look beyond yourself and your mortality. Often we allow ourselves to be near-sighted to the point of blindness: staring hard at a gnat of a problem and missing the elephant-sized solution standing right in front of us.

In this passage, St Paul looks beyond the problem to what Christ can do with it. He looks beyond his strength to the prayers of other Christians and the power of the Holy Spirit at work in both himself and them. He looks beyond his own mortality and counts deliverance not as personal security but as Christ's victory in the situation.

Let us look at the ministry of deliverance not just as a solution to an immediate problem, but the power of Christ being released into the situation. Watch him bring more than we had anticipated out of it.

Action: Whatever problem you face today, look beyond it to Christ's deliverance. Not that you might be relieved of a bit of discomfort. Rather, that you might appropriate the power of Christ to be 'more than a conqueror'.

Prayer: Deliver me, Lord Jesus, from only seeing the problems in life. Help me to learn to look beyond them, trusting that you know all about them and know the perfect solution. Let me see that perfect solution. Amen.

NOVEMBER 8   2 TIMOTHY 4:16-18

THE LORD STOOD BY ME

'At my first defence, no one came to my support, but everyone deserted me. May it not be held against them. But the Lord stood at my side and gave me strength . . . And I was delivered from the lion's mouth. The Lord will rescue me from evil attack and will bring me safely to his heavenly kingdom. To him be glory for ever and ever. Amen'.

Jean: There is a familiar ring in Paul's words, ' . . . May it not be held against them'. Is Paul having a flash-back to the day when he stood by and watched Stephen stoned to death? Did he recall Stephen's prayer, 'Lord, do not hold this sin against

269

them'? He may have also recalled Stephen's cry, 'Look, I see heaven open and the Son of Man standing at the right hand of God'.

When Paul had no advocate, the Lord gave him strength to speak. Two were standing there before the unjust judge, not one. The lion's mouth was closed, but Paul knew it was only a postponement. A day would come when heaven's court, not Rome's, would release him into the heavenly kingdom, safe at last. Jesus would still be standing for him at his throne, as he had for Stephen.

Think of it: If you are in need of a defender, Jesus will stand by you as he stood by Paul.

Prayer: Jesus, thank you for standing by me. Strengthen me so I may speak wisely, honestly and fearlessly. In your name, Amen.

NOVEMBER 9   JAMES 5:14-15

WHERE ARE THE ELDERS?

'Is any one of you sick? He should call for the elders of the church to pray over him and anoint him with oil in the name of the Lord. And the prayer offered in faith will make the sick person well; the Lord will raise him up. If he has sinned he will be forgiven'.

Jean: If the apostle James had written, 'Let them call on the apostles . . .' we might assume the ministry of divine healing ceased with the apostolic age. Praise God, he wrote: 'Call for the elders of the church'. This blessed ministry belongs to the continuing leadership of the church, whether it be in the home, the chapel or the cathedral. Any sickness, serious or trivial, should be attended to by a praying church.

As I lay dying with an incurable kidney disease at the age of sixteen, my mother sought a preacher to anoint for death. To my good fortune, she found one who anointed me to life! I was miraculously healed and soon afterwards converted.

Let us look for a church whose elders are prayerful, gifted and faithful to this greatly needed ministry. Instead of asking, 'Is any one of you sick?', we might better ask, 'Is there any one of you not sick?' The Body of Christ needs healing of every kind. Where are the elders?

Question: When sickness strikes in your family, whom do you call first? The elders or the doctor? Why not put prayer first, before you seek outside help.

Prayer: Bless our family with faith to call for prayer. Bless our church with spiritually gifted leaders who can pray the prayer of faith. In Jesus' name, Amen.

NOVEMBER 10   LUKE 6:8b

GOD WORKS HIS WAY, NOT OURS

'But Jesus . . . said to the man with the shrivelled hand, "Get up and stand in front of everyone". So he got up and stood there'.

Jean: During Jesus' ministry, the most constant and difficult opposition came from the direction where he should have received the greatest support . . . the religious leaders. They were leaders not of a foreign and pagan religion, but believers of his own Jewish faith. Why did they fight him so?

Because he claimed to be Messiah and he didn't meet their expectations of the coming Deliverer. He said he did the works of God. But they were sure God didn't work that way. For instance, to heal a man on the sabbath was not right in their opinion, and their opinion to them was like the law.

Sometimes God comes to meet the needs of the weak in an unexpected manner. He may disturb our rest, break our rules, upset our preconceived notions on how, where, and whom he will bless and not bless. He may ask someone someday to stand up in front of you to show you a miracle. It may be hard to believe it. Not that God couldn't or wouldn't, but you may think he shouldn't. Don't be furious, God is God and no respecter of persons . . . or places.

Discussion: Have you ever seen someone healed in answer to prayer? Were you able to rejoice or did prejudice hinder you.

Prayer: Come, Jesus, have your own way in my home, my church, my business, anytime. Bless anyone who needs your touch. Amen.

NOVEMBER 11   2 TIMOTHY 1:12

REMEMBER AND RELINQUISH

'That is why I'm suffering as I am. Yet I am not ashamed, because I know in whom I have believed, and am convinced that he is able to guard what I've entrusted to him for that day'.

Jean: When we are in circumstances hard to accept as God's will for us, we need to remember, and to relinquish.

Remember you are the Lord's. Are your difficulties due to deliberate disobedience to the Lord you serve? If not, then you are in your present problem within the will of God.

Relinquish your discontent, bewilderment and fear of failure to the Lord. Let go. Think of your tensions and negative feelings flowing out of you from your head to your feet. Relax and rest. Lean, as if you were actually lying in God's lap.

Paul knew he was the King's servant. He knew his sufferings in Rome were in the line of duty. God had to take responsibility for him all the way, right to the end.

It is not your responsibility to change your circumstances, it is God's. He is in charge. Don't take yourself out of his hands.

Say: 'God will take care of me all my life . . . every year, every month, every day, every moment, every second . . . this second, now.

Prayer: Father, I will not be embarrassed by what looks like defeat. It isn't, and you have not made me a failure. I can't be, for I and everything I have is in your hands and you are able to guard what I've turned over to you. Amen.

STRIVING TO OBTAIN

'Not that I have already obtained all this, or have already been made perfect, but I press on to take hold of that for which Christ Jesus took hold of me. Brothers, I do not consider myself yet to have taken hold of it. But one thing I do: Forgetting what is behind and straining towards what is ahead, I press on towards the goal to win the prize for which God has called me heavenwards in Christ Jesus'.

Elmer: Christians look forward to their future which stretches out beyond their present into eternity.

The new life we now live is the eternal life of God himself given to us through Jesus Christ his Son.

We live in the eternal now. Christ has taken hold of us so that we might take hold of our eternal place in the presence of God. God is not static, and we are ever approaching him, ever striving to please him.

We already have obtained much in him. Let us live up to what we have attained and strive for what we have not yet obtained. As we do so, our past becomes a shadow. We live in the present reality of what is to be. We are drawn heavenwards to the Eternal Presence.

Today: Live with eternity in view.

Prayer: Lord Jesus, help me to forget the past problems and sins which are under your blood. Cause me to live in the 'eternal now' of your presence and power. Amen.

PURSUIT OF HAPPINESS

'All these people were still living by faith when they died. They did not receive the things promised; they only saw them and welcomed them from a distance. And they admitted that they were aliens and strangers on earth. People who say such things show that they are looking for a country of their own.

If they had been thinking of the country they had left, they would have had opportunity to return. Instead, they were longing for a better country – a heavenly one. Therefore God is not ashamed to be called their God, for he has prepared a city for them'.

LaDonna: Once I remarked to Alan as we drove down the motorway, 'It seems to me that the greatest need people seem to have today is to attain just the right set of circumstances for happiness.

I have spoken the wistful phrase, 'If only'. 'If only I had a job I'd be fulfilled'. 'If only I had more free time, I'd be happy'. 'If only I had a less stressful occupation'. 'If only I had a better Christian fellowship'. 'If only people understood what I can really do . . . '

The people of whom God was proud were those who recognised they were pilgrims in this world. They knew that complete fulfillment could only exist in a society whose builder is God. They did not grasp at momentary fulfillment which evaporates from one day to another, but travelled through life like pilgrims on their way home.

The 'If only's' on our lips reveal how tied to this life we really are. The people of Hebrews 11 passed through life with their eyes fixed upon the Lord and were able to triumph in life regardless of the circumstances.

Discuss: What are your 'If only's'? Tell each other. Pray for each to see farther ahead by faith.

Prayer: Lord, I thank you that you are at work in me now and the job will finally be completed the day I see you face to face. Help me to be patient with today's turmoils and frustrations because I know you are in control. Amen.

NOVEMBER 14 **HEBREWS 12:1-3**

LIFE IN THE OVERLAP

'Therefore, since we are surrounded by such a great cloud of witnesses, let us throw off everything that hinders and the sin

that so easily entangles, and let us run with perseverance the race marked out for us. Let us fix our eyes on Jesus, the author and perfector of our faith, who for the joy set before him endured the cross, scorning its shame, and sat down at the right hand of the throne of God. Consider him who endured such opposition from sinful men, so that you will not grow weary and lose heart'.

Alan: Eric Liddel was a missionary. He was willing to live a life of hardship and suffer a martyr's death for Christ. He also had a passion for an earthly pursuit — running. The two hardly seem to go together, like many of the things in our lives. But herein lies Eric's witness to us: his passion for running was in submission to the Lord. When required to run on a Sunday, he refused, because he did not believe the Lord wanted him to. 'Chariots of Fire' shows us the victory God gave him.

The witness of this in my heart is that he won a greater victory than that portrayed in the film. He won the crown of life: a crown whose glory would not fade. It was the Lord's glory, the glory which Eric Liddel sought above all else.

Action: We all have things such as sports, social activities, etc. which God has given us to enjoy as part of our Christian lives. The challenge is to put them under God's control, not our own. Talk about the things you love to do. Pray for each other to know God's will.

Prayer: Father, help me as I work in the overlap of life to bring into harmony those things you require of me. Not too fast, nor too slow, but according to your guidance and timing. Amen.

NOVEMBER 15   JAMES 1:2-3

WELCOME TROUBLE!

'Consider it pure joy, my brothers, whenever you face trials of many kinds, because you know that the testing of your faith develops perseverance'.

Jean: 'Welcome, trouble. Come right in!' Is that what James wants us to say? Yes it is, and he means it!

We need to learn the lesson of relinquishment. There are times when we must stop saying, 'This shouldn't happen to me . . . to us . . . to the one I love' and say instead, 'Alright, Lord, you seem to want me (us) to go through this one. I'll not fight it, rather let me take hold of it and find it's hidden joy. I'm not going to let trouble ruin my faith. It will strengthen my faith. Teach me how to hang in there and not give up'.

Hold on. Your faith will pass the test and you'll be stronger to take larger steps forward. God is not out to destroy you. This is a life-giving experience you're passing through!

Belief always faces tests. Promises have to be proven. Why? Belief must be turned into conviction; promises into commitment.

Play a game: One of you be Christian. One of you be Trouble. Trouble comes to the door of Christian. When Christian sees Trouble he is afraid and turns to pray. Then, he answers the door. Trouble enters and says, 'I've come for a while, but when I go you will be a stronger and a more joyful Christian than when I came'. What should Christian say then?

Prayer: Father, my trials are not sent to weaken me, but to strengthen me, if I accept them by faith. Increase my faith to accept your will. In Jesus name, Amen.

NOVEMBER 16   **1 PETER 1:5-7**

SHIELDED BY GOD'S POWER

'You who through faith are shielded by God's power . . . for a little while you may have to suffer grief in all kinds of trials. These have come so that your faith . . . may be proven genuine and may result in praise, glory and honour when Jesus Christ is revealed'.

Jean: When I was a child at home and heard my mother sing, 'God Will Take Care Of You', I knew we were in serious trouble. It was her way of saying 'I don't know what is going to happen, but God does and he'll not let us down'. She had handed over to God.

As I look back now I can see her faith shielded us. We were under God's powerful wings.

Christians are not kept from '. . . griefs in all kinds of trials', but kept through them. Trials are not meant to destroy but to develop our faith. Life's trials are not an end in themselves, but a means towards our completed salvation. We are being saved to be saved forever. We're going to come out of this with something better than gold; genuine faith which will make heaven ring with praise to God.

Family: Encourage one another and say, 'God will take care of you'.

Prayer: Father, help us to shield ourselves and others with our faith from the full blast of life's trials. May the impact of trouble prove our faith and bring to you greater glory. Amen.

NOVEMBER 17   PSALM 23:4

THE SHEPHERD LEADS THROUGH THE SHADOWS

'Even though I walk through the valley of the shadow of death, I will fear no evil, for you are with me; your rod and your staff, they comfort me'.

Jean: When I was a child I would lie on my bed and stare at a painting on my bedroom wall. It was of a shepherd carrying a lamb down a steep mountainside. Far below in a dim valley a river foamed against jagged rocks. At the far end of the valley were green pastures. The sun was almost out of sight. I used to wonder if the shepherd would get the lamb through the valley before it got too dark to see the way.

We go through many valleys in our life time where death shadows fall upon us. Sometimes there are shadows of illness that almost take our life, other times it is the loss of a loved one and we walk a path of sorrow. These are only shadows, not death itself.

But death will come finally for each of us. It may come slowly or suddenly, but first the shadows, then the reality. We flinch from pain or suffering, but our Shepherd will keep us from running away from death. He will hold us steady with his rod and staff. When the shadows become substance, he will be there. Do not fear, he is trustworthy, for he has passed through the valley, shadows and reality, before us. Dying, for a Christian, is walking through a brief valley. It is not lying down into oblivion, but walking into Paradise.

Family: Read or quote the twenty-third Psalm together.

Prayer: Jesus, Shepherd of our Souls, we will fear no evil, for you are with us today and always. Thank you, Father. Amen.

NOVEMBER 18   **ISAIAH 53:9-10**

THE CRUSHING WILL OF GOD

'He was assigned a grave with the wicked and with the rich in his death, though he had done no violence nor was any deceit found in his mouth. Yet it was the Lord's will to crush him ...'

Jean: Jesus was not an unwilling victim of the cross. He willed to do the will of the Father. He was a voluntary sacrifice. 'Lo, I come to do thy will, O God' (Hebrews 10:7).

He was crucified between two thieves and buried in a rich man's tomb. The details of Isaiah's prophecy were perfectly fulfilled. However, it is not the miracle of fulfilled prophecy, but the miracle of surrender by the Suffering Servant that we must recognise. He had done no violence, nor had he deceived, yet it was the Lord's will to crush him!

Suffering is not always a punishment for wrong in our lives. Those experiences where part of us dies are not always identifiable with some past failure of ours. The purpose of suffering can't always be explained. There are times when no lesson can be observed, nothing figures or makes sense. We have to say, not glibly, but solemnly, 'It is the Father's will to crush me'.

Remember: 'The will of the Lord will prosper in his hand'. God will see the result of what is happening and he will be satisfied. And so shall you!

Prayer: Teach me, Father, to be submissive to your will. Then I will be a victor, not a victim. In Jesus' name, Amen.

NOVEMBER 19   MARK 14:36

PLEASE BE THERE

' "*Abba, Father*" *he said,* "*everything is possible for you. Take this cup from me. Yet not what I will, but what you will*" '.

Elmer: Jesus took Peter, James and John, his three most intimate disciples, into his garden of distress. 'Stay here and keep watch' he said.

Each one of us will have Gethsemane experiences. Perhaps we have been taught that in such times of agonising heart searching we should suffer in solitude.

But in his hour of greatest agony, our Lord Jesus asked his dear ones to be with him. He was not ashamed for them to see him crying prostrate on his face. He did not ask their advice. He just asked them to BE THERE.

You will face deep, dark moments of decision. Don't try to 'Go it alone'. Develop close, loving friendships. You will be able to 'watch' with them and they with you in times of distress which lead to deeper commitment.

Today: Think of the one, or those God has given you to share deeply with. Pray for them and for ways to strengthen the bond of love between you.

Prayer: Lord, help me to practice mutual trust with those I love so that we can support one another in hours of crisis. Amen.

NOVEMBER 20   EPHESIANS 5:8-10

NO SHORT CUT TO OBEDIENCE

'*For you were once darkness, but now you are light in the Lord. Live as children of light (for the fruit of the light consists in all goodness, righteousness and truth) and find out what pleases the Lord*'.

LaDonna: The glamour of youth's opportunities can come into conflict with obedience to the Lord's will. Most of the people Alan and I pray with and counsel are young people in their late teens and twenties.

Some come to us in utter confusion. They present us with a tangled knot of circumstances. Apparently they received a leading from the Lord which went wrong. As Alan and I sift through the story, we often come to the same point. Right at the beginning God asked something of them which seemed too difficult. They hesitated, thought about it and finally adjusted the will of the Lord to suit themselves. As a result the circumstances that followed were not under God's authority. Everything crumbled into chaos.

The only way to find peace in the Christian life is to obey the Lord quickly and completely, no matter the cost.

Thought: Is God demanding something of you that seems extremely difficult? Don't hesitate and allow time for confusion to develop. Obey quickly and completely and watch your life respond to the Lord's control.

Prayer: Lord, I accept the challenges you have given me. Help me to do your will completely and joyfully. By faith I thank you for the peace that comes to those who obey. Amen.

NOVEMBER 21   PHILIPPIANS 2:5-8

SURRENDER TO THE FATHER'S WILL

'Your attitude should be the same as that of Christ Jesus: Who being in very nature God, did not consider equality with God something to be grasped, but made himself nothing, taking the very nature of a servant, being made in human likeness. And being found in appearance as a man, he humbled himself and became obedient to death − even death on a cross!'

Alan: A cauldron full of problems boiling on a fire of passion! At the end of the day, it all boils down to one thing, our selfish attitudes!

280

If Jesus' attitude hadn't been one of surrender to the Father's will, he might very well have called down twelve legions of angels in Gethsemane. Such action might have delivered him and might have saved Israel from Rome, but where would it have left us?

No, Jesus' attitude was one of surrender to God. The Father's will meant more to him than his suffering. His attitude was one of trust. He knew the Father's will was love − love towards him and the world. 'For God so loved the world that he gave his only begotten Son'.

Action: Psalm 37:3 says, 'Trust in the Lord and do good'. If there is a situation in your life that is not yet completely surrendered to the Father's will, then do the good thing and trust him with it.

Prayer: Father, please give me patience. Help me to start trusting you more and more. It is my desire to be surrendered to your will and love. Amen.

NOVEMBER 22   **HEBREWS 5:8-9**

THE SAVIOUR OF THE OBEDIENT

'Although he was a son, he learned obedience from what he suffered and, once made perfect, he became the source of eternal salvation for all who obey him'.

Jean: Jesus learned from the things he suffered. He bowed to the experience of absolute submission. Jesus, being very man, possessed his own will. He is our perfect example of human will surrendered to the Father's will. For us he learned obedience. He was made the perfect model of surrender in order for us to learn the same lesson. His whole life-attitude of surrender to his Father's will gives us a living, working model. We are to be like him.

He is the Saviour of the obedient.

Question: If Jesus, Son of God, was not exempt from suffering during his life, then why should we expect to have a non-suffering Christian life?

Prayer: Father, your Son's suffering was not the consequence of disobedience, but obedience. Help me to see that my obedience to your will is not an insurance against suffering, but an assurance of your Son's likeness in my life. In Jesus' name, Amen.

NOVEMBER 23   **HEBREWS 12:7,11**

TRAINED TO BE A CHAMPION

'Endure hardship as discipline; God is treating you as sons. For what son is not disciplined by his father? No discipline seems pleasant at the time, but painful. Later on, however, it produces a harvest of righteousness and peace for those who are trained by it'.

Jean: Champions have to be trained. God desires us to be winners, but that means he has to discipline us. His sons are destined to rule and reign with him. He who would share the throne with his Son must also share his cross.

God's discipline in our lives is not for nothing. The cutting back, the nipping in the bud, the waiting for new growth, are all towards fruitfulness. He has made us with the desire to be productive. His desire is in us. The Father cares that our creativity is not lost. He cares that our inner beauty be revealed. He cares that our talents are not wasted, that our cup of life overflows.

So he trains us and makes us grow in the manner which will bring the fullest realisation of all he has planned for us to be. He wants us to share his holiness.

Remember: Acceptance is the secret of a still and quiet soul.

Prayer: Father, keep me from resentment and rebellion. I see your heart of love behind your hand of discipline. Thank you for treating me as your child. In Jesus' name, Amen.

HEAVEN UPON EARTH

'Your kingdom come, your will be done on earth as it is in heaven'.

Jean: The greatest joy a Christian can know is perfect submission to God the Father's will. The best we can pray for our friends and family is that they will do the will of God. The ultimate, universal happiness will be when God's will is done on earth as it is in heaven.

Oh, that we earthlings were as eager as the angels are to obey him who sits upon the throne of heaven!

But that will come when his kingdom comes. When he returns with his saints; when sin and sorrow and Satan will be cast out of the world.

Until then, in the face of earth's trials and Satan's attacks, we who love the Lord pray: 'Thy will be done in my life, as it is done in heaven. Make me eager to obey you. Reign in my heart'.

Say it aloud: 'My obedience to the Lord Jesus is the beginning of heaven upon earth'.

Prayer: Repeat together the Lord's Prayer.

HOW TO DEVELOP FAITH IN JESUS

'You diligently study the scriptures because you think that by them you possess eternal life. These are the scriptures that testify about me . . .'

Jean: I thank God for the encouragement I had early in my Christian life to search the scriptures. Father, mother and I enrolled into a New Converts' Bible Study right after we accepted Jesus Christ. I still recall the excitement we felt as the time each week drew near.

Jesus highly honoured the Scriptures. He used them as evidence of his identity as the Son of God. If you want to know anything about him, search the scriptures. They are his witnesses. Jesus is there in the Old and the New Testaments. He is in the Law, in the Prophets and in the Poets. He is promised and prophesied.

But he does not come walking out. He is there, but concealed. We must search the scriptures. Read the Bible prayerfully. Use tools like a concordance and a Bible dictionary. It will strengthen your faith in Jesus. The more you know him, the more you'll trust him.

Children: How many of the books of the Bible can you say? See who can say all the books of the Bible perfectly.

Prayer: Holy Spirit, be my teacher and help me to learn more and more about Jesus from searching the scriptures prayerfully. Amen.

NOVEMBER 26   GALATIANS 2:20

THE PRICE OF RESURRECTION LIFE

'I have been crucified with Christ and I no longer live, but Christ lives in me. The life I live in the body, I live by faith in the Son of God, who loved me and gave himself for me'.

Elmer: When the mother of our Lord saw her son dying on the cross, old Simeon's prophetic words were fulfilled. A sword pierced her heart. Had it not been for her faith and total submission to God, the spear that cut the heart of Christ would never have touched her soul.

So it is with us. When we believe that Christ'a awful death on the cross was for us, the agony of the cross pierces our own souls and our sinful selves are crucified with Christ.

Now I no longer live on my own. Christ lives in me. I know that just as the old self was crucified and united with him in death, so my new self is united with him in resurrection life.

Family prayer: Memorise our verse for today.

Prayer: I accept Christ's resurrection life within me. Father, help me to allow this life to flow out, bringing healing and new hope wherever it flows. In Jesus' name, Amen.

NOVEMBER 27   JOHN 6:28-29

I STAND BEFORE A MAN

'Then they asked him, "What must we do to do the works God requires?" Jesus answered, "The work of God is this: to believe in the one he has sent"'.

LaDonna: When I witnessed in a rehabilitation centre for drug abusers, I became involved in a discussion with a boy who believed in reincarnation. He saw himself as a small cell in a vast floating system. His hope of personal spiritual progress was in the tedious evolution of many lives within the huge evolving organism.

I said, 'I'm so glad I'm not cast upon the whims of some cosmic flow. I stand before a man, the person, Jesus Christ, who cares for me as an individual and hears my prayer'.

Sometimes we are afraid if we yield our life to the Lord, all that is precious will be completely taken. We fear we will be torn apart by a vast machine called 'The Will of God'.

What is God's will? It is God's will we believe, or trust, in Christ who died for us. When we hand over our life to him, we put it into the hands of the one who has cared for us more than anyone else ever has. At this moment he knows our deepest needs and longs to comfort our fearful heart.

Think: Can you trust Jesus with your whole life? Yielding to the Lord means believing in who he is, the Saviour and Lover of your soul.

Prayer: Your love for me is overwhelming. Thank you for caring for me as an individual. I give you my life. Take care of it. Amen.

FACT, NOT FEELINGS

*'For everyone born of God has overcome the world. This is the
victory that has overcome the world, even our faith. Who is
it that overcomes the world? Only he who believes that Jesus
is the Son of God'.*

Alan: I don't always feel like an overcomer. When I feel down,
I tend to blame it on my lack of faith. But that is not right, for
I have received the measure of faith God has for me, and it is an
overcoming faith.

On the other hand, it requires action on my part for my faith
to work. Our first moment of faith in Jesus Christ brought us to
a salvation which had overcome death and the world. Relin-
quishing our wills continually to the will of God maintains that
overcoming faith. Jesus is in us, the source of victory, the Victor
himself. If we walk in day-to-day dependence on him, we walk
in overcoming faith.

Pause to think: Feelings come, and feelings go. 'But the Word
of the Lord abides forever'.

Prayer: Father, I thank you that your word is true, no matter
what I feel today. Thank you that your word within gives me
faith to believe. I will overcome the situations that face me.
Amen.

NOVEMBER 29   **1 PETER 1:8-9**

LOVING THE INVISIBLE

*'Though you have not seen him, you love him; and even
though you do not see him now, you believe in him and are filled with an inexpressible and glorious joy, for you are receiving
the goal of your faith, the salvation of your soul'.*

Jean: I've often wished I could have lived when Jesus was on
earth. Just to have been near him!

But then, not everyone was near him. It must have been difficult to have been near enough to touch him. And not many were with him all the time. If I had been alive when Jesus walked the earth, I would probably have seldom seen him up close, perhaps never have spoken to him directly and only would have seen a few miracles. I would have been near him for a short time, in any case. When he died, what a grief it would have been!

Maybe it's better to be alive now. He is with me all the time. He lives within my heart, never to leave me. And I love him, although I haven't seen him. My faith fills me with the joy of expectancy. I shall see him face to face some day. The one I love is coming for me.

Discussion: What do you think? Would you like to have been alive when Jesus was on earth? Would you have followed? Which miracles would you have liked to have seen happen? What would you have done?

Prayer: Father, I thank you that the Holy Spirit makes Jesus so real to me, I can love him even though I can't see him. Amen.

NOVEMBER 30   **HEBREWS 12:2**

JOY AHEAD

'*Let us fix our eyes on Jesus, the author and perfector of our faith, who for the joy set before him endured the cross, scorning its shame, and sat down at the right hand of the throne of God*'.

Jean: Jesus' whole life was a life of faith. His unbroken commitment to his Father's will was the result of steadfast faith.

He wants us to fix our eyes on him and life a life of faith, too. 'He endured the cross'. He trusted his Father. He could not come down from the cross, as his enemies challenged him to; his faith would not allow it.

Jesus was humiliated upon the cross, dying like a criminal with criminals, forsaken by his friends. Yet his humiliation did not keep him from finishing the ordeal with one final cry of commitment. He was still in the Father's hands.

His endurance was due to his expectation. There was joy

ahead. He looked forward to bursting out of the grave, away from hell's domain, into the throne room of heaven announcing, 'Here I am . . . and the children you gave me!'

Remember: The joy of living and the strength to endure are in the faith which expects to finish the race as a winner.

Prayer: Father, I fix my eyes upon Jesus. I am one of the children you have given him. I'm coming too! Hallelujah! Amen.

DECEMBER 1   2 TIMOTHY 3:14

FAITH THAT LASTS

'As for you, continue in what you have learned and have become convinced of, because you know those from whom you have learned it, and how from infancy you have known the holy Scriptures, which are able to make you wise for salvation through faith in Christ Jesus'.

Jean: Paul said to Timothy in so many words, 'Stay in the things you have learned and of which you are convinced. Hold on to your beliefs and they will hold on to you'.

Timothy's teachers lived what they taught. In his home at Lystra his mother and grandmother, Lois and Eunice, had opened up to him the Law, the Prophets and the Psalms. They also told him of Jesus. When Timothy thought of the Scriptures he thought of them. He could see their faces and hear their voices.

Let us create conviction that will hold our children steadfast in the faith. Teach them the Scriptures as the God-breathed Word. Live the word you teach. Put a face to faith. When they are adults, may their memories be full of Scriptures and the faces and voices of those who taught them to love Jesus.

Children: Try to think of all the people in your home, church and school who have taught you to believe God's word and to love Jesus.

288

Prayer: Father, we thank you for those who have taught us your Word and are teaching us now. We thank you for members of our family who believe and live what they teach. In Jesus' name, Amen.

DECEMBER 2   MATTHEW 22:37-38

GREAT LOVE PRODUCES GREAT LIVES

'Jesus replied, "Love the Lord your God with all your heart and with all your soul and with all your mind". This is the first and greatest commandment'.

Jean: The very best training we can give our children is to train them to love God. Love for God is the key to true obedience to God. The children who love God do not find his commandments hard to keep. Those who love him serve him best.

Love for God is the key to right relationships with others. Those who love God find it easier to love people. A child who has a loving respect for the Creator will respect those whom he created too much to hurt them, their property or their name.

Love also motivates service towards others and releases goodness. Lifetime vocations, ministries of mercy, flow out of love for God. Our children's futures will have eternal value and bring glory to God if first, they love him. Devotion to him will release their emotions, intellect and will. Love is creative. Great lives come out of great love.

Parents: Think of all the ways you are training your children. Have you placed training to love God first in your list?

Prayer: Father, we pray that you will make us faithful stewards in the care and training of our children to become men and women who love God. Amen.

DECEMBER 3   EPHESIANS 6:5-8

SERVICE WITH A DIFFERENCE

'Slaves, obey your earthly masters . . . with sincerity of heart, just as you would obey Christ . . . doing the will of God from

*your heart. Serve whole-heartedly as if you were serving the
Lord . . . The Lord will reward everyone for whatever good
he does . . . '*

Elmer: Not all of the Christian slaves to whom Paul spoke had
Christian masters, yet they were told to serve as though they
served the Lord. Since the early Christians lived in a pagan
society, there was not a rest day. So for the slaves it was one day
which began differently. They remembered the Lord's death
and resurrection before sunrise. Then they would return to
serve their masters and others would hurry to their businesses.

As servants of Christ doing the will of God, let us remember
the injunction to be content in whatever state we find ourselves.
Let us serve others in the secular world, not to please people,
but Jesus.

Having the mind of Christ means to respond to situations
spontaneously as Jesus would. Someone has pointed out that
Christian principles are good business. To do the will of the
Father from the heart may be difficult, but it has its rewards as
employer and colleagues respond positively to a kind, joyful
Christian attitude.

At Regent's Park Tube Station in London a kind lady ran one
of the lifts. She always had a smile and a kind word. At
Christmas she decorated the creaky, old lifts with bright
streamers, bells and a Merry Christmas greeting. The public
would give her nothing but a smile and pleasant greeting in
return, but she made a lowly task worthwhile.

Project: You can make a lowly task worthwhile today.

Prayer: Lord, help me to be totally committed to you not in
word only, but in deed. As I serve others, I serve you. Teach me
how to love. Amen.

DECEMBER 4   **ROMANS 8:28**

GOD FIRST

*'And we know that in all things God works for the good of
those who love him, who have been called according to his
purpose'.*

LaDonna: Marriage, I think, is the most difficult thing an unmarried Christian woman can entrust to the Lord. As time slips by, the temptation is to take matters into one's own hands, trying to manipulate and control circumstances to bring about the coveted proposal. The apparent shortage of desirable Christian men can make marriage become the paramount concern. The consequence is that any choice that might hinder a woman's chances is immediately cancelled out.

As a young adult I made the choice to seek God's kingdom first. The Lord began taking me everywhere – Afghanistan, America, Dorset, London and always it seemed, farther away for eligible men! At one point, praying about the anxiety I felt, I realised I was looking for a man to make me happy instead of finding happiness for myself in the Lord.

Then at the age of 27 the right man walked into my life. Only then did I realise how all those experiences had prepared me to be part of a truly happy and steadfast marriage. The Lord taught me how to love with a faithful heart by loving God above all else.

Think: Is there something – or someone – in your life which is very important to you? Does it or he pull you away from pursuing God's will?

Prayer: Lord, you have given me such great love. I give to you those things that are so important to me. Help me to love you above all else. Make me someone who will honour you. Amen.

DECEMBER 5   1 CORINTHIANS 2:9-10

'ABOVE ALL ELSE'

'However, as it is written: "No eye has seen, no ear has heard, no mind has conceived what God has prepared for those who love him" – but God has revealed it to us by his Spirit'.

Alan: This scripture touches me deeply. It teaches me to look beyond what my natural senses tell me and to wait in faith for what God has prepared for me.

Our son Ian was born with a severe sight problem. My mind, full of hurt, questioned God. 'Why did you allow this? Why us?

Why him? What next?' Deep in my spirit and in my heart, however, I did not question Almighty God. There was a looking forward in faith to what our loving Father was going to bring out of this difficulty. Something far greater for Ian and La-Donna and me.

These two parts inside of me battle; at times I'm depressed and hurt, at other times I'm at peace and praising. At ALL times I remind myself that our loving God means more than this or any problem.

Action: Can you love God more than your own pain? Release it to him and allow his solution to be worked out fully in you.

Prayer: Help me to realise, Lord Jesus, that your love for me is stronger than anything else in my life. Cause my love for you to grow equally strong. Amen.

DECEMBER 6   LUKE 7:47

OUTPOURED LOVE

'Therefore, I tell you, her many sins have been forgiven . . . for she loved much. But he who has been forgiven little loves little'.

Jean: It was not out of love that Simon invited Jesus to his house. It might have been out of respect or curiousity. But Jesus accepted the invitation out of love. He came not only to save prostitutes, but Pharisees as well.

One converted prostitute gate-crashed Simon's dinner party. Once in, she did not stay in her place as an uninvited guest. Before anyone was able to stop her, she anointed Jesus' feet as he lay prostrate at the table. Suddenly, she started to weep. Tears streamed down on to his feet. There was nothing to do but wipe them away with her long hair. Embarassed, she apologised by kissing his feet!

Simon couldn't handle it. All the emotion, the broken rules of etiquette! She had spoiled his dinner party. What would people think? What about Jesus? Wasn't he prophet enough to perceive what kind of woman was doing all this?

Jesus knew. He knew she had sinned much. He had forgiven her much. He knew she loved him much. He also knew Simon didn't love him at all!

Question: How is Jesus treated in your home? With mild respect or with deeply felt love?

Prayer: Dear God, we who have sinned so much do not deserve any mercy. But through Jesus Christ you have forgiven all our sins. Because of this, we love Jesus more than anyone or anything. Amen.

DECEMBER 7   ACTS 21:13

COMMITMENT TO THE WILL OF GOD

'Then Paul answered "Why are you weeping and breaking my heart? I am ready not only to be bound, but also to die in Jerusalem for the name of the Lord'.

Jean: At times, it is difficult for even one's closest friends to understand one's commitment to Christ. Every child of God must expect such situations to occur and be prepared to do as Paul did.

The big problem was – Paul was sure it was God's will for him to go to Jerusalem, although he had been warned several times by godly people that it would mean trouble, possibly death.

Observe Paul's conduct under those conditions. He explained his motive. It was no holiday. He was going 'For the name of the Lord'. He was a man under orders. He was committed. His goal was Jerusalem. If he died there, he would die in the Lord's will.

'But what if you're wrong?' his friends might have asked. 'What if it is not God's will?'

Paul didn't allow himself to think that way. He did not waste his emotions on what might happen. Instead, he turned energy and faith towards his goal. He had prayed through all the possibilities. He had considered the risks and the alternatives. He had made his decision. The outcome was in the Lord's hands.

Think of it: When Paul picked up his things and started towards Jerusalem, I'm sure he didn't look back. Not because he didn't love his friends, but because he loved Jesus more.

Prayer: Lord, I am ready to do what I feel in my heart to be your will. Bless my friends who may not understand. In your name, Amen.

DECEMBER 8   1 JOHN 4:19

YOU ARE NOT GOD'S AFTER-THOUGHT

'We love because he first loved us . . . '

Jean: We need to remind ourselves often that our love for God is our response to his love for us.

There are times when we feel we let God down by our lack of ardour, our neglect of Bible reading, our failure to obey his leadings, our rebellion to his authority. Any of these can make us feel unworthy of his love.

Can we ever love God enough, in quality or quantity? When we try to love God more, pray more, work harder, do better ... we find ourselves subtly drawn into the treadmill of self-righteousness. We end up saying, 'God loves me, because I first loved him'!

When my love-response wanes, his still remains. When my heart says, 'God can't love someone as unfaithful as me', I need to say, 'Hold on there, heart. Before I ever started loving him, he loved me. When I had no love at all, his love overflowed to me'.

Family: You can say to each other, 'You are not God's after-thought. You are God's fore-thought. I love you, because he first loved me'.

Prayer: Jesus, you chose to love me. I choose to love you. Amen.

FINISH WHAT YOU START

'However, I consider my life worth nothing to me, if only I may finish the race and complete the task the Lord Jesus has given me — the task of testifying the gospel of God's grace'.

Jean: In modern terms Paul was a goal-orientated man. He was an achiever. He knew his task 'Testifying the gospel of God's grace'. His task gave purpose to his life.

A sense of purpose is important to a person's self-esteem. At first glance, Paul's words 'I consider my life worth nothing' sound as though he felt worthless, of no account. On the contrary! He felt his extreme worth. There was nothing wrong with Paul's self-image! He meant he was so excited about what he was doing, he was willing to spend everything he had, right to the end of his life, in order to hit the finishing line a winner!

Without that achievement, Paul felt his life would be worthless; with that achievement, his life would be worthwhile. Indeed, it was!

Question: Do you have a goal-orientated life? Do you know your task?

Prayer: Father, as I set upon the task you have given me today? May I understand who I am and what my purpose is in life. I want to run in the right direction. Give me grace to finish what I have started, at any cost. In Jesus' name, Amen.

OUR GIFTS AND OUR CALLING

'For God's gifts and his call are irrevocable'.

Elmer: The gifts of God are according to our calling, and our calling is according to our gifts!

In Romans 11:33 St Paul continues, 'Oh the depth of the riches both of the wisdom and knowledge of God! How unsearchable are his judgements and his ways past finding out'.

God understands his servants. He understands you. He knows where your strengths lie. He knows your weaknesses. He calls you according to HIS knowledge of your strength and weaknesses. I have often heard people quote the words 'God's gifts are without repentance'. It is true; he will not take back what he has given. But I haven't heard quite as often 'God's CALLINGS are without repentance'.

I had a dear friend who knew sign language for the deaf. Her words were 'God has called me to the deaf'. For many years she said this but never answered the call. God did not remove the call, for she had a special gift. God removed neither the call nor the gift. That lady is now dead. Many of the deaf which she could have reached have never 'heard'. She loved Jesus and is now with him. I wonder where those deaf people are?

Remember: God will not set us to a task without providing both inner spiritual strength and natural abilities for its completion.

Prayer: Help me, Lord, to recognise natural and supernatural gifts in operation in my life. Help me through constant use to develop these gifts and enable me to recognise and answer your call regardless of how great or small the service might be. Amen.

DECEMBER 11   1 CORINTHIANS 1:28-31

STEWARDS, NOT OWNERS

'He chose the lowly things of this world and the despised things — and the things that are not — to nullify the things that are, so that no one may boast before him. It is because of him that you are in Christ Jesus, who has become for us wisdom from God — that is, our righteousness, holiness and redemption. Therefore, as it is written: "Let him who boasts boast in the Lord"'.

LaDonna: Last year our pastor from America, Dan Sneed, visited us in London. He knew our talents, so he suggested we write a play on the Apostle Peter. We sensed in the Spirit that this was what God wanted. Over subsequent months I worked on it sporadically. After the arrival of our first child, Ian, the rough script was completed. Other projects crowded in and the script remained untouched.

Then mom asked us to do it, with two days notice, to cover for a group who had cancelled. We weren't ready! The script wasn't even typed, nor the last touches given. She said, 'Just read it'. How desperately we wanted the first performance to be perfect. But we knew God wanted us to swallow our pride and do it. He had given it to us, now he wanted it done his way.

So Alan stood and gave a dramatic reading. Out of sixty people present, six asked for salvation and many others came forward to be filled with the Holy Spirit. We could not point to special effects, techniques or equipment to explain the response, only the sovereign blessing of God.

Think: God entrusts to our stewardship talents, money, opportunities, children and property. Are you trying to control how they develop, or have you released them to the Lord's direction?

Prayer: Lord, thank you for giving me those special things to take care of for you. Help me to listen and follow your directions every day so that you will receive all of the glory. Amen.

DECEMBER 12 **2 CORINTHIANS 5:18-20**

RESPONDING TO GOD'S TRUST

'All this is from God, who reconciled us to himself through Christ and gave us the ministry of reconciliation: that God was reconciling the world to himself in Christ, not counting men's sins against them. And he has committed to us the message of reconciliation. We are therefore, Christ's ambassadors, as though God were making his appeal through us – we implore you on Christ's behalf: Be reconciled to God.'

Alan: The idea of God trusting us is a frightening one. The responsibility of responding to God's trust is awesome and more than we can bear alone. Praise God he loved us so much, he sent his Son Jesus to bear that responsibility for us. Now, loving obedience becomes our response. It will take a lifetime of service to give God even a part of what his trust deserves. Let's begin to hand ourselves over.

I do so want to relinquish all to the Father. He trusts me to do so, and I will not willingly fail him, for I love him.

Action: Relinquishment is certainly easier said than done, but we must start somewhere. Put under God's control that person or situation that troubles you.

Prayer: Lord, I allow your power to touch those things I have not quite yet relinquished. I do trust you, Almighty God, the One I know and love. Amen.

DECEMBER 13   PHILIPPIANS 3:13-14

PLACE YOUR FAITH ON THE FUTURE

'Brothers, I do not consider myself yet to have taken hold of it. But one thing I do: forgetting what is behind and straining towards what is ahead, I press on towards the goal to win the prize for which God has called me heavenwards in Christ Jesus'.

Jean: What a picture! The runner is getting close to the finishing line. He strains towards the goal, pressing against fatigue, eyes straight ahead. He's sure he'll make it. He can see himself there, even as his legs carry him faster and faster past the competitors. He's excited! Energy surges through his body as he rushes on. He stretches his legs farther than ever before over the line. In his mind he's crossed that finishing line hundreds of times and felt the exhilaration. What he thought he could do, he has done. Faith has become reality.

What if he'd looked back? What if he had started worrying about his chances? What if he'd thought about all the other races he'd lost. Would he have won had he recalled some unfair criticism by a coach who said he'd never be a winner? No! He would have lost his concentration, his courage. He would have lost the race.

Think of it: Friend, don't look back. Look towards the goals

God has given you. Gear all your thoughts towards achieving them. Place your faith on the future. Run!

Prayer: Lord, help me to see myself a victor, not a loser. Today I look up. I see Jesus. He is my victory. Praise the Lord! Amen.

DECEMBER 14   **1 PETER 4:1-4**

SUFFERING FOR JESUS

'Therefore, since Christ suffered in his body, arm yourselves also with the same attitude, because he who has suffered in his body is done with sin . . . live for the will of God. For you have spent enough time in the past doing what pagans choose to do . . . They think it strange that you do not plunge with them into the same flood of dissipation and they heap abuse on you'.

Jean: Do you suffer abuse because you have chosen not to live the rest of your life as you once lived? If so, God approves of such suffering. It is Christlike. Jesus chose to do the will of God and he suffered.

But because he suffered, sin had no hold on him.

Suffering for Jesus' sake, even to the point of bodily abuse, removes one from the dominion of those sins which once ruled over him. Self-denial draws the follower into the life of a disciple . . . and out of the 'flood of dissipation'. Don't drown in the sewage of a wasted life of sin, but be purified by living for the will of God, even if you suffer for it!

Question: Do you have the same attitude as Jesus about suffering for the will of God?

Prayer: Father, as I take my stand to live a different life from those around me, sin shall have no hold on me. For Jesus' sake, Amen.

HE TRUSTED THEM

' "Come, follow me", Jesus said, "and I will make you fishers of men". At once they left their nets and followed him'.

Jean: The Lord's call had an over-powering effect on the fishermen. They laid down their livelihood and followed him. Why were they so radically affected?

His call meant he trusted them. He could see their possibilities. He would teach them to communicate with people better than they had ever caught fish. He was willing to invest in them his message, his gifts, his power, his faith. He would make them something special.

So they took a chance with him. His call inspired them. They too began to see the possibilities ahead. Soon they began to believe in miracles. They sensed he would make them into something better than they had been before. They felt his trust, so they trusted him with their lives.

Visualise it: What if some of them had tried to carry their boats and fishing gear along! The easiest thing to do was to leave it all. Jesus calls you to follow him. Is there a delay in your response? Is it difficult because you haven't left all? What are you carrying along?

Prayer: Lord, you have trusted me by calling me. I will trust you by leaving all and following you. Amen.

RENEWED DAY BY DAY

'Therefore, we do not lose heart. Though outwardly we are wasting away, yet inwardly, we are being renewed day by day'.

Jean: My spirit reaches towards eternal life as my body forces wane. My spirit leaps upon the mountains towards heaven as my body goes towards the valley of death.

But it takes day by day inward renewal to leap upon mountains! The weaker my body, the more need of renewal. My mind stops learning and remembering unless invigorated by Bible study. Preparation for sermons not only imparts life to others, but to me.

The emotions can become jaded as one ages. After a while, one can feel he has seen and heard it all before. There is no excitement unless one's senses are revitalised by prayer. When one prays, God reveals the purpose of one's days. He sets goals ahead and creates an exciting faith. Where there is vision there is life. Faith creates actual energy. Faith is life-giving.

When God speaks to me about a thing he wants done, my mind clears, my body wakes up and I'm excited. I forget I'm getting older. In fact, I'm not so sure I am!

Think of it: God has work to be done by mature servants who have learned not to rely upon themselves, but upon the Lord. Get out of the rut, shift into the over-drive of faith!

Prayer: Father, I thank you for energizing faith. Renew my mind and my heart. Clarity and courage is what I need today. In Jesus' name, Amen.

DECEMBER 17   1 CORINTHIANS 6:19-20

CARE FOR THE TEMPLE

'Do you not know that your body is a temple of the Holy Spirit, who is in you, whom you have received from God? You are not your own; you were bought at a price. Therefore honour God with your body'.

Elmer: When we travelled through the country of Panama as missionaries, Jean and I would often see a late model car rusting away beside a dilapidated adobe house. No doubt it's owner had suddenly come into a lot of money. Perhaps he had won the lottery. He had purchased an expensive new car at a great price. As a result of ignorance, it had become useless through lack of care.

We have been purchased at a great sacrificial price, the precious blood of Jesus.

Within each blood-bought Christian is the constant presence of the Holy Spirit. We are his temple. Our primary place of worship is within the Holy Spirit's temple. Let us therefore glorify God, not only in our spirits, but in our bodies. We must read God's Word so that we will know how to care for ourselves properly both morally and physically. Let us be careful to give attention to both physical and spiritual health.

The Panamanian could have given his broken-down car a new paint job, but that would not have made it run.

Likewise, let's not use the devil's churchy hypocrisy as 'new paint jobs' for outward appearances. Rather, let us understand God's will from his word and thus keep our 'temples' functioning for true spiritual worship.

Discussion: Advise and help each other to give time and attention to physical and spiritual health. Don't rust out or wear out unnecessarily. You are valuable.

Prayer: Lord, help me to be guided by your word into a better understanding how to honour you with my body. Amen.

DECEMBER 18   JAMES 1:2-4

LEARN TO LAUGH

'Consider it pure joy, my brothers, whenever you face trials of many kinds, because you know that the testing of your faith develops perseverance. Perseverance must finish its work so that you may be mature and complete, not lacking anything'.

LaDonna: There is a very special lady I know who has a wonderful laugh. It begins like the sound of a rocket warming up and then explodes into a cascade of chuckles and giggles. The thing about her amazing laughter is that she laughs in the midst of the most desperate circumstances!

It would be understandable if you thought the woman a little silly, or suspected she had never experienced real suffering. But I know she has withstood some of the most soul-rending circumstances. Not only has she held on, but she has kept her laughter.

302

When I encounter problems and trials, my natural reaction is to struggle to control the chaos. Ultimately, I'm left frustrated and angry. But I am discovering how to let go (relinquish), step back and discover the joy of watching God be victorious over the trial.

Thought: Are the trials of your life impossible to endure? James says 'Count it all joy'. Step back, hand them to the Lord and let the joy of trusting God give you strength to carry on.

Prayer: Lord, sometimes it's hard to trust you in the midst of the problems that arise in my life. I give you today's trials and look for the joy that comes from knowing you will work things out. Amen.

DECEMBER 19   1 PETER 4:12-13

HOLD ON

'Dear friends, do not be surprised at the painful trial you are suffering, as though something strange were happening to you. But rejoice that you participate in the sufferings of Christ, so that you may be overjoyed when his glory is revealed.

Alan: Whenever I've been in the middle of a trying time and someone has glibly quoted this scripture at me, I've felt like pushing that person over the nearest pew! Not that there would be any real satisfaction in such action, but it's hard on me when someone points out what I'm really supposed to be doing.

Peter writes we can rejoice in our trials. It's possible! I may not be able to smile all the time I'm suffering, but I can take hold of my attitude towards it. I can praise God through it all. I can look for his deliverance. It will come and will outweigh the pain.

Action: There is no text-book answer to suffering. I've suffered enough to have learned that power to hold on with joy only comes from trusting God. After all, it is through Christ's own suffering that we are healed. Give God whatever pain you feel and trust him through it all.

303

Prayer: Give me strength, Lord, in my trial, that I might know the joy of a closer union with you. Amen.

DECEMBER 20   1 PETER 4:19

COMMIT AND CONTINUE

'*So then, those who suffer according to God's will should commit themselves to their faithful Creator and continue to do good*'.

Jean: During the periods of preparation for future blessing we will suffer according to the will of God. We will have our faith tested, our love proven, our vision refined. During such times we must commit ourselves into the Lord's hands.

Jesus did this upon the cross. He made full surrender, even of his life, in order to release resurrection life.

Go on serving, even under trying circumstances. Go on loving, even when rejected. Each day you may seem to die a little, but tomorrow you will know the power of his resurrection. You will rise into new ministry.

He who created you knows your frame. He knows how much you can bear. He also can re-create. He is the God of broken things . . . hearts, minds, marriages, ministries and dreams. He makes all things new.

Think of it: Your present suffering is preparation for future blessing.

Prayer: Father, I commit myself into your hands. I will not discontinue doing good. Give me grace. Strengthen my faith. Amen.

DECEMBER 21   HEBREWS 6:18

MY ANCHOR HOLDS

'*God did this so that . . . we who have fled to take hold of the hope offered to us may be greatly encouraged*'.

Jean: God has sworn not to let down those who have put their trust in him. His divine promise to us is an 'anchor for the soul' (v.19). It holds us steady, keeps us from shipwrecked faith in life's storms.

You can count on the word of a very few people in a lifetime, but this is a word of which you can be sure. God cannot lie.

The devil cannot tell the truth, by mouth nor discernment. He lies because he is a liar. Don't believe the lies of the enemy who says you don't have the power to hold on. He tries to make the strongest saint doubt his salvation. Even when it has held him for years!

Believe the truth. Your anchor holds!

Children: Can you draw an anchor? Leave room below your drawing to print MY ANCHOR HOLDS!

Parents: Explain what 'MY ANCHOR HOLDS' means to your children.

Prayer: Father, I thank you for the hope you have offered us through Jesus our Lord. We are encouraged. Our faith will outlast any storm. Amen.

DECEMBER 22   **HEBREWS 12:12-13**

STRAIGHTEN OUT YOUR LIFE

'Therefore, strengthen your feeble arms and weak knees! Make level paths for your feet, so that the lame may not be disabled; but rather healed'.

Jean: Stress and strain causes muscles to fatigue. Often, the weariness one feels is not due to overwork, but to overstrain.

The greatest strain is rebellion. Opposing God's will is exhausting. Resistance to him can actually cause backaches and stiff necks. Also, feeble arms and weak knees.

Our lives are often like a roller-coaster, up and down and in all directions. Uncontrolled tempers and undisciplined minds make us erratic and unpredictable. At times terrifying. We make life hard on ourselves and upon others.

There are 'lame' people, damaged and hurt, who might like to know our Lord but are often turned away by our conduct. If we can get our own lives lined up and smoothed out by surrender to the will of God, we will be healed and so will they.

To those who are sick and tired of struggling against God's will: Give up your whole self to God. Submit. Pour out your rage and let God's peace come in.

Prayer: Father, I'm tired of the up-and-down life I've had. Straighten me out so that I can walk on a level path of healing for myself and for those who relate to me. In Jesus' name, Amen.

DECEMBER 23   JOHN 15:4-5

HE IS THE VINE

'Remain in me, and I will remain in you. No branch can bear fruit by itself; it must remain in the vine. Neither can you bear fruit unless you remain in me. I am the vine, you are the branches. If a man remains in me and I in him, he will bear much fruit; apart from me you can do nothing'.

Jean: Jesus is your Life-Giver. Every day his life goes into yours. Not only does his life go into yours, but your life goes into his. Any branch of your daily life not open to the inflow of his life will not be fruitful.

You cannot impart spiritual life to yourself. You and I are to abide, not in doctrine (though that is supportive), not in church fellowship (though that is edifying), but we are to abide in Christ. That is where life comes from.

Abiding means communion. Real prayer. Less prayer means less of Christ's life in us. Less of Christ means less faith. Less faith means less fruit.

Children: One day, you will be old enough to leave your mother and father. You will go on to live a life of your own. However, you can never leave Jesus and live a Christian life. You will need him always. Never leave him and he will never leave you.

Prayer: Lord, let my communion with you become more constant. As I depend upon you for my life, you can depend upon me for your fruit. Amen.

DECEMBER 24   MATTHEW 2:1,11-14

GOD'S INFINITE PROVISION

'After Jesus was born in Bethlehem in Judea, during the time of King Herod, Magi from the east came to Jerusalem . . . On coming to the house, they saw the child with his mother Mary, and they bowed down and worshipped him. Then they opened their treasures and presented him with gifts of gold and of incense and myrrh. And having been warned in a dream not to go back to Herod, they returned to their country by another route. When they had gone, an angel of the Lord appeared to Joseph in a dream. 'Get up', he said, 'Take the child and his mother and escape to Egypt. Stay there until I tell you . . . ' So he got up, took the child and his mother during the night and left for Egypt . . . '

Elmer: The long awaited day had come. The perfect Son of God was born. God fulfilled his plan with great simplicity, a boy born in a manger.

When God plans he provides. God's provisions are for small necessities as well as major projects. In the Old Testament a prophecy said, 'Out of Egypt have I called my son'. Yet, Jesus was not born in Egypt. He was born in Bethlehem.

Joseph must have had a restless night after the dream. How could he, a working man, plan and find the money for an expensive trip abroad on such short notice? For security, the Holy Family would have to join a caravan. No family could travel alone. He might need to buy a camel. Soon he knew the answer. Mary's son was rich. God had provided.

The wise men from the east had great joy when they worshipped Jesus. Their joy was not only in worshipping, but in giving. They gave abundantly. The Bible says they opened their **treasures** of gold, frankincense and myrrh.

There was gold that could pay for the trip. There were small boxes of frankincense and myrrh which could be easily hidden to help pay living expenses.

Think of it: When God plans he provides. Sometimes, just in time!

Prayer: Lord, help me to trust you for the things I need to fulfil your plan for my life.

DECEMBER 25   LUKE 1:38

LET IT HAPPEN!

' "I am the Lord's servant" Mary said. "May it be to me as you have said" '.

Jean: Mary's submission to God's will demanded a great deal of her. She must have been aware of the terrifying, immediate implications. Her reputation, her relationships, her testimony were all jeopardized by her 'Yes'.

Yet her only question, after the angel's message, was not if it would happen, but how it would happen. After she was told of the Holy Spirit's power, she accepted God's will. She believed the word spoken to her. She accepted herself as chosen to be a special person for a special purpose.

Phillip's translation of her response is beautiful: 'I belong to the Lord, body and soul', replied Mary, 'Let it happen as you say'.

At this Christmas time give the Lord full surrender of body and soul. Believe you have been chosen to be someone special for a special purpose. Receive the Holy Spirit's power. Then, through the coming year, let it happen.

Children: Cut out pictures and make a lovely birthday card to Jesus.

Prayer: Dear Father, as each of us offer ourselves to you anew, let us become a special family for a special purpose in this world, for Jesus' sake. Amen.

Alan: These past two years have brought many times of personal crises for LaDonna and me. Such times have not been isolated nor coincidental. Rather, they have been an integral part of God's work in our lives. LaDonna and I have seen our ministries develop as the Lord brought increase through pruning. There have been definite seasons during these times, showing growth and indicating direction.

Two areas of ministry have specifically developed. One is to teenagers. We long to see committed young Christians entering adult life in the power of the Lord. Jesus Christ is the only hope for this generation. The enthusiasm of youth should be rooted in that hope in order to grow strong and towards new directions.

The other area of ministry we feel called towards is to performing artists. I was an actor in Hollywood when I received a call from God into ministry. I have a special affinity for actors. This ministry includes counselling and teaching (biblical and theatrical) for professionals and non-professionals alike. It also includes a one man play about St. Peter, LaDonna has written and I perform. At the first performance, six people received Jesus as Saviour . . . praise the Lord!

We rejoice in all that the Lord is doing in England. We look forward to many years of service in Britain. We love this place and its people. This is our home. We thank God for it.

Ruby: My early years in Sunday School laid a good foundation of knowledge about God and his love, but at the age of sixteen I felt a restlessness and a hunger to know the Lord personally. I began to attend a Full Gospel church and was converted there. All members of my family subsequently gave their lives to Jesus. During that time, I met John at the youth fellowship of our church. The Lord, in deep heart-searching, showed me that John was to be my husband.

We married in May 1966 and began to develop a godly influence in our own family. Praying together has been a fundamental influence on all our lives. All major decisions have been committed to God in prayer. We have obeyed what we felt God was saying to us – even if, humanly speaking, it has seemed the wrong decision. God has never once made a mistake. The children, too, have prayed about their personal decisions. They have seen the strength and power of prayer at work. This has become a wonderful uniting factor in our family.

At a certain stage, John was instructed by the Lord to pray over the children each night. God gave insights into their individual needs. We prayed for those God would later bring into our children's lives. Such prayer has had a deep influence on their spiritual growth.

There have been times when I have had to go to their schools to discuss difficulties the children were having with their studies. I asked God for a 'key' to motivate and stimulate each child. Every time I have prayed for such a 'key', God has given it, and we've been thrilled to see the results.

We are both elders at Church on the Way, Van Nuys, California. We teach a Married's Class of more than a hundred. We hold interdenominational marriage retreats where couples can strengthen their relationships. John works in his own company and I with him, alongside our church commitments and our responsibilities to the schools our children attend. I look back with gratitude, to a strong, loving family influence which has held us closely knit together.

DECEMBER 28   PERSONAL TESTIMONY

John: The knowledge that my grandparents on both sides of my family have been praying for me all my life, everyday, has had a powerful influence on me personally. I believe it was the primary factor that drew me at an early age to a knowledge of Jesus Christ.

At five years of age I gave my heart to Jesus. Shortly afterwards I was baptised in the Holy Spirit and in water. I grew in the ways of the Lord with the ongoing care of my parents through childhood into my young adult years. I strongly believe that their continual prayers for me and my sister during our childhood, our young adult years and as we moved into our married lives, have kept us from being overcome by the assaults of the enemy.

I was nineteen when I moved out of my parents' home. During the Vietnam War I enlisted in the United States Air Force. Later I attended the University at Long Beach, California. During all those years I suffered no major time of rebellion or turning away from the Lord. I believe such stability is directly related to the fact that my mother, father and my grandparents prayed for me.

In my early twenties I met a beautiful Christian woman who is now my wife. Ruby and I, both from strong Christian homes, combined our lives to form a new Christian family. As our children arrived we continued the pattern of prayer.

Every major and minor phase of our marriage has been covered with prayer. We have found that nothing we plan is done well without it. We search and find the will of God and his directions for the way we are to live. After graduating from Long Beach University with a degree in advertising and graphic design, I began to do free-lance work. Later, I took a position with a Christian publishing company and served four years as the assistant advertising manager. Currently, I am president and part-owner of an advertising graphic design firm in the Los Angeles area. Our clients are widespread both among secular and Christian organisations. We do commercial advertising, graphic design and promotional programming.

Ruby and I have three children: our eldest daughter, Sharolyn, who is fourteen years old; our second daughter, Johanna, who is seven; and our son Johnathan, five.

When Sharolyn was five years old, the Lord directed Ruby and me very strongly to begin to pray in a special way for her each night; not just good-night prayers. After she was asleep we were to pray for her as the Lord would direct us. We have prayed in this manner for all three of our children ever since. Each day I present my wife and my children before the Lord. I pray for Ruby to have time and opportunity to be her own person, as well as my marriage and business partner.

Ruby and I pray specifically for the children whom our children will someday marry. For the two boys who will someday be our son-in-laws. For the girl who will someday be our daughter-in-law. We pray the Lord will give to our children mates who are designed and destined for them. Ruby and I see that we don't have three children, but six! We cover each of our six children with prayer.

We attend the First Foursquare Church of Van Nuys, better known as Church on the Way, pastored by Rev Jack Hayford. We have taught the young married's class for five years, and conduct seminars which deal with issues relevant to young couples rearing children in an urban society.

All three of our children know Jesus. Their conversions mark four generations of born again, Spirit-filled servants of the Lord. I look forward, as a husband and father, to the future when there will be not only children, grandchildren, great-grandchildren, but great-great-grandchildren who will be the result of prayers that began many years ago when my grandmother and grandfather prayed they would have a family who would serve Jesus.

DECEMBER 29   PERSONAL TESTIMONY

LaDonna: Alan and I have been through both exciting and difficult times while writing this book. Through everything, we've felt the Lord's care as we have travelled and ministered at numerous conferences, camps and house-parties. Also, for the last two years Alan has attended Christian Life College three nights a week.

We feel Alan should work only part-time so he can be free for ministry. This caused us to be financially desperate at times. In those times, the Lord has led someone to us with food or has miraculously provided through some other unexpected source. Often we wouldn't have an egg or even an onion, but the Lord never let us run out of coffee! What a sense of humour God has!

There was a time when we began to despair as we faced a long delay in moving house, waiting with a new baby week after week for months. The Lord had put us in a particular area and we felt he wanted us to stay but financially it was impossible. Then out of the blue, someone who had money to invest, told us to find a house. They would buy it and let us live in it. We are now in the house, after a few trials and delays. It is above our wildest dreams and worth waiting for. Yes, God proved again that he knows our needs and cares.

But the most profound personal experience came when our dear son was born. He was just a couple of days old when I saw something white in the pupils of his eyes. The pediatrician was called and they confirmed it as congenital cataracts. They were so dense, it was impossible for him to see. He was blind. Deep feelings of guilt about what I had passed on to my son flooded in as I sat behind drawn curtains in the maternity ward, blinking back tears of anguish.

Then the Holy Spirit reminded me of John 9. Those around the blind man asked Jesus whose sin caused the blindness. He said, 'Neither this man, nor his parents; but it was in order that the works of God might be displayed in him'. Then I knew in the Lord I had the strength to go on and do the best for our son. When Alan came into the hospital room, he had the same verse God had given him before he left the house.

Later, Alan contacted a dear friend in California. Not knowing what the Spirit had said to me, our friend Linda told him months before Ian's birth God had led her to John 9. She had been praying for his eyes continually. God knew and cared.

I went through five weeks in hospital with Ian for operations to remove the cataracts. I have made countless trips to eye clinics and watched huge hands endlessly probe our son's tiny eyes. Alan and I have had to wrestle daily with our baby, prying his eyes open to insert contact lenses and later to remove them. I have had to face the fact of Ian's visual limitations (without a miracle). But through it all I have remembered that before Ian was even born, God knew and cared and someone was praying for him.

Today we have a happy, strong baby who can see enough to reach for things. One special tomorrow, 'The works of God will be displayed in him'.

DECEMBER 30   **PERSONAL TESTIMONY**

'. . . I know whom I have believed, and am convinced that he is able to guard what I have entrusted to him for that day. (2 Timothy 1:12)

Elmer: In 1928 Aimee Semple McPherson conducted an evangelistic campaign in my hometown, Des Moines, Iowa, USA. She preached three times daily, thirty sermons in ten days. The largest auditorium was packed with ten thousand people every night. She prayed for the sick in some of the services. A family friend, Lois Shepherd, was taken to the auditorium dying of tuberculosis. She was instantly, completely and permanently healed. At the close of the ten day mission a new pentecostal church was started with five hundred members from among the converts who had found the Lord during the meetings.

The new church was started in what had been a roller skating rink. It was there, a few weeks later, as a lad of eight, I accepted Jesus as my Saviour. That was 54 years ago. I remember clearly the lady who prayed with me saying, 'That's alright, cry!' I wept bitter tears. I was so sorry for my sins and sorry Jesus had suffered so much for me.

A few months later, on Good Friday, 1929, I received the baptism of the Holy Spirit, speaking with other tongues (Acts 2:4).

In these early years of my life, I was persuaded to give my life to Jesus. God has kept me for himself ever since. Yet to come is 'that day' when I shall see him and be like him.

I will continually receive him as my eternal Saviour. I will continually trust him to keep my life for evermore.

Editors note: Rev Elmer Darnall is now Principal of Christian Life College, London. The college offers a two year evening course in practical Christian service. Elmer Darnall's counselling course emphasizes loving Jesus is loving your neighbour as yourself.

DECEMBER 31   A FINAL WORD FROM JEAN

Our tiny living room was crowded one summer's day last year when both John and LaDonna, with Ruby and Alan and four grandchildren came together to look through five big suitcases full of old photos. It was something I'd been hoping to do with the children for years. 'What's the use of us hoarding all those memories in the garage?' I complained to Elmer. 'We should get the kids together and let them sort out the photos they would like to have as keepsakes'.

What a good family time! We all said it was better than Christmas!

'Hey, Mom, is this where you and Dad lived when I was born?' John asked, holding up a shot of us in Panama.

Alan blew a long whistle. 'Wow, look at this glamorous gal!' waving a glossy publicity shot of me.

'Yeah, I remember that' LaDonna said, 'The photographer erased all her character lines'.

'I'd like that one!' 'Mom, can we have this one?'

Soon almost all the photos were divided among them, reminders of a life we had shared in many parts of the world.

At the end of the evening, my beautiful daughter-in-law, Ruby, put her arms around me and said, 'Mom, to me this has been the best day of our whole month's holiday here'.

Funny how we photograph all the happy times . . . birthdays, anniversaries, picnics and parties. But in the gallery of my memories are sad, terrifying times: times of misunderstanding, times when I worried lest our children might not love God when they grew up because they had seen so much of the raw side of the ministry. Times when we hurt and could not hide it. Times when I feared they might become insecure adults because of changing schools so often, moving not only from town to town, but from country to country. But that evening, surrounded by our children and grandchildren, I watched their faces as they looked through the photos, listened as they reminisced . . . Not a word of bitterness or regret. Not a complaint.

John's voice rose above all the chatter. 'Hey, everybody, you've got to hear this'. He had found our wedding book. There were photos of our wedding and our honeymoon. There were little love-notes from Elmer, and my diary during our honeymoon. John's voice wavered with emotion as he read of our love for one another.

That is our treasure. We have loved one another, by God's grace, through it all. Our son wrote in his testimony how grateful he was for praying parents. Don't confuse that with perfect parents. We prayed because we often felt so inadequate, so afraid, so foolish.

We prayed for more love. We prayed for wisdom, for faith.

Love is our family legacy. Because of God's love, we have given love to our children, and they now to their's. God's love has bound us together.

I have faith for the future of our children. I look forward to the remaining years we have to love all the children God has given us everywhere. Faith for the family, ours and his.